TWENTIETH-CENTURY

SPRAWL

TWENTIETH-CENTURY

SPRAWL

*Highways and the Reshaping
of the American Landscape*

Owen D. Gutfreund

OXFORD
UNIVERSITY PRESS
2004

OXFORD
UNIVERSITY PRESS

Oxford New York
Auckland Bangkok Buenos Aires Cape Town
Chennai Dar es Salaam Delhi Hong Kong Istanbul Karachi Kolkata
Kuala Lumpur Madrid Melbourne Mexico City Mumbai Nairobi
São Paulo Shanghai Taipei Tokyo Toronto

Published by Oxford University Press, Inc.
198 Madison Avenue, New York, New York 10016
www.oup.com

Oxford is a registered trademark of Oxford University Press

Library of Congress Cataloging-in-Publication Data
Gutfreund, Owen D., 1963–
    Twentieth-century sprawl : highways and the reshaping of the American landscape / Owen
D. Gutfreund.
        p. cm.
    Included bibliographical references and index.
    ISBN 0–19–514141–5
    1. Cities and towns—United States—Growth—History—20th century—Case studies.
    2. Middlebury (Vt. : Town)—History—20th century.
    3. Smyrna (Rutherford County, Tenn.)—History—20th century.
    4. Denver (Colo.)—History—20th century.
    5. Interstate Highway System—History—20th century.
    6. Roads—Government policy—United States—History—20th century.
    7. Transportation, Automotive—United States—History—20th century.
    I. Title: Highways transformed America.
    II. Title.

HT384.U5G86 2004
307.76'0973—dc22 2003190050

Book design by planettheo.com

9 8 7 6 5 4 3 2 1
Printed in the United States of America
on acid-free paper

To Victoria, Charlotte, and Willa

Contents

Illustrations, Figures, and Tables

CHAPTER THREE
THE DECENTRALIZATION OF POST–WORLD WAR II DENVER

CHAPTER FOUR
AUTOMOBILES AND A SMALL TOWN

CHAPTER FIVE
BRIDGES, BYPASSES, AND BOULEVARDS

CHAPTER SIX
AUTOCITY: SMYRNA, TENNESSEE

Acknowledgments

While working on this book, I was fortunate enough to receive support and assistance from many people. As the project developed, changed, and finally materialized, I amassed a debt of gratitude that these words of acknowledgment can only begin to repay. First and foremost, were it not for years and years of indulgences from my wife, Victoria, the whole thing may not have gotten off the ground and certainly never would have been completed. She endured too many working weekends, abbreviated vacations, painstaking editing sessions, research-related absences, and repetitive conversations about traffic, highways, and urban planning, while never flagging in her support.

The other person who merits particular thanks is Kenneth T. Jackson, whose probing questions and persistent urgings to answer the question "Who cares?" pushed me to do more than I thought possible. As a teacher, a mentor, and historian, he sets a standard that inspired me as a graduate student and continues to inspire me as a professor and scholar.

I also owe thanks to those who, at pivotal stages in the research and writing of this book, gave me much-needed feedback, sometimes forcing me to rethink entire arguments, sometimes simply helping me to refine ideas that were already sound. While I am sure that I cannot mention all that I should, I will particularly acknowledge the sage advice and feedback provided by Elliot Sclar, Elizabeth Blackmar, Alan Brinkley, Mark Rose, and Bob McCaughey, as well as the many members of the George Washington Plunkitt Benevolent Society. Harold "Slim" Curtis and Abbott Fenn, two long-time residents of the Middlebury area who had been involved in community affairs for decades, were kind enough to read draft chapters, offering valuable insights and corrections. And finally, though they did not know it at the time, many of my students in the Urban Studies Programs at Barnard College and Columbia University forced me to clarify and revise my arguments, as they poked and prodded at my interpretation of urban history in seminar discussions.

The research for this book took me to more than half a dozen different archives, and in some instances I met extraordinary archivists whose dedication and thoughtful assistance were remarkable. In particular, Polly Darnell at the Sheldon Museum Library in Middlebury, the staff at the Colorado Historical Society Library, and at the Western History Department of the Denver Public Library. Also helpful were the staff at the Colorado State Archives, the Vermont Historical Society, the Vermont State Archives, the Middlebury College Library, and the Wilbur Collection of the Bailey/Howe Library at the University of Vermont. Finally, the research in Tennessee, which was in some ways the most difficult, was in the end made possible by the generosity and cooperation of an anonymous clerk at the Smyrna Town Hall.

Abbreviations

American Association of State Highway Officials	AASHO
Bureau of Public Roads	BPR
Colorado Historical Society	CHS
Denver Planning Office	DPO
Denver Public Library, Western History Collection	DPL, WHC
Denver Tramway Company	DTC
Denver Urban Renewal Agency	DURA
Henry Sheldon Museum of Vermont History	HSMVH
Highway Education Board	HEB
League of American Wheelman	LAW
National Highway Users Conference	NHUC
Office of Road Inquiry	ORI
Project Adequate Roads	PAR
Public Works Administration	PWA
Regional Transportation District	RTD
Rural Free Delivery	RFD
Works Progress Administration	WPA

TWENTIETH-CENTURY

SPRAWL

Introduction

In 1896, two bicycle mechanics from Springfield, Massachusetts, built the first automobile in the United States. In the century that followed, Americans spent enormous sums of money expanding and overhauling the nation's transportation network to accommodate the motorcar. This reconstruction, propelled by a multilayered set of private initiatives and government programs, had profound consequences on the landscape, on residential and commercial choices, on occupational patterns, and, most important, on the way that ordinary families went about their daily lives. As the states and the federal government invested in streets, roads, highways, and bridges, the citizenry simultaneously flocked to the open land on the urban periphery. These two related trends—the suburbanization of the nation and the overhaul of the transportation infrastructure—combined to define and shape late twentieth-century America, laying the groundwork for the twenty-first century legacy of ballooning municipal debt burdens, deteriorating center cities, incessant demands for capital improvements, and unstable municipal tax bases.

These changes were not simply driven by technological innovation and cultural preferences—they were also impelled by an overlapping array of unheralded government subsidies and policies. Collectively, these policies reshaped the American landscape and created a crisis in the nation's metropolitan areas. They funded and facilitated fundamental changes in the spatial arrangement of residence, commerce, and industry, tipping the scales in countless ways away from centralization and toward deconcentration. At the same time, they fueled a chronic nationwide need for capital expenditures on highways unmitigated by considerations of expense, efficiency, affordability, or equity.

This book analyzes these changes by focusing on three primary case studies: a major western metropolis (Denver), a small New England village (Middlebury, Vermont), and a sunbelt boomtown (Smyrna, Tennessee). The three case studies are not treated as subjects in themselves, but as illustrations of an historical dynamic. These very different communities, when considered side by side, demonstrate that the consequences of American-style automobility are not limited to any particular region or to any particular type of American settlement. Rather, all were transformed by unheralded federal and state incentives.

Middlebury, at the turn of the century, was a small New England town with a population of only a few thousand, down from a peak of more than five thousand in 1840. It was the county seat for Addison County, a rural region of central Vermont sandwiched between the Green Mountains and Lake Champlain. The county was mainly farm country, with most of the nonagricultural activity concentrated in town, which was home to an assortment of mills, a marble works, and Middlebury College. The main road ran north–south, providing a route for horse-drawn vehicles to get to Rutland (south) or Burlington (north); additional dirt roads led eastward over the mountains or westward down into the Champlain Valley. A railroad also provided both passenger and freight service.

At the beginning of the new millenium, Middlebury is still a small New England town. Agriculture remains a primary component of the local economy. The community is still bisected by the same north–south road, now designated U.S. Route 7. But regular traffic jams occur daily in Middlebury, fueling a relentless debate over projects that pit would-be developers and boosters against defenders of the small town status quo.

Downtown storekeepers now compete with shopping centers. Factories have moved to an industrial park on the edge of town, and retail shops and small offices have taken over the old mill buildings and marble works downtown. On the edges of town, postwar tract housing spreads across the countryside. The railroad now runs only a skeleton freight service, and passenger service was forsaken many years ago. In essence, despite the anti-urban sentiments held by a significant portion of the local community, small-town Middlebury has been transformed into a modern American community, sharing the same auto-related problems as big cities nationwide.

Smyrna, at the beginning of the twentieth century, was one of the countless small towns sprinkled across America's midsection. Local residents were connected to the rest of the nation only by a dirt road to nearby Nashville, a city of one hundred thousand residents. As the century progressed, Nashville grew considerably but remained smaller than its regional neighbors, Memphis, St. Louis, and Atlanta. Smyrna retained its small-town character, even as the dirt road to Nashville turned into paved U.S. Route 41.

Now, however, three major expressways intersect at Nashville. Interstate 40 runs coast to coast, from Raleigh–Durham on the Atlantic coast to Los Angeles on the Pacific, with Winston–Salem, Charlotte, Memphis, Little Rock, Oklahoma City, and Albuquerque in between, as well as numerous connections to other interstate highways. Another new super-highway, Interstate 65, joins the Gulf of Mexico to the Great Lakes, connecting Mobile, Montgomery, and Birmingham in the south with Louisville and Chicago in the north. Interstate 24 provides connections to St. Louis and Atlanta.

This remarkable access to the nation, via the toll-free, federally funded Interstate Highway System, attracted the Nissan Motor company to Smyrna for its first North American factory, completed in 1983. Another attraction in Smyrna was that there was virtually nothing else there: no other major employers; no underfunded and decaying municipal infrastructure; and no cumbersome social welfare bureaucracy supported by local taxes.

Smyrna is now home to the largest auto assembly facility in North America, a factory the size of ninety-two football fields that can produce almost half a million vehicles a year. It provides direct employment to almost six thousand people and indirect employment to twice as many. A whole new infrastructure has been constructed in Smyrna, attracting many other new employers to the area and fueling rapid regional population growth.

Denver, on the other hand, was already a city of one hundred thousand inhabitants before the close of the nineteenth century. Nine different railroads served the Colorado capital, with lines extending east to Chicago, south to Texas and New Mexico, and west to the Pacific. Bicycles were common, and the city's mass transit system reached almost every corner of the metropolitan area, while automobiles were rare. But by 1925, more than a quarter of a million motor vehicles were registered in Colorado, and the state and city governments had begun ambitious projects to adapt the infrastructure to the new vehicles. At the same time, the city's transit system died a painful death, as auto-dependent suburbanization took hold. By mid-century, only one out of every five new residents of the metropolitan area chose to live within Denver's city limits.

Throughout the latter half of the twentieth century, the city sprawled across the open plains, as auto-use skyrocketed and population density dropped. Shopping centers and malls went up at a pace matched only by the speed at which developers laid out new subdivisions along suburban highways. Denverites' journey-to-work time increased, carpooling declined, and bus ridership fell. The metropolitan area grew to nearly two million people, but traffic congestion increased at twice the rate of population growth. A "brown cloud" hangs over the city, caused by truck and automobile emissions, and yet the region's growth remains focused on the fringes. Aurora, at mid-century a small town outside of Denver that counted fewer than four thousand residents, has grown so much that it now rivals its older neighbor and houses a quarter of a million people. Meanwhile, imaginative redevelopment efforts were needed to save down-town Denver from desertion, in the face of the relentless shift toward deconcentration and sprawl.

The diverse histories of Denver, Middlebury, and Smyrna, in the context of the system of highway federalism established early in the twentieth century and continued through present times, illustrate and explain how the American landscape was transformed by the drive to accomodate automobility in the United States, leading to the rapid decentralization of American communities after World War II, the dispersal of the citizenry across previously undeveloped countryside in the pattern now known as sprawl, and the accompanying abandonment of many central cities.

ONE

Highway Federalism

On January 15, 1953, Charles E. Wilson, President and Chief Executive Officer of General Motors testified before the Senate Armed Services Committee, in connection with his nomination as President Dwight D. Eisenhower's Secretary of Defense. When one of the Senators on the panel suggested that Wilson's extensive holdings of GM stock might present a conflict of interest, the auto executive responded thus: "For years I thought what was good for our country was good for General Motors, and vice versa. The difference did not exist."[1]

This statement was—and remains—controversial, not just because it was arrogant but also because it rang shockingly true. By the early 1950s, even before the Interstate Highway legislation was passed, the automobile industry had, for decades, participated in a loosely organized but politically powerful group that could be known as "the highway lobby." By the time of Wilson's inflammatory utterance, carefully orchestrated efforts had already achieved long-lasting success, with the political and social consequences that we live with today. In the preceding half-century the United States had made crucial policy decisions about how to adapt to the new automotive technology, while the American public remained mostly unaware of the stakes. Unnoticed, an elaborate system of highway federalism had taken shape as a dizzying array

of interested lobbying groups insinuated their economic interests into the
fabric of American political and popular cultures, and into the state and
federal legal codes.

Prior to the twentieth century, roads in the United States were built and
maintained almost exclusively by local government. The states did little more
than grant occasional franchises for privately operated turnpikes, and the
federal government did even less. The only exception was a short-lived effort
to support new highways as part of the "internal improvements" movement
early in the nineteenth century; however, most of these regional routes were
privately operated turnpikes in the mid-Atlantic states. By 1821 New York
had authorized over four thousand miles of turnpikes. Pennsylvania, which
had started with the sixty-two mile Lancaster Pike connecting Philadelphia
to Lancaster in 1794, reached a peak of about 2,400 pike-miles in 1832. New
Jersey and Maryland also had turnpike programs during this brief period. At
the same time, the federal government planned a piecemeal series of turnpikes
known collectively as the National Road, which was completed in dribs and
drabs over several decades at a cumulative cost of $6.8 million. However, by
mid-century the federal government had abandoned *all* of its highways, and
the private turnpike operators had deserted most of theirs. In the face of stiff
competition from railroads, they had turned them over to county governments as local roads. For many decades thereafter, railroads were universally
accepted as the basic mode of long-distance transportation, and Americans
relied on roads for local traffic only.[2] Accordingly, the national government
and the states focused their attention on railroad development, leaving roads
and streets under the exclusive purview of local government.

Neither the states nor the federal government became involved in road
building again, even in a limited fashion, until the closing years of the
nineteenth century. Furthermore, it was not until well into the twentieth
century that the renewed commitment became widespread and effective.
Most importantly, though, the twentieth-century version of "internal

improvements" was no longer based on privately operated turnpikes supported by tolls. Instead, roads were recast as a public enterprise managed by new government bureaucracies, and road users were not expected to pay tolls or other user fees to defray their costs. This reconception of free-of-charge roads and highways as a public good began with the Good Roads movement in the 1890s and was institutionalized by the establishment of federal aid for highway construction in 1916.

THE GOOD ROADS MOVEMENT

The Good Roads movement, started by bicyclists in the 1880s, first developed broad momentum during the final decade of the nineteenth century, before a single automobile had been assembled in the United States. The nation's roads were in a pathetic state: muddy, rutted, overgrown, and often washed out, causing enormous difficulties for the growing ranks of Americans trying to use bicycles as a basic mode of personal transportation. Consequently, bicyclists organized the League of American Wheelmen (LAW) to promote better roads. Bankrolled by Albert Pope, a leading bicycle manufacturer from Massachusetts, the LAW generated a persistent clamor for increased government involvement in road building, which could not easily be brushed off by elected officials. This type of corporate sponsorship of highway advocacy was replicated time and again by subsequent highway advocacy efforts, when the auto and road-building industries provided the driving force and the bulk of the funds for a multitude of lobbying groups, which were often deceptively presented as consumer groups and motorists' associations.

The LAW distributed many publications, including *Good Roads Magazine* and the *Bulletin of Good Roads*, and also sought out the support of farmers, who were eager for alternatives to monopolistic railroads. As a part of this effort, I. B. Potter, a civil engineer, published an influential book targeted at farmers, titled *The Gospel of Good Roads: A Letter to the American Farmer*. Potter argued that more efficient transportation would save farmers

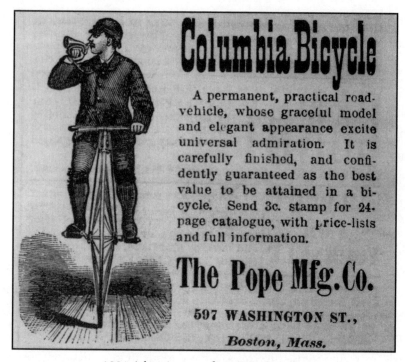

1881 Advertisement for a Pope bicycle,
Leslie's Illustrated Newspaper, April 16, 1881, *Colorado Historical Society*

money, and he supported his case with estimates of cents-saved-per-bushel and cents-saved-per-acre. Many farmers were influenced by this treatise and supported the Good Roads movement in the hope that better roads would enable them to get their goods to more than one railhead, thereby requiring the railroads to compete with each other. Accordingly, the Populist Party supported Good Roads advocacy efforts.[3] Beginning in 1885, the party platform included a plank calling for government-funded rural road improvements. Ironically, the railroads also supported the Good Roads movement to some extent, because they wanted to extend the geographic reach of each station stop, and they overconfidently presumed that rail transportation would remain the dominant mode of long-distance travel for the foreseeable future.[4]

Downtown street at turn of the century, showing widespread bicycle use,
Colorado Historical Society

The first major accomplishment of the nascent highway lobby took place in 1891, when the New Jersey legislature passed the State Aid Act. This unprecedented legislation established state aid to support county-based road projects, offering grants to cover one-third of construction costs. Massachusetts soon followed with its own state-aid law but added an important proviso: the funds could be used only on a system of officially designated state-aid highways that would *connect* the towns and villages of the state. This provision codified the rural slant of the Good Roads movement by establishing the precedent of excluding roads within urbanized areas from government aid while simultaneously funding routes within rural regions. Also, maintenance expenditures were not eligible, another important precedent. By the turn of the century, five other eastern states initiated similar grant programs to support good roads, bringing the total to seven.[5]

Preaching the gospel of Good Roads, 1893,
Colorado Historical Society

At the national level, the Good Roads movement obtained legislation in 1893 to create the Office of Road Inquiry (ORI). In accordance with the rural roots of government highway programs, this new bureau was placed in the Department of Agriculture. The ORI was not yet authorized to fund highway projects but was charged with researching, surveying, and providing technical assistance to the states. In order to make the most of the shoestring budget, General Roy Stone, the agency's first director and a founder of the National League for Good Roads, enlisted a volunteer network of information gatherers. He did this by appointing members of the LAW as "Public Roads Correspondents." In exchange, the "correspondents" were granted liberal use of Stone's franking privileges. The combination of the organization's limited legislative mandate and Stone's initial staffing strategy made the agency into little more than an officially mandated arm of the Good Roads movement.[6]

For the next twenty years, the ORI's main activities included distribution of books and pamphlets to farmers, running public education programs, and organizing publicity campaigns in support of Good Roads initiatives, while simultaneously offering predrafted bills to state legislatures, endorsed with the seemingly apolitical stamp of "expert" approval. A noteworthy example of the collaboration between the ORI and the highway lobby was the publication of a specially prepared book intended to win wider support from farmers, *Must the Farmer Pay for Good Roads?* Otto Dorner, the chairman of LAW's National Committee on Highway Improvement, wrote the book, and the ORI used federal funds to publish it and distribute it widely, making it into one of the best-known official publications of the federal agency, even though it had been written by a private lobbying group.

At the same time, the ORI helped local road clubs by providing model constitutions and recommending committee structures. Within a few years, the Good Roads Yearbook listed thirty-eight nationwide member organizations and 617 state and local groups. The ORI's limited budget kept it dependent on this network of private highway groups for information, maps, and model legislation, much of which was then widely distributed using the government frank. Agency officials were often feted as speakers or guests of honor at Good Roads meetings, with travel expenses paid by the LAW. At one such meeting in 1897, General Stone enunciated the relationship between the ORI and Good Roads groups such as the LAW: "Every Wheelman is a preacher, a worker, and a fighter for good roads. It is only necessary to furnish him texts for preaching, tools to work with, and weapons to fight with."[7]

Meanwhile, America entered the auto age. In 1900 the first auto show was held in New York City at Madison Square Garden, organized by the National Good Roads Association. The first gas station opened in 1901 (also in New York City), and in 1902 the Automobile Association of America was formed, primarily to secure state and federal funding for road improve-

The challenges of early cross-country travel by automobile,
Colorado Historical Society

ments.[8] Fueled by the new support offered by the AAA, the Good Roads movement gained momentum and began to hold regular meetings nation-wide. A 1903 Good Roads convention in St. Louis was conspicuously attended by President Theodore Roosevelt and former presidential candidate William Jennings Bryan.

In 1904 the ORI released the first national survey of road conditions. According to its data only 7 percent of the country's roads were surfaced, mostly with gravel or low-quality macadam not designed for automobiles, which were of course faster and heavier than horse-drawn vehicles. Five years later, a follow-up survey found that this number had risen to only 8.66 percent, with no significant upgrade of surface quality.[9] Statistics such as these were used by Good Roads advocates to cast public discussion in terms that were predicated upon the acceptance of their own objectives and standards. Since this was an age characterized by a great deal of confidence in the ability of "experts," the findings of the engineers employed by the ORI (and its successor agencies) were not questioned. The public officials charged with evaluating and formulating new state highway policies were usually drawn from the ranks of the Good Roads movement and therefore approached the issues with the predisposed objective of providing new roads as a free-of-charge public good.

At a Good Roads meeting in Vermont during 1904, the president of the American Good Roads Association (who was also a member of the Connecticut State Highway Commission) proclaimed that "If it took night and day for a hundred years and the wealth of a Croesus to bring about the reformation of any State in the Union from the thralldom of mud, it was time and money well spent." This statement was met with considerable applause by the assembled acolytes.[10] Despite the fanatical tone of such speeches, the Good Roads movement was by no means a marginal group. On the contrary, it grew rapidly and developed an increasingly broad base of support.

The voices of bicyclists and farmers were now echoed by many other groups. The LAW faded when Albert Pope withdrew his funding and turned his entrepreneurial energies toward a newer transportation device, one that had potential for far more profit than the inexpensive bicycle: the automobile. He was soon the leading auto manufacturer in the United States and by 1907 had eight plants in operation nationwide, making steam-, electric-, and gasoline-powered vehicles. Not surprisingly, as Pope and other entrepreneurs shifted their focus toward autos, the AAA emerged as the successor to the LAW, co-sponsoring the second National Roads Convention in Cleveland during 1909, along with the National Grange, the National Association of Automobile Manufacturers, and the American Road Makers Association, which represented civic engineers, highway contractors, and makers of road-building machinery.[11] One year later, in 1910, Logan Page—a federal official—assembled a new umbrella highway lobby organization to coordinate all these groups, called the American Association for Highway Improvement. This marked the beginning of a public–private partnership that would reach its zenith in the Eisenhower Administration, producing the alignment of interests referred to by Charles Wilson when he tried to persuade Congress that he should be allowed to keep his General Motors stock.

Logan Page, the central figure in the initial formation of this public–private partnership, was ironically known as a "nonpolitical" engineer, appointed by the Secretary of Agriculture as the director of the Bureau of Public Roads (BPR), the successor agency to the ORI.[12] Page stayed in this position for a dozen years, from 1906 until 1918. He ran an increasingly aggressive corps of engineer-advocates, despite the fact that he and his agency were routinely described as "nonpolitical," and eventually secured passage of the 1916 Federal-Aid Road Act, a landmark congressional enactment that established the same basic program of federally funded highway construction that we have today.

Historian Bruce Seely has convincingly argued that BPR engineers from this period, under Page's leadership, were "central figures" in "the creation of popular and political support for a road-building program, [and also in] the determination of the goals highways should serve."[13] Consequently, the policy decisions made during this period should not be presumed to be public choices arrived at via democratic mechanisms. On the contrary, the unelected engineers who made policy decisions remained largely oblivious to the broader political or social dimensions of the issues at hand. Instead, road building was debated and discussed as a set of narrowly conceived technical concerns. Among the most important consequences of this approach was a lack of substantive discussion, at the outset, of an essential question: *Who will pay for the new road-building programs?* For the time being, the amount of money involved in these programs was relatively modest, and it was easy to disregard this question.

All the same, decisions were made and programmatic biases were institutionalized, with long-lasting repercussions.

As a core component of Logan Page's advocacy effort as the director of the BPR, he worked to unite all the various Good Roads supporters. His vehicle was the aforementioned American Association for Highway Improvement, which included (by Page's invitation only) various highway officials, Good Roads associations, the AAA, and railroad executives.[14] The organization sponsored the first American Road Congress in 1911, which featured a keynote address by President Taft and also produced resolutions that later became the basis for the Federal-Aid Highway Act of 1916.[15]

When the federal government made its first direct grant to road construction, one year after the 1911 Road Congress, the emphasis was unequivocally on rural roads. Since 1893, Congress had been expanding "rural free delivery" of mail, but the post office could provide such service only along passable routes. Largely in response to urgings from the Grange, extension of postal delivery became a popular campaign promise, and the only method of accomplishing this was to improve roads. In 1912 a coalition of rural congressmen secured $500,000 for the post office to make grants for one-third of the costs of improving designated post roads. The legislation also directed the post office to rely on Page's road office in the Department of Agriculture to administer the aid program.[16]

Even as these first highway aid programs got underway at the federal level and in some states, the Good Roads movement showed signs of fracturing. When government aid for highways was a theoretical objective, it had been easy for all the various interest groups to work together. However, it soon became apparent that not all of the participants shared the same objectives. While they all agreed on the need for new roads, and they all agreed that these new roads should be public enterprises free of any significant user charges, they disagreed about what kind of roads should be built first.

Not all Good Roads advocates placed a top priority on farmer-oriented rural free delivery and farm-to-market roads. In particular, automobile interests opposed the 1912 post road legislation, testifying before Congress that the rural post road program would produce roads that began "nowhere and ended nowhere."[17] Instead, there was growing support for building regional highways for long-distance travel. There were virtually no such routes at the time. Cal Dowling, an adventuresome traveler who drove from Washington, D.C., to California in 1912, reported (to his wife in a postcard) that on days when the roads were relatively good and the car was running properly, his average speeds were still only twenty-eight miles per hour.[18] Auto-related entrepreneurs recognized that poor road conditions limited the prospects of the nascent industry and responded with proposals for long-distance highways.

Perhaps best known of these efforts was the Lincoln Highway, launched by Carl Fisher in 1912 when the Lincoln Highway Association began a coordinated effort to connect New York to San Francisco, via Pittsburgh, Indianapolis, Chicago, Omaha, and Salt Lake City, with a gravel road. Fischer, later founder of the Indianapolis speedway, had already made a fortune selling Prest-O-Lite auto headlights. The Association's membership roster also included Henry Joy, the president of the Packard Motor Car Company. Fischer proposed that members pledge 1 percent of their gross revenues to pay for materials, with states and localities paying for labor and equipment.[19] There were other similar projects, some long forgotten: the so-called National Highway from New York to Atlanta, by way of Philadelphia and Winston-Salem (1909); the Capital Highway from Washington through Richmond, Raleigh, and Columbia to Atlanta (1910); the Dixie Highway from Chicago to Miami (1915)—another Carl Fisher scheme;[20] the Robert E. Lee Highway from New York to New Orleans via Philadelphia, Washington, Knoxville, and Birmingham (1921); and the John Bankhead National Highway, which included Washington, Charlotte, Atlanta, Birmingham, Memphis, and Little Rock on the way to San Diego (1921).[21]

These endeavors were fundamentally different, in both strategy and organization, from the earlier thrust of the Good Roads movement. In contrast to the formalized lobby groups working to secure general government support for roads, each individual regional highway was championed by a separate, narrowly focused ad hoc association. These loosely bound groups of private-sector businessmen and local officials would coordinate on routing, signage, and maps, leaving the actual construction and financing of the highways to a helter-skelter patchwork of segment-specific initiatives. Some sections were built by local boosters and tourist-oriented businessmen along the route; others were completed as town or county roads; other portions were never actually finished at all, until they were later taken over by the federal-aid highway system. Another important difference is that these roads were not farm-to-market, nor were they postal delivery routes. Instead, they were planned as long-distance travel routes that would provide interregional connection and stimulate specific local economies and the nationwide auto-tourism economy. The lists of supporters often included owners of hotels, gas stations, repair garages, and manufacturers of auto parts, as well as developers of real estate along the routes.[22] For their part, farmers denounced these projects as "cross country trunk lines or boulevards for those who have the money and time to idle away in long distance tours," and instead voiced continued support for efforts to make "more local roads available for farm-to-market purposes and which are of service to all the people."[23]

At the same time that this apparent schism in the Good Roads movement was emerging, the advocates of federal subsidies for highway construction achieved an enormous success: the passage of the Federal-Aid Highway Act of 1916.[24]

ESTABLISHING HIGHWAY-FINANCE FEDERALISM, 1916–1939

In 1914, with Logan Page's encouragement, leading highway officials joined together to form the American Association of State Highway Officials (AASHO). Page wanted civic engineers to present a unified front when highway matters came up for debate, and the AASHO was the ideal vehicle for such efforts. Later, as state and federal governments increased their commitments to highway building, the AASHO developed into "one of the most important, least-known political groups in the country . . . part lobby, part professional association, part quasi-political agency. No effective national highway policy could be enacted without its agreement."[25] It is not surprising, therefore, that one of the AASHO's first official actions was the submission to Congress of draft legislation for what would become the Federal-Aid Highway Act of 1916, the legislation that first established a comprehensive system of highway-finance federalism.

After the AASHO first proposed the new federal highway initiative, the other highway lobbies stepped in to offer their support, as well as their suggestions for modifications. The AAA launched an aggressive campaign, along with the National Automobile Chamber of Commerce and the American Road Builders Association. Many railroads, still mistakenly convinced that road construction would expand rail traffic, sponsored itinerant lobbying trains that would take Good Roads evangelists across the countryside to give lectures and stump speeches pushing road improvement programs. Beleaguered legislators, under the pressure of the 1916 election campaigns, turned to Logan Page and the engineering staff of the BPR to sort out the various proposals and make a "nonpolitical" recommendation.[26] Nevertheless, the resulting legislation had political and policy consequences that lasted for many decades.

The Federal-Aid Highway Act of 1916 established important precedents, by its most general provisions and by some of its narrowest. It created a system for federal highway aid distributed through an independent bureaucracy controlled by "expert" engineers in the Bureau of Public Roads and in the newly reformulated state highway departments. Logan Page had learned from the experiment with aid to Rural Free Delivery (RFD) that many states lacked constitutional or administrative structures capable of accepting, directing, or managing federal highway grants, so he made certain that the Act required the states to create highway departments that fit a prescribed format before they could apply for the dollar-for-dollar matching grants that were the centerpiece of the legislation. Details about these requirements were published, immediately after passage of the Act, in the *Rules and Regulations for*

Carrying Out the Federal-Aid Road Act.[27] Furthermore, the BPR published another set of mandates titled *Standards Governing the Form and Arrangement of Plans, Specifications, and Estimates for Federal Aid Projects.* These technical edicts prompted *Engineering News* to report that, despite the political rhetoric that lauded the novel federal-state partnership created between the state highway departments and the BPR:

> the rules and regulations governing surveys, plans, specifications, estimates, contracts, construction work, costkeeping and payments are so comprehensive that the [BPR] will have a dominating influence in all work for which application for federal aid is made.[28]

Thus, this important piece of legislation created a formalized mandate for the states to administer federal grants in accordance with technical regulations and congressionally legislated formulas, overseen by a strong centralized federal agency. Eight states formed new highway departments after the new rules were promulgated, three of which needed constitutional amendments to do so. Nine states revamped their existing highway departments to satisfy the BPR guidelines, and eighteen others reorganized their highway departments to take maximum advantage of the new system. Engineers and other experts from the BPR provided expert testimony, model laws, and other guidance to twenty-seven state governments as they worked through these changes.[29] As a harbinger of the new federalism that would be forged during the New Deal twenty years hence, this component of the Act and the subsequent regulations are noteworthy, but no more so than some of the details buried in the actual aid provisions, many of which had enduring ramifications.

Sections of the 1916 Act further institutionalized the rural emphasis of the Good Roads movement. Not only was this emphasis explicitly stated in the Act's legal description, "An Act to provide that the United States shall aid the States in the construction of *rural post roads* [emphasis added], and for other purposes" but it was also built into the restrictions on projects eligible for aid. The Act limited aid to $10,000 per mile, which had the effect of underfunding projects in settled areas, where roads would be more expensive because of higher land values or more demanding traffic flow (along many portions of the Boston Post Road connecting New York City to Boston, for example). A related anti-urban regulation prohibited grants for segments of roads within towns of population greater than 2,500, unless houses were more than 200 feet apart, on average.[30] Since the exclusive focus of the new subsidy was Rural *Free* Delivery routes, tolls were forbidden on any roads that received the new federal aid. Finally, the 1916 Act contained a precedent-setting formula for dividing the $75 million five-year authorization among the states. This same formula, which was based upon a combination of population, area, and existing road mileage, would be used for the next half-century. By giving the same weight to a mile of single-lane dirt road as to a mile along a main thoroughfare near a city (urban streets did not count at all in this formula), and simultaneously adjusting for each state's geographic size (with the area calculation and again with the adjustment for existing nonurban road mileage), the formula effectively stipulated a strong funding bias in favor of sparsely settled states, at the expense of those states that were more urbanized.[31]

World War I, which came on the heels of the passage of the 1916 Act, precipitated a broader agenda for government road programs. During the war the military used increasingly heavy trucks to haul troops and manufactured war material from inland bases and factories to coastal ports for transport to Europe, so that by the end of the war it was not unusual for convoys of vehicles weighing over ten tons each to travel long distances over roads that were designed for much lighter horse-drawn vehicles. At the same time, there was explosive growth in the use of trucks to transport nonmilitary goods, largely as a response to the inability of the war-burdened railroads to provide adequate service. Herbert Hoover, who was serving as U.S. Food Administrator at the time, stated that half the country's farm produce did not make it to market before it spoiled because of woefully inadequate transportation.[32] With the official encouragement of groups like the National

Highway Council, a federal body responsible for rationing state and local governments' use of economic resources (including labor, material, and railroad capacity), truckers stepped into the breach—transporting goods that the railroads could not. The nation's roads were often not up to the task, even those that were paved, and there were numerous reports of military truck convoys leaving crumbled road surfaces in their wake.[33]

At first, the BPR responded by raising engineering standards and requesting even more funds for increased construction costs, since war-induced inflation had also raised costs. Not surprisingly, the highway lobbies lent their support to the Bureau's request, and Congress quadrupled the aid allotment for 1919–1921.[34] These appropriations were part of the annual post office appropriation measures, indicating the continued centrality of RFD projects and the corresponding exclusion of projects in or near heavily populated areas. However, the wartime trucking experiences also raised renewed questions about whether federal aid should be expanded to include long-distance connecting roads ("primary routes"), instead of only rural farm-to-market roads ("secondary routes").

Dwight D. Eisenhower, only twenty-eight years old at the time, participated in a military exercise that underscored the inadequacy of the nation's trunk lines. During the war the military had placed large orders for automotive equipment, much of which didn't arrive until after the war ended. In 1919 the army assembled these unused new vehicles for an overblown road test: The First Transcontinental Motor Convoy. The expedition was staffed by 24 officers, 258 enlisted men, and 15 war department staff officers, one of which was Lieutenant Colonel Eisenhower. Ike later recalled that the adventure had been "in part prodded by the enthusiasts for a transcontinental highway." The convoy included dozens of brand-new military vehicles, including heavy trucks, light trucks, machine shop vehicles, a blacksmith truck, a tow truck, spare-parts vans, tankers, tractors, kitchen trailers, and about twenty cars and motorcycles. Goodyear Tire and Rubber Company provided a specially designed truck that carried a fifteen-piece band, and Packard lent a touring car. Not surprisingly, the group ran into repeated road trouble. The tractors were frequently used to haul trucks from mud, sand, streams, and up some of the steeper or hard-to-negotiate hills. Sometimes bridges that were too weak to support the heavy trucks had to be temporarily rebuilt. The vehicles themselves broke down frequently, needing replacements of broken belts, spark plugs, bearings, and head gaskets. On its best day, the convoy traveled only ninety miles, and on at least one occasion it made only four miles of headway in an entire day. Average speed, coast to coast was six miles per hour. Interestingly, the official report of the convoy, in addition to noting the military advantages of an improved road network, also concluded that

> the necessity for a comprehensive system of national highways, including transcontinental or through-routes east and west, north and south, is real and urgent as a commercial asset to further colonize and develop the sparsely settled sections of the country.[35]

That interior highways could be justified on military grounds, but would have the primary effect of developing underdeveloped regions, did not escape young Eisenhower's notice.

Meanwhile, there was leadership change at the BPR, after Logan Page died unexpectedly in 1918 from a heart attack suffered while attending an AASHO meeting. His replacement in Washington was Thomas H. Mac-Donald, former chief highway engineer of Iowa and president of the AASHO. MacDonald, who remained at the helm of the BPR until 1953, was a diplomatic engineer-*cum*-bureaucrat.[36] Known to highway engineers and officials nationwide as "The Chief," MacDonald was instrumental in building further consensus among the disparate highway groups and assembling a political juggernaut that dominated transportation policy for decades. He worked assiduously to close the fissures within the Good Roads community and simultaneously to forge new alliances and broaden the movement's support base. Throughout his tenure he maintained close ties with his former colleagues at AASHO and stayed on its board even after he took over the helm at the BPR. One observer noted that under MacDonald, "in practice, the Bureau of Public Roads almost never adopted standards except on the recommendation of the American Association of State Highway Officials."[37] Not surprisingly, Commissioner MacDonald embraced many of the core components of the association's philosophical platform, first and foremost of which was the conviction that "Free Roads are the Ideal of a Free People."[38]

MacDonald created the Highway Education Board and the Highway Research Board, which were intended to look like independent education and research groups, respectively. He used them for disseminating highway-booster propaganda and for providing seemingly impartial expert testimony at legislative hearings. The Education Board sponsored essay contests, with a college scholarship as prize (funded by tire maker Harvey Firestone), on such topics as *"How Good Roads Help the Religious Life of My Community."* It also made movies and pamphlets describing how autos could improve Americans' everyday life, if only there were more good roads. Taking the public-private partnership to a new level, most of the Board's expenses were paid for by the National Automobile Chamber of Commerce and the Rubber Association of America.[39]

Meanwhile, MacDonald's desire to build consensus among highway boosters was also manifest in federal policy changes. He shifted the direction of the federal highway program away from an exclusive focus on secondary farm-to-market roads toward a dual commitment that included primary long-distance routes as well. This shift was manifest in the Federal-Aid Highway Act of 1921, which created a system of formally designated primary highways and extended the 1916 Aid program with a one-year budget of $75 million (the original five-year appropriation was the same amount).

The 1921 Act required each state to designate 7 percent of its total road mileage as "federal-aid highways," divided into two categories: primary (interstate) routes; and secondary (intercounty rural) routes.[40] The primary routes received 60 percent of the money, while secondary routes got 40 percent, and the per-mile aid limitation was increased to $20,000 because of higher construction standards and inflation. There was still no urban component to the program. Adding to the array of important precedents set by earlier highway legislation, the Act mandated that state highway departments maintain all roads built with federal aid, although it did not permit federal funds to be used for such maintenance. Finally, the Act adjusted the matching ratio for states with large tracts of federal land, ostensibly to make up for the exemption of such lands from the state and local property taxes used to raise road funds. The formula for computing this adjustment, which followed very closely the one that the AASHO had suggested two years earlier, produced considerably more favorable terms for rural and western states than for more urbanized eastern states. For example, while the Act authorized federal aid on a 1:1 matching ratio for most states, after these new adjustments Nevada benefited from an 8:1 aid ratio, Utah 3:1, Wyoming 2:1, and six other states (Arizona, California, Colorado, Idaho, New Mexico, and Oregon) got about one and a half federal dollars for each one of their own.[41]

While the federal government set precedents that would shape the nation's transportation system for the twentieth century, America moved farther into what historian Kenneth T. Jackson has called the "New Age of Automobility."[42] Whereas in 1910 there had been less than half a million cars in the United States, or one car for every 201 people, this figure rose to 8 million (plus 1 million motor trucks) in 1920. By 1930 there were 22 million automobiles in the nation, or one for every 5.3 people. In 1921 alone, Americans purchased 1.6 million new cars. There was a corresponding decline in the use of horses and mules for transportation, which peaked in 1918 when there were 26 million such animals in use nationwide.[43] During this transition to the automobile, each decision about roads and highway policy influenced how the new mode of transport would be used and who would pay for it.

The coordinated Good Roads movement had successfully lobbied government to provide better roads as a free-of-charge public good, ostensibly to get the farmer out of the mud. One of the most significant aspects of the landmark 1916 legislation was that there were no federally imposed user charges associated with the Federal-Aid highway program. Furthermore, motorists were protected from toll charges, and attempts to levy a federal gas tax had been repeatedly defeated by the lobbying efforts of motorists groups, oil companies, and other highway lobbies, despite support from the White House.[44] As a result, there was an enormous government subsidy of auto use, and the technical provisions of the Federal-Aid Highway Acts directed these subsidies exclusively toward rural areas.

In effect, the federal government established a system of transfer payments, from urbanized regions to rural regions, and from all taxpayers to those who drove automobiles. In 1921 users of the 9 million motor vehicles in the nation paid only twelve percent of *all* highway costs. In the mid-1920s, $1.5 billion went into *new construction* of roads and highways each year, while user fees collected at all levels of government were only $472 million.[45] The difference, over $1 billion a year, was a stimulus for expanded auto use, adding impetus to the rapid growth of the auto industry. By 1923 the auto business already accounted for 10 percent of the nation's iron and steel output, 10 percent of tin, 12 percent of lead, 14 percent of lumber, 53 percent of plate glass, 69 percent of upholstery leather, and 80 percent of rubber.[46] As the industry expanded, so did its political strength, providing Good Roads advocates with powerful partners, since industry leaders knew that growth in auto-and-related businesses was tied to increases in road capacity.[47] Most state governments were persuaded to supplement federal-aid programs, "modernizing" their infrastructure and increasing automobility. Just as at the federal level, the techniques used to finance these programs and the states' mandated portion of federal-aid projects produced additional subsidies for automobility and decentralization.

New York was the first state to charge motorists a registration fee, in 1901. This charge was not intended to defray any of the general costs associated with automobiles but was instead a "processing fee" to cover the costs of administering the registration system itself. Nevertheless, it stands as the first modern instance of a *user fee* or *user tax* on motorists. Other states followed New York's lead, and by 1917, when all states had created highway departments to conform to the new federal legislation, all had also imposed registration fees.[48] Some states took a broader view of the costs of accommodating the automobile and attempted to charge higher fees. In these instances, vigorous efforts by the AAA produced requirements that the revenues be exclusively devoted to auto-related expenditures. This revenue, however, did not come close to matching the increasingly expensive commitment to road programs pushed through state legislatures by the Good Roads movement.

To close this gap, the states taxed gasoline sales. Oregon was the first to do so, in February 1919, followed closely by New Mexico (March 1919) and Colorado (April 1919). It was no accident that these three states simultaneously came up with the same mechanism to close the ever-widening gap between highway expenditures and revenues: State highway officials had discussed the possibility of imposing gas taxes among themselves, presumably through AASHO channels and undoubtedly with the blessing of BPR Commissioner MacDonald. In these three states, and in many others in years following, it was the state highway engineers acting as "agents of dissemination" that spread information about the gas tax. By 1925 forty-four states and the District of Columbia raised about $150 million annually from gasoline taxes, and in 1929 New York became the last state to impose such a levy.[49] The tax rates were relatively low, often starting at one cent per gallon, but they climbed quickly, so that six states were charging six cents per gallon by 1928, and another twenty-seven states charged three or four cents per gallon. The distribution of revenue raised by these levies was influenced by the anti-urban provisions of the federal mandates, so that even though urban residents paid about three-quarters of all state gas taxes, only 5 percent of the state funds were spent in cities, and then only on extensions of primary routes through the unpopulated sections of municipalities.[50]

Meanwhile, as gas taxes rose, organized opposition to additional increases grew proportionally. While the imposition of these user fees raised motorists' share of costs (by the early 1930s they raised about $500 million a year, or 40 percent of *state* expenditures), the oil companies, the AAA, auto manufacturers, car dealers, tire makers, service station owner-operators, truckers, and bus operators allied against additional gas taxes. At the same time, costs ballooned (for example, the 1930 BPR standard for road width was 15 percent wider than the 1920 standard, and minimum surface thickness had similarly increased), and these same groups pressed for even more road construction, with the added support of the American Roadbuilders Association, the AASHO, the American Society for Municipal Improvements, and the American Society of Civil Engineers.[51]

The Good Roads movement had been remarkably successful at recasting highways as a public enterprise that ought to be unencumbered by user fees. Gas taxes, as long as they were kept very low, were viewed as a relatively painless exception. With the aggressive support of the newer highway lobbies, this thinking became enshrined in the canons of highway engineering and planning. For example, a 1927 special issue of the *Annals of the American Academy of Political & Social Science* contained more than thirty articles written by an assortment of government officials, corporate spokesmen, planners, engineers, think-tank representatives, and private sector emissaries, all focused on how to plan for ever-increasing traffic. There were articles about lighting technologies, route planning, traffic flow engineering, off-street parking, implementing new signs and signals, traffic regulations, zoning rules, elimination of grade crossings, and building pedestrian crossings, without a single mention of financing these projects or imposing user fees to charge motorists for their expenses. There was no consideration of using fees to influence consumer choices and thereby direct automobility, let alone fund it.[52]

As a result of the simultaneous pressure *for* more expenditures and *against* user fees, the auto subsidy widened. Between 1921 and 1932 American governments spent $21 billion on streets and highways and collected only $5 billion from motor vehicle users. This meant that motorists were directly contributing less than one quarter of the *direct* costs of adapting to the automobile.[53] In the early 1930s, as the highway programs continued to balloon, it became increasingly difficult for state and local governments to fill this yawning gap with depression-strained budgets. Into this breach stepped FDR and the New Deal.

More than a third of all New Deal work-relief jobs were on road and highway projects, many within the nation's urbanized areas, a departure from previous policies. New Deal initiatives added more than $5 billion in special authorizations for automobility projects. Work relief was the main purpose of many of these projects, so they were not necessarily overseen by the BPR. Also, since unemployed Americans had flocked to big cities in search of work, the new jobs could not practically be focused on exclusively nonurban projects. Furthermore, the 1933 National Industrial Recovery Act specifically required the BPR to spend part of its $400 million allocation on projects previously excluded from federal aid. For political balance, FDR included some farm-to-market rural routes that had not qualified for designation as secondary routes, as well as urban connections to rural primary routes, and grade-crossing elimination projects in both urban and rural settings.[54]

Thus, the New Deal put huge new sums of money to work building new roads and highways and at the same time undermined the long-sought aid system that was governed by formulae, oriented almost exclusively toward rural regions, and dominated by engineers in the BPR and state highway departments. The three-way conflict between the supporters of primary highways, proponents of secondary roads, and advocates of urban streets escalated during this period; as cities became more congested, farmers were still literally stuck in the mud, and intercity highways were still fragmentary, inconsistent, and jumbled. At the same time, since most New Deal projects were driven by a combination of economic concerns and pork-barrel politics, engineers and state highway officials no longer dominated highway policy. In yet another sign that consensus was crumbling, the Public Works Administration and the Reconstruction Finance Corporation worked together to support Pennsylvania's ground-breaking plans for a major toll-financed turnpike, thereby undermining the commitment to *free* highways. In sum, the New Deal's politicization and dispersal of government road building efforts brought to the forefront many of the submerged schisms between the various highway lobbies. Now, however, the nation was preoccupied, first by the Depression and then by World War II, so these conflicts and disagreements remained unresolved (and undiscussed, to some extent) until after the war.[55]

In the interim, despite the New Deal largess, highway boosters pressed for further expansion of government programs, demanding more and better roads. In 1937, as the next step in this relentless push, the auto industry launched the strategically misnamed Automobile Safety Foundation to promote more highway construction under the guise of safety-advocacy. The Safety Foundation, which was funded by the Automobile Manufacturers Association, was routinely invited to testify at legislative hearings as a consumer-oriented safety group. It also regularly put out press releases, but its testimony and press statements consistently and invariably argued that the solution to all auto-related safety concerns was the construction of newer and wider highways.[56] AASHO followed with the announcement that 100,000 miles of primary roads did not meet the standards of the Safety Foundation and would have to be relocated or rebuilt. The funds needed to do so would amount to more than all the federal aid since the 1916 Federal-Aid Highway Act. In 1940 a highway official complained that "in spite of the prodigious efforts and the expenditure of vast sums of money, the work has never caught up with the actual requirements and needs *of the motoring public.*" [emphasis added] The AASHO wanted governments to spend more general revenues on roads. There was scant recognition of the inherent wealth transfer produced by spending money raised from *all* taxpayers for the benefit of the subset of the public described here as *the motoring public.*[57]

Simultaneous to these aggressive strategies to "up the ante," the highway lobby pursued defensive strategies to protect existing revenue streams. But state governments still faced prodigious budget gaps, strained by these incessant demands and the need to provide matching and supporting funds for the federal-aid highway programs. At the same time, they struggled to raise revenue for the expanding array of government responsibilities that arose from the Depression and the subsequent new initiatives of the New Deal. One revenue-raising measure that many states turned to was the general sales tax, and there was some pressure to recast the sales tax on gasoline as general revenue, alongside the other new sales taxes.[58] For example, Tennessee avoided bank-ruptcy by pledging gas tax revenues to refinance general obligation state bonds.[59] Similarly, the federal government imposed a special tax on gasoline (one cent per gallon), which was not conceptually tied to highway funding whatsoever but was instead considered a new general revenue.[60] This was already common practice in other developed nations. In response, highway groups lobbied to "protect" gas tax revenues from what they called "diversion." They vigorously pushed measures to require that gas tax revenues be expended on highways, and they also fought to exempt gasoline from the new general state sales taxes, arguing that because gasoline sales were already taxed to raise money for highways, collecting any additional levy for general purposes would be unfair. The end result was that retail sales of gasoline were, and still are, treated as fundamentally different than all other retail sales.

General Motors president Alfred P. Sloan, mentor of Charles E. Wilson, started the most aggressive new highway lobby in 1932, the National Highway Users' Conference (NHUC), a group that survives to this day. With auto industry funds, Sloan built this organization into a powerful force—again, clothed as a consumer advocacy group—that focused on any state or federal legislation related to gas taxes or auto-related fees.[61] His efforts produced results quickly, in the form of the Hayden-Cartwright Act of 1934, which threatened to reduce aid to any states that increased "diversions" of revenues from gas taxes to nonhighway purposes. The preamble to this act of Congress serves as an excellent example of the insertion of auto subsidies into the fabric of American political culture:

> Since it is unfair and unjust to tax motor-vehicle transportation unless the proceeds of such taxation are applied to the construction, improvement, or maintenance of highways . . . [62]

With this federal legislation as motivation, supplemented by the local activities of the NHUC and other highway lobbies, many states passed legislation requiring that all gas-tax revenues be used to directly benefit

Summary of the Officers and Permanent Committees of the National Highway Users Conference (NHUC)—1941

Chair	Alfred P. Sloan, General Motors Corporation
Vice Chair	President, A.A.A.
Secretary-Treasurer	Master of the National Grange

Advisory Committee	Representative, Automobile Manufacturers Association
	Representative, American Petroleum Institute
	Representative, National Automobile Dealers Association
	Representative, National Association of Motor Bus Operators
	Representative, Rubber Manufacturers Association
	Representative, Farmers Educational Cooperative Union

Steering Committee	Representative, General Motors Corporation
	Representative, Automobile Manufacturers Association
	Representative, American Petroleum Institute
	Representative, National Grange
	Representative, A.A.A.
	Representative, Rubber Manufacturers Association
	Representative, National Automobile Dealers Association
	Representative, National Sand and Gravel Association
	Representative, Council of Private Motor Truck Operators
	Representative, National Association of Motor Bus Operators
	Representative, American Trucking Association
	Representative, Portland Cement Association
	Representative, International Harvester Corp.
	Representative, National Rural Letter Carriers Association

motorists. Within a few years, twenty states had enacted *constitutional* provisions to "protect" highway revenues, and others had amendment procedures underway.[63]

As a result of the Hayden-Cartwright Act and the related measures enacted at the state level, gasoline consumption could not be taxed to support nonhighway expenditures, even though virtually no other type of consumption was similarly privileged. Highway construction was now sheltered, at least partially, from the need to compete with education, law enforcement, prisons, or welfare programs for scarce government funds, unlike virtually all other government endeavors.

Great Britain had established a much different precedent for taxation of gas consumption. In 1926, then Chancellor of the Exchequer Winston Churchill explained his use of gas taxes as a general revenue:

> Entertainments may be taxed; public houses may be taxed; racehorses may be taxed . . . and the yield devoted to general revenue. But motorists are to be privileged for all time to have the whole yield of the tax on motors devoted to roads? Obviously this is all nonsense . . . such contentions are absurd, and constitute an outrage upon the sovereignty of Parliament and on common sense.[64]

Nevertheless, the lobbying and "public education" efforts of highway booster groups, spearheaded by the NHUC, overwhelmed any American proponents of Churchill's "common sense" approach. To make matters worse, road advocates turned the tables altogether, contending that it would be unfair for motorists to pay the full cost of highways, since they conferred a "general benefit" and therefore should be funded out of general revenues.

After the successful antidiversion efforts, Sloan's group focused on preventing gas taxes from increasing and lowering them if possible, bolstered by the "general benefit" argument. For example, to combat attempts to raise the Tennessee gas tax, they dispatched representatives to a Knoxville highway conference to testify that the current levy was too high and that license fees should only support the administrative cost of issuing licenses and need not support new construction at all. Less muscular conference participants pointed out that European countries had higher gas taxes (Great Britain imposed a national gas tax in 1910 and had increased it regularly since, for example), and nationwide studies found that in the United States "automotive vehicles *do not* bear their full burden of taxes."[65] The NHUC arguments prevailed, and the increase in the Tennessee gas tax never materialized.

That same year, a University of Denver study found that the cost of operating a car over paved roads was nearly half the expense on dirt roads (1.73 cents per mile vs. 3.17 cents), not even taking into account saved time or increased safety and comfort. Nevertheless, the NHUC continued to fight efforts to increase user fees far and wide, trumpeting the "general benefit" rationale to great effect.[66]

The "general benefit" argument was fundamentally flawed. The general benefit was attributed to the connection highways provided between and among producers and their markets. Goods could be more efficiently transported for consumption, resale, or integration into higher-level products, and the economy as a whole benefited. Therefore a portion of the highway costs should be funded out of general revenues. The flaw in this argument can best be understood by considering a passage from Adam Smith's *The Wealth of Nations*:

> When the carriages which pass over a highway . . . pay toll in proportion to their weight or their tunnage, they pay for the maintenance of those public works exactly in proportion to the wear and tear which they occasion of them. . . . This tax or toll, too, though it is advanced by the carrier, is finally paid by the consumer, to whom it must always be charged in the price of goods. As the expense of carriage, however, is very much reduced by means of such public works, the goods, not withstanding the toll, come cheaper to the consumer than they could otherwise have done; their price not being so much raised by the toll, as it is lowered by the cheapness of carriage.[67]

By calling the benefit "general," lobbyists obscured the fact that it was distributed unevenly, in proportion to individuals' use of the roads, both directly by personally driving over highways and indirectly by buying and selling goods and services transported on them. However, there was no effective voice offering this counter argument, so the NHUC was able to spread the gospel of free roads, often without rebuttal.

With gas-tax revenues constrained by the lobbying efforts of the NHUC, the states had to find alternative means of financing highways. The other major source that they relied on (to augment federal aid, general revenues, and user fees) was the issuance of bonds, borrowing against future revenues. New York was the first state to fund highways this way, borrowing $50 million in 1906 and again in 1912. By 1920 many other states had followed suit. In elections during 1918 and 1919, voters approved highway bond issues in Illinois ($60 million), Pennsylvania ($50 million), Michigan ($50 million), and Mississippi ($60 million), and there was legislation pending for another $300 million of such borrowings in other states.[68] Even though some states resisted this practice, preferring to maintain pay-as-you-go policies, by the mid-1920s almost half of outstanding state debt in the United States was for roads and highways. By 1931 there were $1.2 billion of state-issued road bonds outstanding, up from only $124 million in 1916. Furthermore, local governments had another $3.5 billion in these loans outstanding, compared to $287 million in 1914.[69]

Two very important side effects resulted from the use of municipal bonds to finance highway projects. First, the interest on these bonds was exempt from income taxes, so investors were willing to accept much lower interest rates than prevailing market rates. In effect, the costs of borrowing money to finance highway construction were subsidized, or "bought-down," by the federal government. In an ironic twist, this tax exemption enabled state and local borrowers to borrow money on more favorable terms than the federal government itself.[70] One recent attempt to quantify this subsidy estimated that for each $1 billion in municipal bonds issued, the federal government lost as much as $30 million each year that those bonds remained outstanding.

The second important consequence of highway-related borrowing by state and local governments was another powerful (albeit subtle) subsidy to automobility. Virtually all the highway debt of local governments (counties, townships, cities) was backed by pledges of future revenues, mainly property taxes. Even at the state level, where user fees were levied, 20 percent of state road bonds were serviced by general revenues (in addition to the use of general revenues to fund road construction and maintenance).[71] This meant that *all* taxpayers were bearing the burden of accommodating automobility, regardless of how much they used automobiles (if at all) or how much they benefited from lower transportation costs.

Thus, in the first decades of the automobile age, the gap between motorists' demands and their contributions was filled by a combination of federal aid, subsidized state and local debt, and New Deal grants. Still, highway boosters clamored for more, while the NHUC kept user fees and taxes down. The incessant pressure, in opposite and conflicting directions— for more highway spending and lower user fees—backfired, thus fracturing the highway lobby. In particular, there was growing pressure for new long-distance express highways, despite the continuing requirement that much of the federal aid go toward rural farm-to-market secondary roads. Something had to give. The result was a mid-century explosion of toll-road construction.

CREATING THE INTERSTATE HIGHWAY SYSTEM, 1939–1960

Before the United States entered World War II, a handful of important toll roads opened, laying the groundwork for a postwar boom in turnpike construction. In 1937 the Pennsylvania legislature created a Turnpike Commission to build limited-access toll roads that would traverse the entire state, despite the opposition of the BPR, which was left out of the project altogether. At first, it seemed that the BPR engineers' efforts to block the toll road would be successful, when they convinced the financial community that toll revenues would be insufficient and the road would be a financial failure. However, with support from FDR, the commissioners were able to secure a $35 million loan from the Reconstruction Finance Corporation and an outright grant of $29 million in work-relief funds from the PWA. They were vindicated when the first major section of the

Turnpike opened, in 1940. It was hugely successful, discrediting the pessimistic forecasts of the BPR. The Turnpike's chief engineer proudly boasted that "contrary to widely disseminated information by responsible public officials, the Turnpike is paying its own way and will be able to finance the eastern and western extensions from tolls charged." Even though truckers were asked to pay a $10 toll to travel the full length of the highway, they crowded onto the new road, since their operating costs were reduced by more than $27 over the same distance.[72]

Meanwhile, Connecticut had similar success with its Merritt Parkway, an express alternative to the traffic-clogged U.S. Route 1. Then, eyeing the revenue stream generated by the Merritt, Robert Moses retrofitted the Hutchinson River Parkway (which connected to the Merritt at the New York border) with tollbooths and used the toll receipts to finance additional parkway construction. By 1941 New York, Maryland, Massachusetts, Maine, Florida, and Illinois all were planning or studying major new turnpike projects.[73]

President Roosevelt stepped forward as a proponent of toll roads. In 1937, the same year that his New Deal agencies pushed the Pennsylvania Turnpike forward, FDR called for the construction of six federally sponsored nation-spanning toll roads, three running north–south and three running east–west. He summoned BPR's MacDonald to a meeting at the White House, during which MacDonald agreed to conduct a full-scale feasibility study, despite his personal opposition to toll roads as a matter of principle. The following year, Congress joined the fray and also directed MacDonald to compile a comprehensive report evaluating a nationwide system of toll roads.[74]

Advocates of toll-free roads reacted to this new trend with alarm, as did BPR highway engineers and many state highway officials who were often left out of the toll-road construction process, which was usually carried out by private consulting engineers retained by specially created turnpike "Author-ities" or "Commissions." Amid cries of "We must stop this epidemic now," the highway officials moved to protect their own centrality by vigorously challenging the shift away from the established paradigm (free roads, planned and administered by the bureaucracy created by the 1916 Act), and they engaged in a protracted debate that continued well into the postwar era, only to be resolved by the Interstate legislation of the mid-1950s. For example, Michigan State Highway Commissioner Charles M. Ziegler proclaimed that toll roads were "undemocratic" because they impinged on American freedom and hampered the free movement of citizens. He also offered the strangely illogical argument that if projections indicated there would be enough demand for a toll road to support a bond issue, then the road should be free.[75]

For his part, MacDonald shrewdly used the study mandated by Congress and FDR as an opportunity to produce a manifesto for a nationwide system of *free* highways. The resulting pamphlet, *Toll Roads and Free Roads*, was published in 1939. It concluded that the six toll roads proposed by the President could not collect sufficient toll revenues and would thus be a failure. Instead, the report (which was endorsed by many highway lobby groups, including the AASHO, the AAA, the American Trucking Association, and the National Association of Bus Operators) proposed a more comprehensive network of lower cost highways that would not have tolls and (in an important policy shift) would include links to the downtown of each of the country's major cities.[76]

MacDonald hoped that he could rebuild consensus within the ranks of highway boosters by bringing advocates of urban road building into the fold, much as he had co-opted long-distance advocates in 1921 by adding primary routes to the federal system. In addition, there were two other reasons for this new-found commitment to urban routes. First, the BPR engineers found that in order to make its proposed new network appear more viable than the six trans-national toll roads, their network of free highways would have to be easily accessible from the nation's center cities. The vast majority of vehicular traffic involved either an urban origin or an urban destination. Also, a quarter century of pro-rural and anti-urban funding mechanisms had produced a tangible imbalance that was beginning to affect highway policy debates: urban streets and highways were now worse off than their rural counterparts. Speaking for the AASHO, the head of the Ohio highway department proclaimed that "It is a well established fact that the major part of the cost of our highways outside of our municipalities is paid by people living in the urban areas," but the lack of adequate arteries in and out of the cities now presented an inconvenient bottleneck for motorists, a shortcoming that should be rectified using "general" highway funds. Second, inclusion of urban links was a politically prudent move by MacDonald, one that broadened the congressional support for the project and helped to secure the President's endorsement of the BPR plan (which FDR chose to view as a revision to his own 1937 proposal). In 1941 Roosevelt appointed the National Interregional Highways Committee to develop a more detailed blueprint for implementing the plan in *Toll Roads and Free Roads*, with the technical assistance of MacDonald's staff.[77]

Meanwhile, GM executives Alfred Sloan and Charles Wilson went straight to the public, producing one of the crowning achievements of the highway lobby. In the midst of the Depression, while the developed nations of the world were poised on the brink of World War II, General Motors spent a small fortune on its famous Futurama exhibit at the 1939 World's Fair in New York City. With a theme of "Building the World of Tomorrow," the fair was meant to tangibly and forcefully demonstrate that the bleak global circumstances could be followed by a wonderously prosperous and pleasant future. The fairgrounds were billed as a "working model of the future," full of hope and promise. GM's Futurama was one of the most successful exhibits, attracting an estimated 25 million visitors. Visitors rode in Epcot-style cars along a track around a 35,000-square-foot panoramic model, simulating a trip across GM's version of what America would look like in 1960. The centerpiece of this vision was a system of seven-lane superhighways with one hundred mile-per-hour speed limits. The panorama and the accompanying audio program script were designed, according to Walter Lippman, the well-known columnist of the *New York Herald-Tribune*, "to convince the American public that if it wishes to enjoy the full benefit of private enterprise in motor manufacturing, it will have to rebuild its cities and its highways with public enterprise." As visitors left Futurama, they were given a lapel pin that said "I have seen the future."

Besides Futurama, another important and popular exhibit at the 1939 World's Fair was Democracity, a scale model of a city of the future. The model, displayed within a two-hundred-foot-diameter globe called the Perisphere and viewed from the top of the Helicline, the world's longest escalator, depicted a metropolis of 1.5 million inhabitants, spread out over 11,000 square miles. None of the residents lived in the central city, Centerton, but instead commuted from suburban Pleasantvilles and Millvilles along highways. There was no mass transit. And, paradoxically, Democracity was described as pollution free.

An additional highlight of the 1939 Fair, besides the models of the future and demonstration projects showing off cutting-edge technological achievements, was the abundance of documentary films. Film, still in its formative stages as a mass media, was a novelty for many fairgoers and attracted a great deal of attention. Given the problems of the Depression and the future-oriented theme of the fair, many of the documentary films were designed to promote slum clearance, planned satellite towns, and decentralization. Among the films shown were *Housing Problems, Miracles of Modernization* (the Federal Housing Administration), *Housing in Our Times* (the United States Housing Administration), and *The Other Side of Town* (the Pittsburgh Housing Authority). However, the film that was seen by more fair visitors than all the others combined was titled, quite simply, *The City.* This movie was reviewed in newspapers nationwide, receiving widespread publicity and praise. Produced by a group that included many luminaries in the field of city planning, *The City* was funded by the Carnegie Corporation and directed by three highly acclaimed documentary filmmakers. The score was composed by Aaron Copland, the leading American composer of the era. And, last but not least, the well-known public intellectual and urban critic, Lewis Mumford, wrote the narrated commentary. The result was a superbly effective manifesto for anti-urban city planning, centered around an outright rejection of existing urbanization patterns in favor of new-construction suburban subdivisions in the garden-city tradition, beyond the limits of existing metropolitan areas, linked to other settlements by newly built highways.

Depression-era Americans, faced with low living standards and crowded cities, enthusiastically embraced the visions of the future presented in Futurama, Democracity, and *The City*. Millions of visitors left the fair spreading the highway-construction gospel, convinced that renewed and expanded public spending on highways would lead Americans to the rosy future depicted at the New York fairgrounds. This marketing effort, targeted at the American public, coincided with MacDonald's release of *Toll Roads and Free Roads* and FDR's subsequent creation of the Interregional Highways Committee, establishing a new mandate for federally funded road building.

Armed with this mandate, the BPR and the state highway departments began to map the new network of toll-free highways. Even after the United States entered the war, the surveying and planning efforts continued apace, under the rubric of identifying "strategic highways" with "defense importance." During this time, the proposed highway network was often referred to as the "military system." The Automobile Manufacturers Association periodically published tentative maps of the system in its serial, *Automobile Facts and Figures*, alternately referring to it as the "Interregional Highway System" or the "Strategic Defense Highway System," while the BPR published similar maps in *Public Roads*. By 1944 a thirty-thousand-mile network of these new highways had been planned and formally presented to Congress and the President in a report from the National Interregional Highways Committee. This report, *Interregional Highways*, formed the basis for the Federal-Aid Highway Act of 1944, which created the Interstate Highway System.[78]

The congressional hearings for the 1944 Act were a forum for the various highway boosters to present their arguments. However, the testimony submitted during the hearings revealed none of the growing disagreement among many of the road-building groups. Two years before, in 1942, a semiformalized group had convened in Detroit for private, invitation-only lunch meetings to discuss transportation planning and to formulate collective lobbying strategies.[79] To some extent, these meetings were successful, generating enough agreement for the 1944 Act to become law. But consensus crumbled again almost immediately thereafter. While all the participants agreed that they wanted more asphalt, they disagreed about who should pay for it and where it should be located. The testimony offered at the hearings in 1944 thus delineated only a bare-bones consensus, advocating more and better highways without any more taxes or fees. For example, the National Automobile Dealers Association made three basic suggestions:

> First, the deficiencies that have accumulated must be corrected; Second, programs already planned and deferred should be completed; and Third, additional projects actually needed should be implemented . . . within the limits of the income available for such work through Federal aid and the present rate of highway taxation, existing bonds, etc. . . . . We are very sure that highway users will very seriously resist any proposed increases in general highway taxation.[80]

Likewise, testimony jointly submitted by a consortium that included the AAA, the American Trucking Association, the National Grange, and the National Council of Private Motor Truck Owners, among others, supported additional construction but simultaneously opposed any new revenue-raising measures:

> The highway user taxes that already prevail are unnecessarily burdensome . . . [cars and trucks] are employed in competition with other modes of transportation which [gain] an unreasonable competitive advantage when the tax burden of highway users is made heavier . . . any talk of increased user taxes is manifestly ill-advised."[81]

There was scant reference during the hearings to the contentious underlying questions that were dividing the highway community.

When President Roosevelt forwarded *Interregional Highways* to Congress in 1944, his enclosed letter supported the newfound urban emphasis that had been implied in *Toll Roads and Free Roads* and was now explicitly built into the proposed new program. He noted "the special importance of those sections of the system located within and near our larger cities and metropolitan areas" and he pointed out that, in contrast to previous federal-aid highway programs, "over-all expenditures would be approximately evenly divided between urban and rural sections of the system."[82] In the main body of the report, the committee (which included Rexford Tugwell, the chair of the New York City Planning Commission, and Harland Bartholomew, a well-known city planner) urged first priority be given to routes into, through, and around big cities, because:

> It is within and in the vicinity of the cities and metropolitan areas that through travel now experiences its most serious resistance and delays. . . . Now, with congestion of transcity routes replacing rural highway mud as the greatest of traffic barriers, emphasis needs to be reversed and the larger expenditure devoted to improvement of the city and metropolitan sections of arterial routes.[83]

However, FDR and the majority of the MacDonald-led committee supported these urban segments only out of political expediency, not because of a new commitment to genuinely aiding urban transportation.

For Roosevelt, not only did the urban extensions ensure broader political support for the initiative, but they also fit into his plan for new urban work projects to offset anticipated postwar unemployment in the cities. In this instance, as during the prewar New Deal, FDR's main objective was the actual *construction* of public works as economic stimuli, not as ends in themselves. In his message to Congress, he specifically urged Congress to approve the highway initiative "to utilize productively some of the manpower and industrial capacity," which would become available when the war ended. It only made sense to have the largest portion of the projects close to the biggest population centers of the nation.[84]

Highway engineers' rendering of new highways bypassing cities,
with an urban extension, 1938, *Colorado Historical Society*

On the other hand, MacDonald's commitment to the urban extensions was born from a different sort of political expediency. He needed the city-related traffic to justify the ambitious scope of the proposed *free*way network and almost admitted so in the body of the report: "The cities and metropolitan areas of the country are known to include the sources and destinations of much of the great part of the heavy flow of traffic that moves over the nation's highways." In another section of the report, MacDonald acknowledged with surprising candor that the urban components of the system were not designed to alleviate urban congestion, except to the extent that they would provide relief to those motorists for whom the city was an inconvenient obstruction.[85] There continued to be no apparent support, from any quarter, for funding transportation initiatives that would facilitate travel *within* cities. The inclusion of cities into the network that would soon

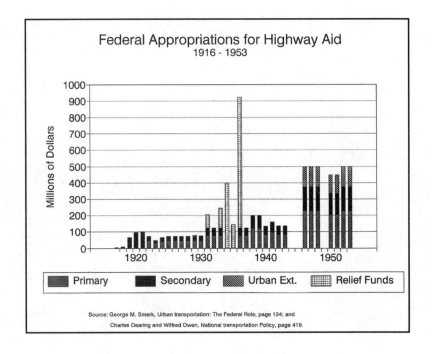

Federal Appropriations for Highway Aid
1916 - 1953

Source: George M. Smerk, Urban transportation: The Federal Role, page 134; and
Charles Dearing and Wilfred Owen, National transportation Policy, page 419.

become the Interstate System was derived from a planning paradigm oriented solely toward making it easier to get into and out of cities.

Even the commitment to urban extensions was soon undermined in Congress. Subtle changes to the proposed legislation were affected by the same rural predispositions in the legislature that had facilitated the anti-urban slant of the earlier highway programs.[86] While the 1944 Act officially created a forty-thousand-mile highway network that promised to connect all of the nation's major cities and metropolitan areas, the details of the funding and implementation provisions indicated that the urban emphasis had been all but eradicated.

The Federal-Aid Highway Act of 1944 provided for $1.5 billion in road-building funds over the first three postwar years. Almost half the money, $225 million per year, was dedicated to primary routes. About a third, $150 million per year, went to secondary routes, farm-to-market feeder roads, RFD routes, and rural school bus routes. The smallest allocation, $125

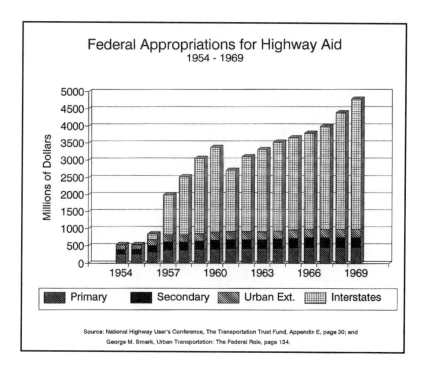

Federal Appropriations for Highway Aid
1954 - 1969

Legend: Primary | Secondary | Urban Ext. | Interstates

Source: National Highway User's Conference, The Transportation Trust Fund, Appendix E, page 30; and
George M. Smerk, Urban Transportation: The Federal Role, page 134.

million each year, was allotted to urban extensions. This ratio (45 percent for primary, 30 percent for secondary, and 25 percent for urban extensions) indicated that urban highways were ranked as a third-of-three priority, a precedent that governed highway aid distributions for the next three decades. Furthermore, ordinary urban streets were still not eligible for any federal aid whatsoever, even though they too functioned as feeder roads, postal delivery routes, and school bus routes.[87] Even though Congress did include urban highways in the federal system for the first time, it accorded them third-class status and severely limited the roster of eligible urban routes.

As in the past, Congress built in numerous other anti-urban provisions into the Act. While construction costs could be matched on a dollar-for-dollar basis, the Act stipulated that there were a few exceptions to this ratio, each of which had the effect of penalizing urbanized areas or benefiting rural projects. For example, right-of-way acquisition costs, which were higher for urban projects than for suburban or rural projects, required two dollars of local funds for each federal dollar. This made urban projects a less-efficient use of state funds than other projects. On the other hand, grade-crossing eliminations, the vast majority of which were not in cities, were allowed higher than usual matching ratios, covering construction costs entirely and half of right-of-way costs.[88] Furthermore, following the practice established in 1916, the primary and secondary aid was allocated to the states according to formulae that benefited rural states and penalized urbanized states.

This anti-city funding bias was compounded by the extremely broad definition of "urban" used by the BPR and by the replication in most state governments of the same structural pro-rural predilections as in Congress. The BPR classified any settlement of five thousand people or more as "urban," which meant that the largest cities in the nation had to compete with relatively tiny towns for "urban" funds controlled by the state governments that had historically devoted a mere 5 percent of state-collected auto user-fees to city streets.[89] As a result, only a tiny portion of the newly created "urban" component of the federal-aid program went to projects in major metropolitan areas. This misappropriation of the "urban" moniker for a program that would barely have an effect on the nation's largest cities did not go unnoticed. One study cautiously warned of this divergence of substance from rhetoric:

> Urban areas are in a position to benefit more substantially in this program than they have in the past, although traditional distribution patterns in some states may continue to deprive many major metropolitan areas of their share.[90]

Not surprisingly, city streets continued to fall behind the rest of the country's transportation network. A report on "State-City Relations in Highway Affairs" published by Yale University in 1950 started with the initial observation that "city street systems had become totally inadequate. As a result, all larger cities today are plagued by a near paralysis of traffic."[91]

So, the United States entered the postwar era in the midst of an increasingly divisive debate about transportation policy. There was growing disagreement about what kinds of roads should be built, where, and with whose money. Even while the policy debate continued and as soon as the war ended, the states renewed their rush to build toll roads—either unable to stave off pressure to build more highways or unwilling to wait for the new national system to come to fruition.

The success of the Pennsylvania Turnpike had discredited the draconian traffic forecasts assembled by the anti-tollroad engineers at the BPR, and a dizzying flurry of new similar highway projects ensued. Maine built a state turnpike, Robert Moses added the toll-financed Saw Mill Parkway to his famous network of Westchester County parkways, New Hampshire announced plans for a turnpike that would connect to the Maine pike, and Oklahoma started work on the Turner Turnpike between Oklahoma City and Tulsa. Pennsylvania soon built two extensions to its Turnpike, and New York started a 535-mile toll-financed Thruway system stretching from New York City to Buffalo, via Albany. Ohio, North Carolina, Indiana, Colorado, and Texas began work on their own toll roads, as did Kentucky, Connecticut, and Massachusetts. New Jersey began its mammoth Turnpike project, as well as the toll-financed Garden State Parkway. In addition, there were new smaller, privately operated toll roads, like the Equinox Drive in Vermont, the Mount Washington road in New Hampshire, and the Medina Lake road in Texas. Within a few years there were thousands of miles of toll roads in use across the United States.[92]

Money to build most of these new highways was raised by the sale of tax-exempt bonds backed by anticipated toll revenues: The constrained realities of highway politics had left no other alternatives. For example, while sections of the New Jersey Turnpike cost as much as $8 million per mile, the state highway department had only $30 million available each year for new construction of primary routes. A state official summed up the scenario: "Increasing the tax structure, as it relates to gasoline, registration fees and excise taxes to the point necessary to finance needed construction is not feasible. Moderate increases have been tried in several instances and, in general, have been defeated."[93] The Turnpike Authority then had to borrow

$225 million by selling long-term debt backed by tolls, as did other states building new turnpikes.[94] More and more turnpikes reported revenues in excess of projections, so market enthusiasm for similar bonds grew. As a result, each year between 1947 and 1954, more toll-road bonds were issued, and by 1954 there were over $4 billion such securities outstanding.[95]

The rapid toll-road construction prompted the three major auto manufacturers to join with the oil industry, the AAA, and the trucking industry to start Project Adequate Roads (PAR), a redoubled effort to push "free" highways through a coordinated nationwide lobbying campaign. PAR brought together more than forty national associations and was headquartered in Washington at the National Press Building, in the offices of Alfred Sloan's NHUC. As a part of its marketing and publicity initiatives, the group organized gala events across the country. For example, in 1952 more than five hundred executives from business and industry attended a gathering in Philadelphia sponsored by PAR and underwritten by the Greater Philadelphia Chamber of Commerce and the National Council of Private Motor Truck Owners. The main speaker, a top executive of Goodyear Tire and Rubber, spoke to the assemblage about the supposed links between free roads and American liberty, symbolized by the nearby Liberty Bell.[96]

From the start, PAR reiterated the long-standing opposition to *any* increased gas taxes, while also denouncing the new trend toward toll roads. In connection with this, the AAA passed a widely publicized resolution supporting new and expanded highway programs with no new user fees. Likewise, the Petroleum Industries Committee complained that the motorist had been made into a "whipping boy, and he'll keep on being one until the country's seventy million licensed drivers stand up and declare that they won't take any more tax punishment."[97] For its part, the NHUC continued its longtime practice of complaining about what it called "indirect diversion" of user fees to "street cleaning, highway lighting, construction and maintenance of sidewalks . . . and other marginal uses." Despite the obvious connections between these expenditures and highways, the NHUC claimed that "Highway users regard this as unfair and discriminatory . . . they do not feel that they should be singled out as a class for special taxation for general purposes."[98] They also tried to claim new revenue streams as "highway revenues" that should be protected from diversion. In Tennessee, for example, a study commissioned by the NHUC suggested that inspection fees for the transportation of kerosene, heating oil, gasoline, and other combustibles, currently classified as revenues supporting public safety, should be reclassified as highway revenues and expended solely on constructing new highways. The same report also complained that highway revenues were funding half of the state highway patrol's budget and offered the questionable argument that the highway patrol "performs a general protective function not closely related to highway traffic, and should, therefore, be financed out of general revenues."[99]

Meanwhile, public sector highway officials were also pushing hard to obtain increased funding for toll-free roads. Echoing the PAR rhetoric, Hal Hale, the executive secretary of the AASHO, proclaimed that road building had a special importance to Americans. Speaking at a conference on "Highways of the Future," he pointed out that one of every seven jobs in the United States was linked to the automobile industry (including construction, operation, maintenance, and design of both roads and motor vehicles) and then continued:

> True, there might be other industries of comparable nature but, certainly, these exist by virtue of the presence of the roads which we have built in this country. Therefore, I submit to you that the highway program in the United States is a basic element of our national economy. As such, it is not subject to the customary conception of public works.

Hale went on to bemoan the near-crisis status of the nation's highways, as indicated by pseudoscientific "sufficiency ratings" from the BPR and many state highway departments, and concluded with a call for new federal highway legislation: "Certainly, the program made possible by the Federal Highway Act of 1944 does not begin to meet that need. . . . Obviously much money is required and the only possible source is taxation."[100]

Not surprisingly, this final suggestion of Hale's—that an expanded highway program should be funded by *increased* gas taxes—did not meet with agreement from all quarters. While there were many groups willing to make liberal use of a shared rhetoric of crisis, talking of "dangerous backlogs" and an urgent need to "catch-up," there was equally widespread disagreement about how to pay for crisis-resolution measures.[101]

PAR's inflexible insistence that new highway funds come *entirely* from general revenues was considered by many to be unrealistic and ultimately proved to be the project's undoing. Furthermore, AASHO members preferred a federal gas tax over state levies, since they counted on a strong federal program to maintain their own centrality, while PAR viewed federal taxes as the most objectionable, since they were not—as state gas taxes had been since the Hayden-Cartwright Act—constitutionally protected from diversion "for the support of foreign nations, housing and development, and diversified other federal objectives and expenditures which have no connection with highways."[102]

BPR Commissioner MacDonald finally severed the public-private lob-bying partnership when he joined the AASHO in calling for additional gas taxes and therefore opposed Project Adequate Roads. In "The Gasoline Tax in Relation to Automobile Operation and Highway Costs," an article published in *Public Roads*, the official agency publication, BPR officials argued that motorists were undertaxed and that gas-tax rates had not kept up with inflation.[103]

The lack of support from the AASHO and the BPR handicapped PAR but it was the AAA that delivered the crippling blow when it withdrew support in 1953. Again, this disagreement revolved around gas-tax policy. In this case, the AAA was protesting the group's support of additional tax relief for truckers, whom the AAA believed were already undertaxed by state gas taxes. By 1954 PAR collapsed entirely, and its members became embroiled in the loud and rancorous public debate over how to finance highways and where to build them.

In the absence of an effectively unified lobbying effort, the ambitious highway network established by the 1944 Act received virtually no federal funding. Three times during the Truman administration, Congress enacted highway legislation that gave the new Interstate network a token $25 million annual allocation. Meanwhile, congressional attempts to rectify the anti-urban funding bias by increasing the population-oriented component of the allocation formulas were regularly defeated in the Senate, where rural states had as much vote as more populous states. To make matters worse, the 1952 rollover legislation actually curtailed the ability of urban projects to qualify for federal aid.[104]

In these circumstances, just as before World War II, the states responded by borrowing for streets, roads, and highways. Between 1952 and 1955, the total amount of such debt exploded, from $5.8 billion in 1952 (already a substantial sum) to $10.1 billion by the end of 1955. Unfortunately, this practice solved financing problems only in the short term and actually exacerbated the long-term imbalance by mortgaging future highway revenues, even though it was clear to contemporary observers that demand for highway construction would continue to escalate for many years to come.[105]

The fault lines within the highway-boosting community now extended in all directions. The bitter divisions over financing methods (gas taxes vs. tolls vs. general revenues vs. borrowing) meant there was not enough support for any one method to prevail, so there were not sufficient funds to quell the incessant jostling between advocates of rural roads, primary highways, and interstate highways. Groups that had been united under Logan Page and Thomas MacDonald in a common quest to secure government subsidies for roads were now pitted against each other. Everybody seemed to want something different: truckers, farmers, oil companies, state officials, urban officials, developers, road-building contractors, commuters, and auto manufacturers. BPR commissioner Mac-Donald, whose trademark had been his ability to forge consensus among the disparate highway boosters, resigned.

Incoming President Dwight D. Eisenhower, who had requested
MacDonald's resignation, reconstructed the prewar public-private highway lobbying partnership, starting from the top. As MacDonald's replacement, Eisenhower appointed Francis Dupont, a man who had grown up
in the twin worlds of automobile manufacturing and highway building.
He had run the Delaware highway department, and his family owned a
substantial portion of General Motors. In 1924 his father, T. Coleman
Dupont, had given Delaware a ninety-seven-mile multilane paved road that
spanned the state from Wilmington to Dover (he had built it in 1912, with
$4 million from his personal fortune).[106] So, when Francis Dupont joined
the Eisenhower Administration, he became yet another vital link between
the White House and Detroit. Already, Ike had appointed Charles E.
Wilson (Alfred Sloan's protégé and the GM executive who uttered the
famous quote at the beginning of this chapter) as Secretary of Defense.
Later, another GM board member, Lucius Clay, was put in charge of the
President's Committee on highway policy.[107] With these close ties with the
auto industry, the White House was ready to break the logjam of
disagreement and launch what would be the largest public works project
ever undertaken by the United States.

The auto industry had resumed its explosive growth after the war,
becoming a political juggernaut. There were 64,000 car dealers in the United
States, more than 200,000 gas stations, 10,000 commercial parking lots or
garages, 5,000 car rental agencies, and about 3,000 car washes. Millions of
jobs were directly tied to automobiles, including over two million jobs in
sales or service of cars and trucks, 650,000 autoworkers, 340,000 oil
company employees, nearly 500,000 highway workers, and millions more
that drove their own trucks or worked for trucking companies. The United
States had about 6 percent of the world's population, and two-thirds of the
world's automobiles. Yet, at the same time, the automobile had not yet
become entirely ubiquitous. While Charles Wilson's congressional testimony
aptly summarized the convergence of the national interest with the auto
interests, there was still substantial room for growth. Over one-quarter of

American families did not own a car and 60 percent of women did not have driver's licenses.[108]

In 1954, as a core component of his domestic agenda, President Eisenhower made a commitment to resolve the differences among highway groups and gather broad support for the 1944 Act's 42,000-mile National System of Defense and Interstate Highways, which now carried a price tag of $26 billion. Highway boosters from all quarters hailed the President's commitment, hoping that leadership from the White House could forge a new consensus on how to finance highway expansion. Their hopes were well founded, and after two years of hard-fought political wrangling, Congress passed the Federal-Aid Highway Act of 1956, a landmark enactment that turned the 1944 Act's highway network from a theoretical plan into a steel-and-concrete reality, facilitating the continued suburbanization and decon-centration of America.[109]

The Highway Act of 1956 simultaneously preserved the status quo, established new precedents and boosted highway funding by a quantum leap. On the one hand, the primary, secondary, and urban aid programs were allotted money by the same formulae and in the same relative proportions as always, at a moderately increased level. On the other hand, the allotment to the new *toll-free* Interstate system was greater than for the other three categories put together, starting at $1 billion per year and climbing to over $2 billion by the third year. The old programs maintained their 1:1 matching grants, while the Interstates benefited from a new 9:1 ratio.[110]

At the heart of the legislation was the new Highway Trust Fund, which simultaneously satisfied the demands of the two biggest components of the highway lobby, the public employees of AASHO and the private corporate interests behind the NHUC. Even though the expensive new aid program was funded by an assortment of new federally levied user fees, the NHUC was satisfied because the Trust Fund formally protected this revenue from "diversion" or other undesirable congressional meddling, ensuring that it would be spent solely on highway construction. Furthermore, the new program would be administered in parallel to the existing federal-aid program, as it had been formulated in 1916, under the direction of the purportedly apolitical experts at the BPR and the state highway departments. Thus, the AASHO and the BPR were reinstalled at the hub of the nation's highway-building program as the mandated gatekeepers and overseers for the billions of new highway dollars authorized by the Act, as the bureaucrats that would control the planning and execution of this enormous new undertaking. The NHUC and its members (including the AAA) finally won the same special legal protection for federal gas taxes that they had previously garnered for state user fees. Also, the prohibition against toll roads continued, despite an obvious willingness on the part of many motorists to pay tolls, when necessary.

It is important to note that most of the subsidies to automobility that had been built into the prewar highway aid legislation were renewed by the 1956 Act but now involved even greater sums of money. Perhaps most importantly, the apportionment formulae among the states were not substantially changed, nor were the anti-urban/pro-rural definitions of eligible projects. The wealth-transfer effect of these provisions was actually increased. The newly increased user fees, which would raise billions of dollars each year, would be disproportionately collected in cities and disproportionately spent outside of cities.[111] For example, the funding adjustment for states with publicly owned land allowed the matching ratio to be increased from 9:1 to 19:1 for states with large tracts of federal land. In effect, this meant that many western states benefited from a ratio that was more than twice as favorable as the one applicable to more urbanized eastern states.

In a reprise of the 1939–1944 debate over *Toll Roads and Free Roads*, the Eisenhower Administration obtained congressional support from urban delegations by paying generous lip service to the urban segments of the new Interstate System.[112] However, just as had been the case in 1944, these urban segments were designed to make it easier to get in or out of cities, with little regard for easing transportation *within* cities. In fact, while the BPR engineers claimed that half of all Interstate funds would be spent in "urban areas," this was grossly misleading, since these were mainly suburban segments that fell under the BPR's anachronistic definition of urban as any area with a population of 5,000 or more. In effect, the lavish new Interstate Highway grants would make it easier for Americans to get from their homes to an urban workplace, marketplace, or cultural attraction, but only if they lived outside of the city and owned a car. Likewise, the transportation of raw materials and manufactured goods between rural and suburban locations would be subsidized by this new program, but the movement of the same items between urban sites would not.

Even though the Interstate Highway program created new sources of highway revenues and handed out these funds to the states on an unprecedented scale, it also had the paradoxical effect of hobbling the states' ability to satisfy motorists' demands. In the first year after the 1956 Act went into effect, the aggregate matching requirement for all the states was $954 million, 30 percent higher than for the previous year. Some individual states faced an even higher increase. Vermont, for example, needed to double its entire highway budget to match the available federal grants.[113] However, despite the continuing clamor for more road building, the NHUC and its members maintained their overpowering opposition to increases in state user fees, causing severe budgetary problems. In Indiana, efforts to raise the gas tax had been defeated since 1929, despite demand for dual-lane roads in the 1940s and limited-access four-lane roads in the 1950s. As a result, the state was unable to match all of its federal-aid grants after the Interstate legislation and ultimately was forced to forfeit some of its federal-aid allotment.[114]

At statehouses all across the country, this type of budgetary crisis was not uncommon. Indiana's state gas tax, which couldn't generate enough revenue to match federal aid, was only slightly lower at 4 cents per gallon than the national average of 4.8 cents per gallon.[115] The states had no choice but to borrow more or to increase their gas taxes, or risk losing their federal aid. Effectively, this meant that the states could not afford to fund any projects that were not eligible for matching grants. As seen from the state capitol, projects with Washington's blessing cost one-tenth as much as projects that were not on the official Interstate map. Likewise, country roads eligible for aid as part of the secondary program cost half as much as their urban counterparts. Furthermore, it turned out that the Interstates dominated the budgets of state highway departments in other ways, too. Some of the expenses related to the Interstates were not fully eligible for aid payments, so the states' share often turned out (in retrospect) to be about one-seventh (14 percent), not the projected one-tenth. Also, the states were obligated to give first priority to improving the primary and secondary routes that served as feeders and access roads to the Interstates.[116] In effect, the states could scarcely afford to support any highway projects beyond the Interstates, leaving responsibility for funding all of the remaining roads and streets in the hands of local authorities, who were usually not authorized to collect *any* user fees. Instead, these other needs had to be funded exclusively out of general revenues.

CONCLUSION

The Interstate Highway legislation was the latest in a succession of laws that established and perpetuated a skewed American system of highway finance. Generally considered one of the signtaure accomplishments of the Eisenhower Administration, the Act went a long way to closing any remaining gap between what was good for General Motors and what was good for the country. But, as much as it was the beginning of a new era of automobility for the United States, it was also the culmination of a process that had begun with the creation of the LAW more than half a century before. It followed precedents set in previous legislation, some of which dated back to the late nineteenth century, and all of which were shaped under the influence of Good Roads rhetoric and lobbyists connected to the automobile industry. Over time, these measures established, and then institutionalized, two related subsidy patterns. First, they undercharged motorists by a wide margin, penalizing the nonmotoring majority while simultaneously inducing more and more Americans to adopt the automobile as the preferred mode of transport. In contrast, other developed nations in the world chose to impose user charges far in excess of road expenditures. A study of fourteen industrialized European nations found that, on average, user fees were nearly three times the amount of direct highway costs, while in the United States they were only about half.[117] Second, American highway legislation consistently favored construction in unpopulated areas while impeding investments in urban transportation networks.

These measures provided powerful incentives by themselves, but they were also augmented by other complementary government programs, particularly the income tax code and federal housing policies. As Kenneth T. Jackson showed in *Crabgrass Frontier: The Suburbanization of the United States*, federal banking and housing regulations sanctioned and subsidized suburban investments while obstructing the flow of capital into urban areas. The deductibility of mortgage interest was certainly a major component of this policy, but there were also other related incentives built into the income tax code as well. For example, the sales tax on automobiles (which was invariably dedicated to state highway programs) was tax deductible. Likewise, employers could deduct the (often substantial) costs of providing free parking for workers, a benefit that was not taxable for the recipients.[118] Company cars were similarly privileged. In contrast, any reimbursement for commuting by mass transit was fully taxable. More arcane tax provisions like the Investment Tax Credit, and Accelerated Depreciation also favored corporate investments in new, unbuilt locations, instead of reinvesting at existing urban locations.

As marginal tax rates rose during the postwar era, the power of these inducements grew, even as the Interstate Highway legislation sent automobility incentives to new highs. Taken together, these decentralizing forces became virtually irresistible, pushing and pulling at the fabric of American communities everywhere. Cities and towns in all regions of the nation, of all shapes and sizes, were affected as resources were persistently directed to the periphery, away from downtowns and town centers.

Denver Meets the Automobile

BACKGROUND

At the end of the nineteenth century, Denver was an important regional center. It had grown from a mining town of less than five thousand residents in 1870 to a railroad hub with more than thirty-five thousand inhabitants in 1880, making it the largest settlement between Kansas City and the West Coast. Nine different railroads served the city, with lines extending eastward to Chicago, southward to Texas and New Mexico, and westward to the Pacific. Over the next decade Denver's population tripled, surpassing one hundred thousand by 1890.[1]

Boosters and local politicians knew that Denver's success would be short-lived if they failed to invest in the future. The cycle of boom and bust was all too familiar in nineteenth-century America, as Denver experienced firsthand when President Grover Cleveland repealed the Sherman Silver Purchase Act in 1893. In the resulting Silver Crash, 400 nearby mines closed, twelve local banks went under, and 50,000 Denver-area workers were unemployed.[2] Even though the Cripple Creek gold rush revived the local economy soon afterward, civic leaders of the 1890s recognized that the city's long-term viability was fragile and thus undertook a deliberate civic improvement effort, starting with a paving and bridge-building initiative, so that

Denver could retain its dominant role in the region. Farther east, Chicago had surpassed St. Louis as the unofficial capital of middle America, a scenario that Denverites did not wish to be repeated in the West.

The Denver city council dispatched a special delegation to visit more than a dozen larger eastern cities to study ways that Denver could remain competitive. After the committee issued its report, *Public Improvements: Report of the Special Committee on Public Improvements,* the city council began paving downtown streets. Over the next decade, as the economy recovered, the target area was expanded, until more than twenty miles were paved. Similarly, by the opening years of the twentieth century, new bridges and viaducts spanned the city's main train tracks and the two waterways that flowed through Denver, Cherry Creek and the South Platte River. Without these new links, the rivers and rail yards would have confined the city and impeded local transportation and communication. These projects were financed by a mixture of property taxes, bond issues, and railroad levies.[3]

At the time, the bicycle was a common form of private transportation, and automobiles were still rare. The first car in Denver arrived in 1899 by mail, an unassembled Columbia Electric. That same year, the Annual Cycle Show featured one vendor of electric autos, the American Electric Vehicle Company of Chicago. In contrast, more than 25,000 of the city's 133,859 residents were members of a local bicyclists' organization, the Denver Wheelmen.[4] Bicyclists convened a Good Roads Convention in October 1900, rallying for state and federal funding for roads and urging the State to expand its use of penal labor for highway construction, which had been tried experimentally the year before on a "state wagon road" from Pueblo to Leadville.[5]

While the initial impetus for good roads in Colorado came from the Denver Wheelmen, automobile owners quickly made their presence known. By 1902, even though there were still only two hundred automobiles in the city, Denver had already experienced its first reported auto theft, its first lawsuit arising from an auto accident (seeking $2,000 in damages), and its first auto show. City officials passed a registration law, as well as a speed limit

(8 mph downtown, 15 mph elsewhere). The Denver motorists formed the Colorado Automobile Club and joined the Wheelmen's crusade for good roads as a full co-sponsor of the 1905 State Good Roads Meeting.[6] Denver's "Automobile Age" had begun.

ROBERT SPEER'S DENVER, 1904–1912

Modern Denver was created in 1904, after the state constitution was amended to permit home rule. Denver voters adopted a new charter, creating the consolidated City and County of Denver. Previously, the city overlapped a handful of counties, and its government was dominated by two committees appointed by the governor: the Board of Public Works and the Fire and Police Board. Robert W. Speer, the leader of the local Democratic machine and former president of the Board of Public Works was elected the first mayor of the new city government. Speer's importance in party politics, and his city's status as an emerging metropolitan center led the Democratic Party to choose Denver to host the 1908 nominating convention. Likewise, the city's national profile rose when the federal government announced plans to build a new mint facility in Denver in 1906, second only to the main mint in Philadelphia. Under Speer's leadership, Denver was changing from an Old West mining town into a city of national importance. This change was captured by the *Denver Post* in a special supplement distributed to delegates and other conventioneers attending the Democratic Convention, when the editors defensively joked that "We can read, lots of us, and we don't know a woman in Denver who carries more than one revolver when she comes downtown shopping."

Mayor Speer dominated the Denver political scene for a decade and therefore oversaw the city's early attempts to accommodate automobile transportation. His rise to power had been fueled by patronage jobs related to public works, so as mayor he relied on a steady program of civic improvement to sustain his political machine. He championed a City Beautiful movement, and during his tenure in city hall he oversaw construc-

Mayor Robert W. Speer, 1904,
Denver Public Library, Western History Collection

tion of parks, museums, a zoo, and a new civic center. He paved and widened streets, buried downtown power lines, and distributed over 115,000 shade trees throughout the city.[7]

In a flamboyant and popular move, Speer *gave* the shade trees, for free, to any Denver citizen willing to take responsibility for planting and maintaining them, with a limit of three trees apiece. Since Denver's image suffered from a well-deserved reputation as a treeless town, Denverites were pleased to plant "Mayor Speer's trees" along the street in front of their homes and businesses.[8]

The two biggest components of Mayor Speer's public works initiative were the new civic center and a citywide network of parks and parkways. While the civic center was promptly completed and emerged as a lasting legacy of Speer's tenure, progress on his parkway system was uneven. In 1907

Speer retained landscape architect George Kessler to draft detailed plans for this initiative. Kessler had been trained at the Olmsted firm and had worked on parks systems for Kansas City, Dallas, Memphis, Indianapolis, Cleveland, Syracuse, and Salt Lake City. His plans were based on a Denver Art Commission report, written by Charles Mulford Robinson for an unsuccessful 1906 referendum on a City Beautiful plan to revamp the entire city. Even with Speer's support, Kessler's imprimatur, and the backing of the *Denver Post*, voters rejected the far-reaching plan again in 1910. The mayor resorted to a piecemeal approach, pushing through a few components of the plan and leaving most of the parkway network on paper.

By the time Speer was temporarily forced out of office by a reform movement in 1912 (he was returned to office the following year under a new "strong mayor" charter, after the collapse of the commission-type reform government that had ousted him) only twelve miles of new parkway had been finished, mainly on Marion and Downing Streets, and along the banks of Cherry Creek. The latter, completed in 1910, had become one of Speer's best-known projects. Prior to his reclamation effort, Cherry Creek had been lined by shanties, dumps, and industrial remnants. The city spent nearly a million dollars reconstructing the creek walls, installing new landscaping, and building a modern roadway now known as Speer Boulevard. At the time, there was considerable public outcry surrounding the new drive, since Speer and his "associates" reportedly had owned land adjacent to the improved tracts. Over the next fifty years, similar political considerations occasionally motivated the completion of additional fragments of Kessler's parkways. By 1965, after numerous revisions and extensions to the city's parkway plans, there were about fifty miles completed; as testament to the machine-oriented roots of the system, there were twenty-one segments less than a mile in length. With a few exceptions, the Denver Parkways turned out to be a system of patronage delivery and sporadic neighborhood beautification, not a transportation network.[9]

During Speer's tenure, the city developed auto "camps" (camping areas designed for motorists, a precursor to RV parks) in public parks throughout

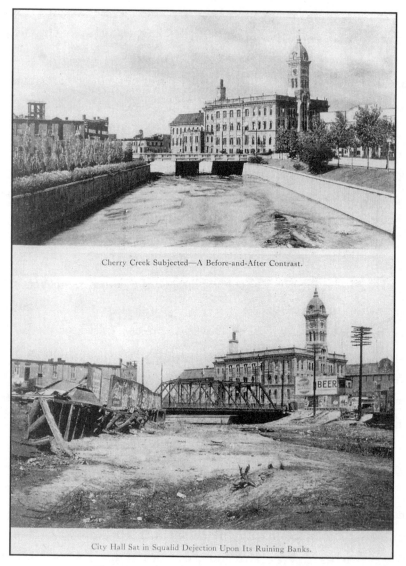

Cherry Creek Subjected—A Before-and-After Contrast.

City Hall Sat in Squalid Dejection Upon Its Ruining Banks.

Cherry Creek, before and after renovation,
Colorado Historical Society

the city. The largest of these, in City Park, had four hundred lots with free services for camping motorists, including running water, mail delivery, an adjoining golf course, and daily concert performances by the municipal band. During the summer, at least three hundred carloads of people camped out every night. Intended to encourage motor-tourists to make Denver a prime stopping-off point in their travels, the autocamps amounted to an outright subsidy for motorists, paid for directly out of city coffers.[10]

One of the legacies of Speer's improvement projects was an increase in the city's debt burden. After a decade of Speer rule, the total value of municipal debt had ballooned six-fold.[11] These loans were almost entirely supported by general revenues and supplemental property-tax assessments. To partially defray these costs, Speer levied annual license fees for all cars, trucks, and horse-drawn vehicles.

But, the state of Colorado soon prohibited the city from charging motorists such fees, as the auto lobby began to flex its growing political muscles. There were only four thousand automobiles registered in Denver in 1910, compared to a population of well over two hundred thousand. Nevertheless, motorists' ranks were growing rapidly, as was the economic strength of the automobile industry, a fact that became more immediately apparent to local politicians when Ford opened a production plant in Denver during 1913.[12] The swelling political clout of automobility fans was manifest over the ensuing decades, as the state's highway policies took shape.

COLORADO AUTOMOBILITY POLICY, 1909–1945

The Denver Good Roads Convention in 1900 and the Colorado Good Roads Meeting in 1905 had pushed hard for state-funded highway construction. Finally, in 1909, the legislature created a State Highway Commission to administer highway grants-in-aid. The initial budget allocation was small but was soon supplemented by distributions from the Internal Improvements account, funded by a 5 percent impost on all government land sales. In 1913, after a $10 million highway bond was rejected by referendum, the State Highway Department (which replaced the Commission) began to collect a registration fee to partially cover the costs of processing registrations, distributing plates, and administering the state-aid program. The fee ranged from $2.50 to $10, depending on the horsepower rating of the vehicle in question. Concerned that Colorado was moving toward a user-fee funded system, the AAA and Good Roads groups obtained legislation in the following session (1914) that imposed a statewide property tax for highway construction and a prohibition against locally levied user fees. This established a precedent that increased user fees should go hand-in-hand with increased general revenue commitments, a combination that was repeated in 1919 when the property tax levy was boosted and a one cent per gallon state gas tax was instituted to match federal-aid grants.[13]

This period was marked by repeated battles over highway finance. On the one hand was pressure for stepped-up construction and the need to match federal grants. On the other hand was resistance to each and every attempt to raise revenues through user fees. As a result, the state repeatedly went into debt to raise highway money, although even this strategy caused disagreement. In 1916 the Colorado Auto Club proposed a large bond issue to fund a north–south highway. The measure was defeated because it would have been repaid entirely from statewide property taxes and yet did not seem to provide benefits to Coloradans that lived far from the proposed route.

The highway boosters were not easily discouraged and returned in 1919 with a bigger bond proposal, this time for unspecified projects. Calling themselves a "committee of boosters," they secured the governor's approval of a scheme that would divert revenues from the state inheritance tax into the highway fund to repay the bonds. This measure failed, but many more modest bond issues passed in the following years, including a $5 million loan in 1920 and one for $6 million in 1922. More than three-quarters of these borrowings were used to match federal-aid grants. Throughout the 1920s, the state and counties spent in excess of $10 million each year on new highway construction. Soon, three-quarters of the state's outstanding debt was for highways and about a third of the state's annual budget went to the Highway Department.[14]

By 1925, more than a quarter million motor vehicles were registered in Colorado, a formidable political base for the AAA to draw on in its campaign to boost services for motorists while holding down user fees. For example, when the legislature was considering raising the state gas tax to four cents per gallon, the auto club arranged for newspaper stories with headlines like "Prevention of Heavier Taxes is Chief Problem of Autoists: Serious Handicap Threatens Owners of Cars—Motorist Carrying All the Burden He Can Stand." These efforts were successful and the increase was fought off until 1927, and even then the new levy was only three cents per gallon, not the sought-after four.[15]

However, the rhetoric describing overtaxed motorists did not correspond to the actual situation. Up until 1936, Colorado drivers were charged only fifty cents for a lifelong drivers' license. When this fee increased, it only went up to one dollar. Likewise, even after the gas tax was finally raised to four cents per gallon in 1935, the average motorist paid a total of only $25.50 in user fees over an entire year (including the gas tax on an average year's consumption), or seven cents per day. According to contemporary newspaper reports, one of the most-evaded taxes in Colorado was the personal property tax on cars. At the same time, all the major highways in the state were continually monitored by the Colorado Highway Courtesy Patrol to assist stranded motorists free of charge, and thousands of miles of mountain highways were "kept free of snow in winter months, an enormous burden to the state."[16]

In addition to battles over fee increases and the use of general revenues to benefit motorists, there was also bitter disagreement over how road funds would be distributed within the state. In 1921 Denver sued the state to block a bond issue approved by voters the previous fall. Denverites were furious that none of the funds would be allocated to projects within Denver. In response, rural coalitions threatened a boycott of Denver goods and trade. Of course, since the main purpose of the bond issue was to match federal grants, which explicitly excluded cities, the suit was not winnable and was soon dropped.

The issue remained unresolved. According to the formula used to distribute state gas-tax revenues, after debt service, 70 percent was reserved for state highways, 27 percent for county highways, and a mere 3 percent for routes within cities and towns.[17] This unbalanced allocation persisted in Colorado for many decades, despite repeated complaints. For example, a report by the University of Denver in 1940 suggested that

> In as much as a sizable portion of gasoline taxes is collected from residents of cities and towns on gasoline purchased for use on city streets, there is point to the contention that cities and towns should be given a larger share of the revenues obtained from this source.[18]

Such comments fell on deaf ears at the rurally dominated state legislature and within the rurally oriented highway department.[19]

In a report on bringing Colorado transportation infrastructure up to "desirable standards," the highway department recommended spending nearly forty times more in rural areas than in cities.[20] Furthermore, the 3 percent of state gas tax revenues allotted to cities was restricted to urban segments of state highways, leaving Denver with no funds collected from motorists to use for other roads, streets, and bridges.[21] There was no choice but to use general revenues to accommodate the demand for automobility, even though two-thirds of Denverites did not drive cars. They relied on mass transit, which never received the same government support as private cars.

THE DENVER TRAMWAY CORPORATION

On the eve of the twentieth century, in 1899, Denver's extensive mass transit facilities were merged into one company, the Denver Tramway Company (DTC). The resulting system employed more than one thousand workers and transported approximately 36 million passengers each year over 150 miles of track. This translated to about 250 trips each year, per capita. As with many other urban transit systems in the United States, mass transit in Denver had started in the 1870s with a few horsecar lines, many of which were later converted to cable-car lines before final conversion to electricity in the 1890s, when electric traction technology surpassed cable-driven systems, especially for flat cities like Denver.

Streetcar suburbs developed, starting with Curtis Park in the 1870s. As the transit system extended tendrils past the settled areas of Denver, new neighborhoods sprouted, attracting those settlers who could afford the fare. The Tramway continued to expand, launching a five-mile commuter line to Littleton in 1907. Similarly, the Denver and Interurban Railroad initiated service to Boulder in 1908. By 1917 DTC ridership had grown 77 percent, to 62 million trips per year.[22] However, even as the transit system's reach was expanding, it was also beginning its ultimate demise.

As a private company operating under a public franchise, large portions of DTC's cost structure were governed by its franchise agreement, as were fares. For example, one of the oldest provisions of the contract required the company to pay half the maintenance and repair costs on streets with two-way operation and one-fourth on streets with one-way operation. Similarly, outside of the city, DTC paid the state a passenger-mile tax. As more and more streets were paved and improved and subjected to the pounding wear-and-tear of thousands of automobiles and trucks, which were much heavier than the horse-drawn vehicles in use when DTC had made this financial commitment, the company had to contribute more and more money to street projects. Likewise, inflation raised the cost of materials and put upward pressure on wages, problems that were exacerbated when the United States joined World War I. However, the franchise agreement capped fares at five cents, and in 1917, despite record ridership levels, DTC was unable to pay a dividend and reported an annual loss of half a million dollars. Not surprisingly, the company's rolling stock was woefully undermaintained.

Since all but a small percentage of Denver voters rode the Tramway regularly, the prospects for obtaining approval for a rate increase from elected city officials seemed dim, so the DTC petitioned the state Public Utilities Commission for permission to raise fares. An increase to seven cents was granted in 1917, prompting a public outcry. The city council tried to control the situation by passing a six-cent fare and simultaneously suing in state court

Denver Tramway strikers, 1920,
Denver Public Library, Western History Collection

to have the seven-cent fare nullified on the grounds that the state Public Utilities Commission had no authority over the Tramway Company. Many Denverites objected to even the one-penny increase passed by the city council, and in 1919 Dewey Bailey was elected mayor partially on the strength of a campaign promise to restore the nickel fare. The DTC responded with layoffs and wage cuts, which led to a brief strike ended by a temporary return to a six-cent fare, pending a full referendum on fare increases. Voters rejected the raise, and the five-cent fare was automatically reinstated. Again, the Tramway Company responded with layoffs and wage cuts, and the result was the notoriously bloody and hard-fought Denver Tramway Strike of 1920. By the end of the year, the strike had prompted numerous riots, the company had attempted to hire replacement workers protected by private "guards," and the

Denver Tramway strike destroyed trolley, 1920,
Colorado Historical Society

government was forced to intervene with armed troops. In the end, the DTC filed for bankruptcy and mass transit in Denver never recovered.[23]

The bankruptcy court authorized an eight-cent fare, restrained the city from enforcing lower fares, and allowed the Tramway to resume operations. The city appealed this fare hike, but it was upheld by the Supreme Court. The DTC was able to get back on its feet, and ridership temporarily resumed its pre-strike climb, reaching new highs in 1927. But usage soon resumed its decline, as more and more Denverites chose to use cars and buses to get around. By 1935 Tramway ridership amounted to only 42 million rides per year, two-thirds of the 1917 level, while the city's population had grown by 20 percent to about 300,000. But even this relatively low ridership figure indicated that Denverites still rode the Tramway, on average, about 140 times a year. Nevertheless, the final collapse of the system had begun.

The ridership plunge can be explained simply. On the one hand, Denver's rail-based transit system was hampered by a woefully neglected fleet (the fare increase had been too little, too late, and subsequent increases were rejected, despite inflation during and after World War II), a damaged reputation, and the burden of maintaining a far-flung route system without government assistance. By comparison, subsidized automotive transportation was more attractive. Beginning in 1928 the DTC gradually converted its rail lines to bus routes, replacing burdensome street-maintenance obligations with the opportunity to benefit from subsidized infrastructure (gas taxes and registration fees were much lower than the franchise fees and paid only a small fraction of the street maintenance and construction costs). Similarly, many Denverites now chose private cars over the decrepit Tramway system, aided by the artificially low marginal cost of operating the affordable mass-produced vehicles pioneered by Henry Ford (by 1930 the price of a Ford Roadster in Denver had dropped to $435, or about $4,500 in 2000 dollars). The DTC's last streetcar route was closed in 1950.[24]

City planners accelerated the decline of mass transit in Denver. A major planning publication from 1932 called for removing trolley tracks from some of the major routes, because the streetcars got in the way of automobiles. The planners presumed that automobiles were meant to be the primary mode of transportation and that mass transit should be provided only to accommodate "citizens who do not have automobiles of their own, or visitors to the city." In the planners' view, mass transit was a necessary but inconvenient afterthought. As such, it benefited from supportive lip-service in official planning documents but was accorded a low priority.[25] In contrast, accommodating automotive transportation was arguably the primary goal of planners during this period.

BEN STAPLETON'S DENVER, 1923–1947

At the end of World War I, Denver was a highly centralized metropolis. Long-haul railroads, commuter trains, and DTC's streetcars were radial, meeting near the city center, with virtually no circular connecting routes.

Sixteenth Street before paving, ca. 1888,
Colorado Historical Society

Consequently, even though residential growth occurred along the radial spurs, the central business district grew, attracting offices, hotels, and retail stores. The city served as a regional center, with particular strengths in agriculture, mining, manufacturing, and wholesale trade. As a main transportation hub, Denver was along the planned routes of many of the regional highways proposed between 1909 and 1921, including the Lincoln Highway, the Dallas–Canada–Denver Highway, the Santa Fe Trail, the Omaha–Denver Road, and the Pike's Peak Ocean-to-Ocean Highway ("The Appian Way of America"). The war had fueled a new burst of growth, in part because there were many lead mines in the vicinity. With this prosperity and the completion of some of the regional highways came a sharp increase in trucking activity and increased downtown congestion. This prompted, as in other parts of the country, a clamor for road improvements.[26]

The city was ill equipped to deal with the rush of heavy trucks and increased auto use. As late as 1922, there were virtually no paved streets beyond downtown, which had been surfaced after the 1892 *Report of the*

Sixteenth Street looking north, with trolleys, horse-drawn traffic, and early automobiles,
Colorado Historical Society

Special Committee on Pubic Improvements. Elsewhere in Denver, the new
heavier vehicles were constantly bogging down on soft, muddy streets. Even
in the paved sections, the streets were overburdened. Downtown, roadways
were eighty feet wide and in pre-automotive years had been praised as
"excellent, broad, and regular." But the car changed everything, and this
width now seemed inadequate. Two 16-foot sidewalks used 32 feet, leaving
48 remaining. Parking used another 16 feet (8 on each side), streetcars used
approximately 20 feet, which left room for only one unobstructed lane of
moving traffic on streets that permitted two-way traffic. Parking itself was a
problem—a 1924 study found that there was room at the curb for only five
thousand cars to park downtown, when there were over 70,000 cars
registered in the city.[27]

    Thus, in 1923 when Ben Stapleton was elected mayor by a two-to-one
landslide, he took charge of a city in transition, a Denver that had risen to

Congestion on Sixteenth Street, ca. 1936,
Denver Public Library, Western History Collection

regional dominance in the pre-automotive era and was now struggling to adapt its infrastructure to accommodate ever-increasing demand for auto-mobility. His administration reflected this duality and was therefore charac-terized by the coexistence of old-fashioned, ward-based machine politics and an attempt (albeit abbreviated) at modern city planning. On the one hand, Stapleton never had a formal budgeting process, his city electrician served as *de facto* chief personnel officer, almost every city job was a patronage job, and he appointed a Klansman as head of public safety, publicly promising to cooperate with Klan activities. On the other hand, he formed the Denver Planning Commission, oversaw the completion of the first comprehensive plan, and championed the construction of a municipal airport so that Denver could compete with other cities as an aviation hub.[28]

In the first years of Stapleton's tenure, he tripled the number of paved streets and set about regrading, repairing, and re-oiling those streets that could not yet be hard-surfaced. Traffic volume leapt as soon as each individual improvement project was completed, sometimes even reaching twice as high as before. This was a clear indicator of how much motorists valued the improvements, which were provided without any usage fees.[29]

Stapleton appointed Saco Reink DeBoer to assemble the city's first comprehensive plan. DeBoer, born in Holland in 1883, had worked for the city since 1910, when he was hired by Mayor Speer to oversee the conversion of a city dump along Cherry Creek into the new Sunken Gardens Park. He served until 1931, spending only five years working for the Denver Planning Commission after its formation in 1926. He left a long-lasting mark on the city, via *The Denver Plan,* which was completed under his guidance in 1929. Although it was loosely based upon Kessler and Robinson's maps from 1906–1907, DeBoer's Plan was more comprehensive. It contained detailed plans for a citywide modernization effort, including suggested changes and additions to the city's parks, public buildings, parkways, streets, and highways.

The first volume of *The Denver Plan*—and its keystone—was DeBoer's transportation scheme. It contained no mention of mass transit or any nonautomotive transportation. Instead, it offered a blueprint for adapting Denver's infrastructure to facilitate automobility. DeBoer recommended circumferential bypass routes, radial feeders, diagonal highways, widened downtown streets, and new parkways and boulevards, all of which would be oriented exclusively toward cars and trucks. He based the plan on projections that accepted decentralization and auto-dependency as unalterable trends. Accordingly, population growth was presumed to be on the periphery, and it was taken as a foregone conclusion that new residents would use cars to get to work, shopping, and recreation. In a subtle attempt to skew the empirical data, *The Denver Plan* presented traffic counts that were all conducted on Saturdays, when automobile use was higher than on weekdays and mass transit ridership was lower.[30] A bias in favor of decentralization and increased automobile use was built into the plan.

Stapleton and his Planning Commission, under DeBoer's guidance, placed a high priority on making Denver more amenable to automobility. The

Busy pedestrian traffic on Sixteenth Street, ca. 1938,
Colorado Historical Society

administration's official publication, *Municipal Facts*, complained of "interference between street cars and automobiles" and suggested that the streetcar tracks should be removed to solve the problem, even though there were approximately the same number of street-car commuters as auto-commuters. A 1931 Planning Commission report proclaimed that the costs of congestion amounted to $1 million per day ($4.1 billion per year, in 2000 dollars). In its fervor to reduce this congestion, the city tore down the landmark Welcome Arch (dedicated just prior to the 1906 Democratic convention as a symbol of

The Welcome Arch,
Colorado Historical Society

turn-of-the-century Denver's status as a major city) because it obstructed the free flow of automobiles and was blamed for congestion.[31]

Meanwhile, the automobile business in Colorado had grown even stronger politically. By 1930, in Denver alone there were 113 dealers of new cars, plus additional used-car dealers, tire sellers, gas stations, repair mechanics, custom body shops, liveries, and driving schools. They allied with the Rocky Mountain Highway Association (the merger of the Colorado Good Roads Association and the Colorado Automobile Club) to push for increased public funding of roads. As a result, 25 percent of the state budget went to roads. The state spent 50 percent more on highways each year than it did on education. Only one-third of this state money was raised from motorists.[32]

However, since only a tiny portion of these funds could be spent within city limits and local user fees had been prohibited since 1914, none of

Stapleton's automobility initiatives could be financed by user fees. Instead, they were financed by special property-tax assessments on adjoining and nearby property through the use of "street improvement districts." This became increasingly unfair, as many of these projects were along major streets used mainly by commuters who didn't live close enough to be taxed. Meanwhile, outside the city, motorists found it easier to get around, because state funds paid for grading, graveling, and paving rural post roads and major connecting routes. A double standard prevented those same funds from supporting similar projects in Denver.[33]

The reliance on property taxes to fund city street projects had cultural and political side effects. For example, working-class residents of Barnum, a streetcar suburb in the southwestern reaches of the city, voted against a ballot proposal to place parking meters on downtown streets. Barnumites would not have been directly affected by the measure, but they feared that the precedent might lead to meters on their own residential streets. They believed that because streets were built and maintained with property taxes, citizens were entitled to park their private vehicles on public streets without additional charge.[34] While this may not seem like a very important notion, it would have long-lasting consequences. Americans who purchased cars could count on other Americans, even those who did not own cars, to share the cost of vehicle storage (in addition to the shared costs of usage built into the highway finance system). If this had been the case in pre-automotive times, urban residents would have been entitled to stable their horses and carriages on the public street in front of their homes.

During the Great Depression, Ben Stapleton was unseated by reform candidate George Begole. To balance the budget, Begole opposed all city-financed public works, an entirely unpopular approach. Voters returned Stapleton to office in the next election. However, Saco DeBoer did not return with Stapleton, and the Planning Commission fell into near dormancy. Instead, the mayor appointed George Cranmer, a Speer disciple who had already worked for Stapleton on the new municipal airport, as chair of the county commissioners of Denver County and placed him in charge of

Improvements and Parks, giving him free rein over public works projects of all types and making him the second most powerful public official in the city.

Cranmer boasted that he had no need of a master plan, instead just going "from one thing to another. . . . They had a planning commission, but I never did anything the planning commission planned. I just decided what ought to be done and I went ahead and did it." Cranmer's decisions were guided by the short-term imperatives of machine politics, keeping large numbers of supporters employed on neighborhood projects in targeted districts. Unfortunately, this approach governed the deployment of most New Deal money in Denver, since Cranmer oversaw all CCC, PWA, and WPA projects, in addition to locally financed or bond-financed improvements.[35] While Cranmer used public works funds to sustain Stapleton's political machine, the city's fundamental transportation problems went unaddressed. Beyond the city's boundaries, though, circumstances were not as grim. Aided by decades of government road-building efforts, Denver's suburbs were growing five times faster than the city itself.[36]

Stapleton and Cranmer's status quo-oriented, "old-fashioned" political style wore thin, and in 1947 Denver voters, eager to live in a more "modern" city, elected thirty-five-year-old Quig Newton by a landslide four-to-one margin. With the editorial support of both the *Rocky Mountain News* and the *Denver Post*, Newton swept into city hall with an entourage of young administrators determined to shake up Denver, bringing it into the modern age. As a main component of his campaign, Newton promised to replace Cranmer's haphazard and reactive approach to planning with a proactive effort to prepare Denver for the second half of the twentieth century, guided by a comprehensive city plan assembled by professional planners.[37]

WORLD WAR II AND THE MILITARIZATION OF DENVER

The Denver that Quig Newton took over from Ben Stapleton had been altered by World War II. Beginning in the late 1930s, the federal government spent millions of dollars on major military installations in the metropolitan area, adding more than 50,000 jobs directly, and many others indirectly.[38] These federal investments were widely dispersed along the metropolitan fringe, speeding deconcentration.

Lowry Field was one such facility, established as an Army training school in 1937 along the Denver–Aurora border east of the city, on the site of an abandoned tuberculosis sanitarium. Expanded in 1939 to cover 65,000 acres and including a bombing range, Lowry remained active throughout the Cold War.[39]

On the opposite edge of the city was the Denver Ordnance Plant, built in 1941 on a two-thousand-acre campus eight miles from downtown. To ease access for the twenty-thousand workers employed by the plant at its peak, the federal government helped the city build the area's first modern superhighway along west Sixth Avenue. After the war, the complex was renamed the Denver Federal Center and converted into a government office park, housing more than twenty government agencies that employed almost five thousand people.[40]

In 1942, Washington spent $62 million to build the Rocky Mountain Arsenal on 20,000 acres at the city's northeastern boundary. The Arsenal served as the main repository for chemical and incendiary weapons for World War II, the Korean War, and the Vietnam War, including mustard gas, nerve gas, napalm, and phosphorous bombs. Later, the Shell oil company operated a pesticide plant on the grounds, and NASA used the Arsenal to make and store rocket fuel for Titan missiles. The Arsenal and its attendant ecological horrors became the trigger that prompted activist-author Rachel Carson to write *Silent Spring*, the apocalyptic environmentalist treatise. In addition, toxic waste dumping at the Arsenal spawned numerous lawsuits involving the state of Colorado, the Army, Shell, and insurance concerns.[41]

The Navy built its own suburban air base, Buckley Field, at Aurora, near the Army's Lowry Field. Fitzsimons Army Hospital in Aurora was expanded to cover more than five hundred acres. After the war, as the United States became embroiled in the Cold War, defense contractors like

Martin Marietta opened plants outside of Denver, and in 1953 the Pentagon erected Rocky Flats, a facility for producing and storing plutonium triggers for the nation's atomic arsenal. This complex, located in suburban Jefferson County, grew to comprise one hundred buildings employing more than six thousand workers; it was the site of a dangerous radioactive fire in 1969 that spread radiation downwind and inspired not only a wave of protests but also a poem by Beat writer Alan Ginsberg titled *Plutonium Ode.*[42]

The influx of workers brought in during the war to staff the new federal facilities created a housing shortage. In response, the city asked Denverites to take in boarders and convert empty bedrooms into rentable rooms, and announced a blanket waiver of zoning provisions that had formerly prohibited such practices. Unfortunately, while this was meant to be a temporary measure, some neighborhoods in the city (Capitol Hill, for example) were permanently changed, as entire blocks of spacious single-family homes were converted to rooming houses or subdivided into rental apartments.[43] But while some city neighborhoods declined, suburban growth was brisk and vibrant.

The Denver region grew at twice the national average for metroplitan areas during this period, but the city itself captured only a small portion of the new prosperity. The widespread military facilities acted as decentralizing magnets, made all the more powerful by the accumulated investments in roads and highways, and the government subsidies to suburban home ownership, drawing settlement to subdivisions oustide the formal city limits and outside the city's taxbase.[44]

CONCLUSION

By mid-century, only one out of every five new residents of the metro area chose to live within Denver's city limits.[45] The anti-urban slant of state and federal policies, the collapse of mass transit, and Mayors Speer and Stapleton's initiatives to accommodate automotive transportation had undermined the sustainability of the city itself, fundamentally altering settlement patterns. These trends, established in the first half of the twentieth century, continued in the latter half, transforming the metroplitan region.

THREE

The Decentralization of Post–World War II Denver

Roads rule the world—not kings, nor courts, nor constables; not ships, nor soldiers. The road is the only royal line in a democracy, the only legislature that never changes, the only court that never sleeps, the only army that never quits, the first aid to the redemption of any nation, the exodus from stagnation in any society, the call from savagery from any tribe. . . . The road is umpire in every war and when the map is made it simply pushes on its great campaign of help, hope, brotherhood, efficiency, and peace.

—Anonymous quote, from frontispiece of
Denver Planning Office publication, ca. 1966

Every informed person is aware that adequate highways are the keys which will unlock the doors of social and educational growth, the expansion and development of agriculture, commerce, and industry and the fulfillment of our hopes for progress and prosperity in the future.

—Walter Cooper, President Colorado Good Roads Association, 1955

PLANNING FOR AUTOMOBILITY IN DENVER

In 1945, the Denver metropolitan area counted twice as many motor vehicles as in 1930, but the city's streets were ill equipped to handle the traffic.

Parking, which had traditionally been free on all Denver streets, was a particular problem. Mayor Stapleton was voted out of office before he could address the issue, but his successor, Quig Newton, launched three simultaneous initiatives to foster increased automobility. He established a traffic engineering department, built off-street parking facilities, and created the Denver Planning Office (DPO).[1]

Newton brought in Henry Barnes from Flint, Michigan, to run this new traffic engineering department. Barnes widened streets, often at the expense of lawns, sidewalks, and many of Mayor Speer's trees, hailed as civic improvements by previous generations. His efforts continued those of George Cranmer, Mayor Stapleton's manager of Parks and Improvements, who had considered tree-lined streets a maintenance and street-cleaning hindrance. Under Cranmer's tenure, streetside trees all over Denver had been cut down. Barnes also made downtown streets one way and installed traffic lights throughout the city (previously, there had been only a handful of traffic lights, managed by the fire department). Soon celebrated nationwide for his work, Barnes became a leader in his field, working next in Baltimore and then in New York City, where he died from a heart attack at the age of sixty-one.[2]

Mayor Newton's off-street parking projects were also extensions of previous initiatives. Following recommendations made by outgoing Mayor Stapleton's special parking committee, voters approved a 1948 bond referendum for two downtown garages, to be owned and operated by the city. Presumably, the bonds would be repaid from meter revenue collected at the new sites. The assumption was persuasive, and in the next half century, more facilities were financed by the same method. But there was a little-noticed subsidy built into this system. The meter revenue paid for the operating costs and debt service for the parking facilities, but not the foregone property and sales tax revenues, now that the land would never be occupied by private enterprise. As in many other motor vehicle programs, the general budget absorbed these costs while benefits accrued only to commuting motorists, most of whom lived outside of Denver's city limits.[3]

Ben Stapleton (left), and Quig Newton,
Colorado Historical Society

When Quig Newton created the DPO to replace the semidormant Denver Planning Commission and appointed Maxine Kurtz as its first director in 1949, he fulfilled his campaign promise to make professional planning part of his administration. This was the third component of his automobility policy.[4] Over the next decade, the DPO formulated the *Comprehensive Plan,* the first installment of which was the *General Street Plan,* published in 1952.

Under Kurtz, the DPO's goal was clear and simple: "to give the automobile maximum freedom of direction and speed."[5] The plan accepted as assumptions that more families would own more cars by 1970, that each vehicle would travel more miles per year, and that all metropolitan growth

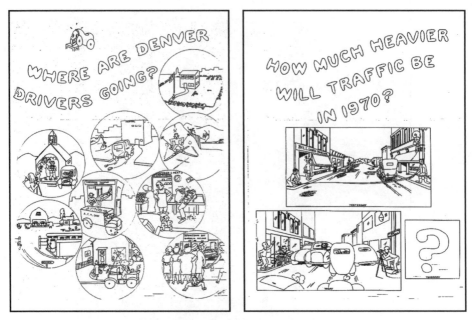

Denver Planning Office cartoons, 1952

would be at the periphery. Reporting that "the metropolitan Denver area is in the forefront of large American communities in the relative number of automobiles owned by its citizens," the DPO suggested that the city should make every effort possible to accommodate these developments: "Denver faces the challenge of how to permit easy movement from place to place, and of providing drivers with places to store their vehicles at the end of their trips."[6] Not only did the planners accept auto-dependency as an unalterable fact, they also embraced the notion that it was the government's responsibility to meet the resulting demands without question, without alteration, and without charging motorists directly. As a result, their assumptions and forecasts became self-fulfilling prophecies.

The 1952 General Street Plan, which delineated a twenty-year transportation blueprint, illustrated this approach. To answer the question "Where are Denver Drivers Going?" the plan offered cartoon-style sketches of a church wedding, a ski resort, a dairy farm, a single-family house on a

suburban-style plot, an industrial manufacturing facility, and a merchant holding a "downtown day" sale. Absent were downtown office workers, persons driving to trains or bus stations, or apartment dwellers. The DPO offered a vision of new six-lane divided freeways with cloverleaf intersections (and a median strip too narrow to accommodate mass transit), augmented by new parking rules, modified traffic regulations (no left turns at downtown intersections, additional one-way designations, etc.), designated truck routes, re-timing certain traffic lights, and numerous street-widening projects.

The mechanisms proposed by the DPO for financing this vision were similarly illustrative. On another page of the 1952 Plan titled "How to Get Tomorrow's Street System," there were four more cartoons: a handout from Uncle Sam; a smiling politician returning from the statehouse with a handful of cash; a cashier at the City Tax Department collecting money from a citizen at a walk-up window; and an investment banker selling tax-exempt General

Obligation bonds and Special Assessment bonds. These tongue-in-cheek drawings referred to more detailed provisions contained in other sections of the Plan: a hoped-for boost in the urban component of the federal-aid program; adjustments to the state highway program to distribute more highway money to local governments; increases in the city's property tax and sales tax; and a lifting of the city's debt limit to allow for additional general obligation borrowing. Conspicuously absent was any mention whatsoever of tolls or increases in license, registration, gas, tire, or parking fees.[7] In other words, even though the plan was geared toward the automobile, the DPO did not expect motorists to pay for it.

This planning approach persisted for decades. A 1963 downtown plan focused almost entirely on increased automobility. Even though one-quarter of work trips and one-third of shopping trips into the central business district were via mass transit, the report dismissed this mode as too expensive because it was not self-supporting. Instead, it concluded that freeways "must be built" to facilitate the flow of private automobiles between residential areas and downtown. Private transit companies could "step into the picture" on their own and operate rubber-tired buses on the same pavement built primarily for cars and trucks. In addition, the report urged that access streets be widened and limited to one-way traffic, and called for $80 million of new off-street "parking terminals."[8]

In the same vein, a 1966 Plan proclaimed that "the need for additional freeways within the urban area is acute and irrefutable when future traffic projections are examined." This report, the first of extensive revisions to the earlier *Comprehensive Plan*, was meant to provide the "structural framework around and within which the other Plan elements assume their dimensions." Despite its claim to comprehensiveness, the focus was exclusively on "street and highway systems and related highway-oriented transportation facilities for motor vehicles . . . [alternative modes of transport] are not treated." It called for the expenditure of $200 million on freeways and $50 million on streets, with the city's share of costs paid for by a bond issue that would be repaid out of property and sales tax collections.[9]

These DPO plans of the 1950s and 1960s were designed to facilitate suburbanization. Denver planners projected that the suburban population would double in the next decade, while the city's population would grow by only 5 percent, and more than two-thirds of the metropolitan area's residents were expected to live in single-family housing.[10]

While the city's planners indicated that suburbanization was inevitable, they in fact actively encouraged it. They planned to eliminate agricultural land use, increase low-density residential development, and limit high-density areas.[11] Operating under the principle that "the situation in older eastern cities is a lesson for Denver," the DPO staff believed that "the mistake to avoid is over-concentration" and "the advent of the private automobile liberated urban growth from central congestion." They were slow to abandon this planning approach, which had been born of the overcongested cities of the pre–World War II era. Accordingly, they intentionally inhibited downtown growth, instead encouraging development on the periphery.

However, to "prevent overextension and sprawl," the DPO suggested aggressive annexation to the geographic limits of efficient municipal services (water, sewer, etc.), combined with a commuter tax to prevent "an artificial tax exemption from expenses of the central city."[12] These limiting strategies proved ineffective, while the inducements to decentralization turned out to be overwhelming.

A commuter tax was politically unworkable, and annexation was impossible, since much of the growth was within previously incorporated towns like Aurora, Boulder, Arvada, Littleton, and Longmont.[13] Even unincorporated areas were removed from Denver's grasp in 1974 when the state legislature passed the Poundstone Amendment requiring the acquiescence, by referendum, of the *entire* host county before Denver could annex. Previously, it had been sufficient for the residents of the annexed territory to agree, a more customary arrangement.

The Amendment, named after suburban politician Freda Poundstone, applied only to Denver, since it specifically restrained city-county combinations, and there were no others in the state. Scholars have argued that

Poundstone and her followers were reacting to court-imposed efforts to integrate Denver's school system, which was coterminus with the city's legal boundary. After school integration legislation had been defeated in 1969, civil rights activists filed a federal desegregation suit that was finally decided in their favor in 1973, prompting suburban legislators to push through the Poundstone Amendment.[14] The measure put an abrupt end to Denver's annexation efforts.

In these circumstances—the combination of defensive incorporation by suburban towns and the limitations imposed by the Poundstone Amendment—it was impossible for Denver to collect any revenues from its swelling suburban population. The city's borders, which encompassed 66.8 square miles in 1950, had extended only as far as 111 square miles when the Poundstone Amendment took effect, in a metropolitan area that sprawled over four thousand square miles. Whereas in 1950, 74 percent of Denver area residents lived in the city, this had dropped to 42 percent by 1970.[15]

As decentralized population growth continued, fueled by highways, Denver struggled to adapt. Auto-dependency rose, and the anti-urban funding bias of federal highway programs strained municipal resources, a problem exacerbated by state highway policies.

For example, in 1950, the state charge for a title certificate was one dollar, not even enough to cover administrative costs. Likewise, the fee for a three-year driver's license was also one dollar. Over the next thirty years, it increased only once, to $2.25.[16] When the state tried to boost truck registration costs in the 1950s to raise matching funds for federal interstate grants, the Colorado Motor Carriers Association hired former gubernatorial candidate Ben Bezoff to lobby on its behalf. He was able to reduce the top fee from almost $800 for heavy duty tractor-trailers to a maximum of $18.50 per year.[17]

Meanwhile, even though Colorado's urbanites contributed two-thirds of state gas-tax receipts, only 3 percent was redistributed back to cities for street improvements. To make matters worse, the formula for dividing these funds among local governments favored less densely settled municipalities, as did the rule for distributing highway funds at the county level. As a result, even though Denver had well over half a million registered cars in 1953, more than three-quarters of the statewide total, its share of state road-fund allocations to counties and cities together amounted to only 5 percent. Furthermore, the state required cities to maintain all state highways within their borders. As the final blow, automobiles and trucks used by city governments were not exempt from gas taxes, while those used by county governments were.[18] Even though many of Denver's street improvement projects benefited commuting motorists who lived beyond the municipal limits, one of the city's only effective means of financing these projects was through special assessments levied on abutting landowners, using more than a thousand special assessment districts.[19]

In these circumstances, public investments in transportation infrastructure worked against the city, advancing the viability of suburban communities while undermining the sustainability of the older urban core. To make matters worse, subsidized superhighways provided added inducement for people and capital to migrate outward.

THE VALLEY HIGHWAY (I-25)

In a report to the Colorado state highway department prepared by consulting engineers Crocker and Ryan in 1944, the relationship between Denver and the Valley Highway project was summed up as follows: "The city interposes a traffic obstacle measured by a time loss of fully one-half hour. It is the function of the proposed new thorough-fare to remove this obstacle."[20] This attitude was typical of the highway engineering community nationwide, which often referred to cities as "obstacles" and subsequently coined the term "bypass." In 1960 the Colorado state highway department went so far as to complain about the need to maintain sections of state highways passing through cities and towns after a bypass is built, arguing that the bypassed urban portions should be abandoned by the state.[21]

The Crocker and Ryan report estimated that motorists would save millions of dollars if such a north–south highway "through or around"

Denver were built. Truckers would save about two and a half cents per minute of reduced travel time, and drivers of personal cars would save about one-half cent per minute. In the first five years of operation, the report continued, savings would amount to twice the construction costs. However, since the study had been commissioned by the anti-toll state highway department, and Crocker and Ryan wanted to be retained for the design and construction phases of the project (if it received approval from the anti-toll federal Bureau of Public Roads), they advised that motorists benefiting from the project need not pay for it, because their savings would contribute to the general welfare.

Crocker and Ryan also advised that the Valley Highway would need "distributing facilities" and street widenings, but that any such projects must be built and paid for by the city "in its own interest"; the municipality should pay for policing the new highway; and "city buses [must] be excluded from the highway."[22] These declarations set the tone for the project. Even after construction started, no decisions had been made on how the highway would connect to downtown.[23] This was consistent with the approach taken by state and federal highway officials on many such "urban extension highways," which had been grudgingly included in the nation's highway network only out of political necessity.

The Crocker and Ryan report, with its anti-urban presumptions, was mere window dressing, meant to add luster to strategies formulated by bureaucrats in the BPR and the Colorado Department of Highways. For example, buried in the report was an acknowledgment that the consultants' proposed route exactly followed the path mapped out by the state and federal road agencies during the survey work for the landmark 1944 *Interregional Highways* study. The firm was rewarded for playing this rubber-stamping role when it was awarded the contract to prepare bid specifications for the subsequent construction of the project.

There was a short-lived campaign in opposition to the Valley Highway, led by Gordon Tamblyn, publisher of *Municipal News*, a reform newsletter. In particular, Tamblyn objected to the financing of the project. In addition to previously mentioned costs that the city had to pay for itself with general revenues, the state also required Denver to pay for all right-of-way acquisition costs not covered by federal aid. However, Tamblyn's crusade had limited support from the start and was further marginalized by his overzealous religious fervor, which drove him to declare that supporters of the Valley Highway would not be "accepted into the kingdom of God until, like Zaccheus, they repent and restore any assessment made [for] the Valley Highway without the people having a chance to vote on it."[24]

Construction began in 1948, and the first sections were completed in 1950. Almost immediately, the daily traffic count climbed to forty-four thousand. However, the entire 11.2-mile stretch within Denver's boundaries was not open until 1958. By this time, the costs had nearly doubled, and the project would not have been finished until well into the 1960s were it not for the increase in federal aid from 50 percent to 90 percent in 1956, when the highway was officially designated I-25 and began receiving Interstate funds.[25]

Partially because of the suburban expansion it facilitated, and also because of the short shrift given to connecting it to the city, I-25 was soon known as "the highway Denver commuters *hate to love.*" It was routinely used by over 60,000 vehicles a day by the early 1960s, and was widened to six lanes.[26]

George Wallace was the first Denverite to realize that the Valley Highway had opened up a new frontier for real estate development. Wallace, a New York-born engineer and inventor with his own firm headquartered in downtown Denver, had an epiphany in 1962:

Things were going well enough, so I bought a new car. My first one in seven years. It was a big black Mercury. And then some son-of-a-bitch in a white car opens his door and leaves a big white scratch on my car. You know some people are just plain [expletive deleted]. But I decided by that night that I was through with downtown Denver. . . . I was so goddammed mad, [I decided to] find a little piece of land outside Denver where I'd build my own office, with parking spaces twenty feet wide."[27]

Wallace needed only one acre to relocate his company, but all the parcels along the Valley Highways were large farms. He bought a forty-acre farm at the southern border of the city, adjacent to an exit of the Valley Highway, and built a small office building with a parking lot big enough for his new car to be safe. Wallace, later hailed as a visionary leader and larger-than-life innovator in the Denver-area real estate business, recalled that at the time "I didn't know what to do with all that land." However, one of his acquaintances that worked at the Denver office of Hewlett-Packard heard of the move and convinced his bosses that H-P should become Wallace's first major tenant. The Denver Tech Center, as Wallace christened his new office park, was on the map.

Wallace built on this success and soon built a reputation as a tireless and tough businessman, a leader in his community. Within a few years, by 1968, he had acquired an additional seven hundred acres of land for expansions to the Tech Center and built his first six office buildings. In the 1970s he added a shopping center, some residential areas, and a heliport. His vision for what the Tech Center could be was so expansive that in an interview in 1988, even though it had grown so fast that it housed 700 companies with 12,000 employees in 60 buildings on 850 acres, he said that the Tech Center was only one-third complete. When he finally retired in 1994, it covered almost a thousand acres and housed more than 900 firms in 165 office buildings, including more than a dozen glass-and-steel towers. Copycat developers bought up nearby land and launched their own office-park developments, riding George Wallace's coattails: Meridien International Business Center, on 1,200 acres; Greenwood Plaza, on 400 acres; and Inverness, on 1,000 acres.[28] The resulting agglomeration of office buildings stretched out along I-25, almost entirely outside of Denver's city's limits, rivaling the central business district.

As suburban complexes like the Tech Center sprouted, fed by subsidized access via I-25 (and later by the completion of I-225), they created an ever-increasing traffic problem on the Valley Highway.[29] As one observer noted, "It is always congested, no matter how many lanes are added—and new lanes it seems are forever being added . . . there are eight lanes in some places and twelve in others, but they never seem to be enough." Traffic counts eventually approached two hundred thousand vehicles per day, and almost three hundred thousand flowed through the "mousetrap," the intersection between the Valley Highway and I-70, precipitating an expensive overhaul in the 1990s.[30]

THE DENVER–BOULDER TURNPIKE

Another of the metropolitan area's major highways, the Denver–Boulder Turnpike was planned and completed at the same time as the Valley Highway, in the late 1940s and early 1950s. It too was projected to save time and money. However, it was not on the *Interregional Highway* report's official map and was therefore opposed by state and federal highway officials. Nevertheless, it became one of the trend-setting toll roads that sprouted up across the country at this time, where highway users willingly lined up at toll plazas to pay for the convenience and efficiency of a limited-access highway.

Roderick Downing, an engineering professor at the University of Colorado, first proposed a direct road from Boulder to Denver in 1927. He used his students to map, plan, and survey potential routes, and he also assembled a technical analysis of demand, costs, and benefits. He concluded that motorists would have lower maintenance and repair expenditures and would save time and fuel. The value of these benefits would be sufficient to amortize the costs of construction in only nine years and also provide for routine maintenance and a reserve fund to rebuild the road in the future.[31]

Nevertheless, Downing made no headway until 1946 when, buttressed by the *Rocky Mountain News* and the Boulder Chamber of Commerce, he obtained the support of Colorado Governor Ralph Carr, who hoped to use federal aid to build a new primary highway along Downing's route. Mark Watrous, a senior state highway official, told the governor that the highway department and the BPR were giving first priority to ensuring that even the smallest town in the state had paved access and therefore could not afford to build the express route. Carr then suggested a toll road, the Denver–Boulder Turnpike.

Watrous, like most of his fellow members of AASHO, was vehemently opposed to toll roads and set out to undermine the proposal. To refute Downing's report, he hired outside consulting engineers to evaluate the project.[32] He selected Crocker and Ryan, the same firm that had been retained for the Valley Highway project, and instructed them to prepare a feasibility study, based upon traffic measurements and projections supplied by his Planning Division. The supplied data was narrowly defined so as to predetermine the outcome of the study. It assumed that there would be *no* growth in traffic between Denver and Boulder if the new expressway were built and that less than three-quarters of the existing traffic would be willing to pay for the faster, shorter, and more convenient route, even if the toll was only twenty-five cents. Based on these assumptions, Crocker and Ryan concluded that the project would not generate sufficient revenues to repay toll-backed bonds. The report scared potential lenders, blocking the project.[33]

The governor, however, was politically committed to the Turnpike project, so he secured a state pledge to cover any shortfall in toll revenues, enabling the bond sale to proceed.[34] This commitment would never be needed.

The Denver–Boulder Turnpike opened in January 1952, the first modern toll road outside of the northeast.[35] It was immediately successful. Within two years, the route that state highway engineers had described as "marginal" was carrying more traffic than had been projected for twenty years hence.[36] After a dozen years of operation, usage was four times the forecast rate. The bond issue was repaid by 1967, thirteen years ahead of schedule. At that point, however, instead of using toll revenue to establish a reserve fund for repairs or replacement as Downing had originally proposed, state highway officials removed the tolls and converted the Turnpike into a federal-aid freeway. They had the loud and vocal support of the AAA, which campaigned vigorously for the highway's conversion to toll-free status.[37]

Denver–Boulder Turnpike, tollbooth removal, *Colorado Historical Society*

Soon, local motorist groups demanded improvements and expansions to the Denver–Boulder freeway, even though they had been unwilling to contribute a modest twenty-five-cent toll to pay for them. The condition of the roadway began to deteriorate and routine maintenance was deferred, so that by the late 1980s virtually the entire highway needed to be replaced. Because the AAA and the state highway officials opposed the reinstatement of tolls, the Turnpike (now officially known as U.S. Route 36) continued to crumble, even while it served more and more traffic.[38]

By the 1990s, the Denver–Boulder freeway served a markedly different traffic stream from when it first opened. The undeveloped land between Denver and Boulder had become peppered with new residential subdivisions, and Boulder itself had changed from a sleepy university town nestled under the Rocky Mountains, where the biggest traffic crushes were caused by college football games on Saturdays, into a rapidly growing suburban city, with an ever-increasing base of corporate and commercial enterprises. Morning rush-hour traffic on the highway became just as heavy flowing "outward" toward Boulder as "inward" toward the city. This type of change was happening elsewhere in the metropolitan area, wherever highway corridors were built.

THE BELTWAY BATTLEGROUND: I-470, C-470, AND E-470

Soon after the toll gates were removed from the Denver–Boulder Turnpike in 1967, attention in Denver shifted to a different highway project: a new outer-loop Interstate highway. The Federal-Aid Highway Act of 1968 authorized the addition of over a thousand miles to the Interstate System, mostly for suburban beltways. Accordingly, a twenty-six-mile segment skirting Denver's southwestern quadrant, on the drawing boards since 1958, was officially added to the Interstate map and designated I-470. By 1972, the state Department of Highways finished a corridor location study and community impact studies, and submitted an "Environmental Impact Statement" to Washington.[39]

The road lobby was now no longer an unstoppable juggernaut. During the late sixties and early seventies, community opposition blocked highway projects in the Princeton, Portland, Boston, New York, Tulsa, New Orleans, and San Francisco areas.[40] In Colorado, Richard Lamm was elected governor in 1974 on a limited-growth platform that opposed I-470.[41] The Colorado Department of Health and the Environmental Protection Agency in Washington also opposed the project because of air pollution concerns. The project was rejected by Washington and sent back to the Colorado highway department with requests for additional information about regional planning, land-use policy, mass transit alternatives, and air quality effects.[42]

What appeared to be a political victory for the newly elected governor quickly turned into a liability. Motorists' groups, real estate developers, and road builders mounted an aggressive campaign to save the project. The

Colorado Highway Commission (a state agency) took Lamm to court, hoping to force him to submit a revised proposal to Washington. To limit the political fallout and appease the project's proponents, Lamm appointed an ad hoc commission to work out a compromise. In 1976, the commission recommended that the governor invoke a technical provision of the Federal-Aid Highway Act of 1973 to formally withdraw I-470 and transfer the corresponding federal-aid funds to substitute projects. The largest share would be transferred to C-470, a four-lane parkway along the same route previously slated for the six-lane I-470, with at-grade intersections controlled by traffic lights instead of grade-separation cloverleafs. Lamm proceeded with these recommendations, and all the requisite approvals for the withdrawal-substitution were obtained by 1977.[43]

Anticipation of the circumferential route had already shaped development along the designated corridor, where real estate investors planned to capitalize on the new easy-access beltway. The Mission Viejo company had already bought land and announced plans for Highlands Ranch, a 22,000-acre development that was expected to house 90,000 residents. Company spokesmen frankly acknowledged that the planned conversion of barren land into subdivisions and gated communities was made possible by the new highway.[44] Nearby, plans for another pair of developments were underway, Ken Caryl Ranch and Ken Caryl Meadows, with homes for 34,000 people. Other developers were hoping to build over 9 million square feet of office and commercial space, plus another 22 million square feet for industrial use. Land values along remaining sections of the route were climbing at annual rates as high as 50 percent.

These developers, with the support of the state highway department, convened a "C-470 Task Force" to coordinate lobbying efforts on behalf of the project. The task force was soon able to change the planned route back into a full-fledged superhighway, with no at-grade crossings, although it was still called a "parkway" for publicity purposes and came to be known as the Centennial Parkway. To deflect anticipated criticisms, the revised plans called for an adjacent bicycle/jogging path along the entire twenty-six-mile

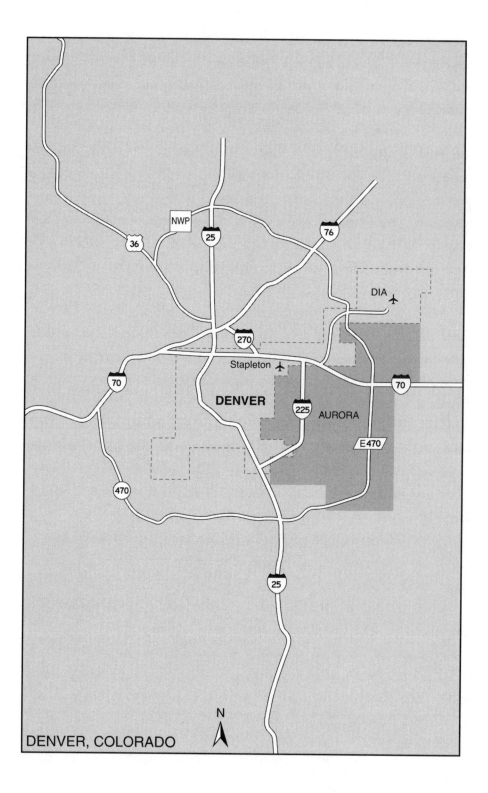

NWP

36

25

76

DIA ✈

270

Stapleton ✈

70

DENVER

225

AURORA

E470

70

470

25

N

DENVER, COLORADO

length, as well as three park-and-ride facilities linked to mass transit. However, these amenities were deferred, with "funding sought at a later date from other sources."[45]

High inflation made financing the highway difficult. Even though the transfer had been "authorized" in 1977, subsequent changes to federal statutes required that transfer funds come from general revenues, instead of the Highway Trust Fund, and as such they were subject to annual appropriation by Congress. The trickle of cash approved by Congress was barely enough for engineering and advance planning, while inflation pushed the construction cost estimates over $200 million. In 1982, when ground was broken for the project, the local chapter of the AAA complained that at current funding levels it would take thirty-two years to complete C-470. Efforts to accelerate the project with a regional registration surcharge failed. Instead, state highway officials made maximum use of available federal highway programs, and each year the C-470 task force sent a delegation of developers, highwaymen, and local politicians to Washington to cajole and persuade Congress to approve special authorizations for the transfer project.[46]

The first section of the Centennial Parkway opened in 1985, covering about one-third of the total length, and within a few months daily traffic averaged 20,000 vehicles. Two years later, traffic counts exceeded 41,000, 40 percent higher than initial forecasts. Boosted by this new toll-free expressway access, area employment had exploded to more than 42,000 jobs from about 5,000 a few years earlier. Additional segments opened in the next few years, and the entire highway was completed by the early 1990s. The surrounding landscape was transformed, from brown uninhabited plains to steel-and-concrete office parks, densely packed subdivisions, and retail shopping malls. Between 1990 and 1995, Highlands Ranch captured one-quarter of the Denver area's new home sales, and Douglas County became the fastest growing county in America. In 1996, the area's largest shopping mall, billed as a "retail resort," opened on the previously barren land at the intersection of C-470 and I-25. Known as Park Meadows Mall, the center is anchored by four department stores (Nordstrom's, Dillard's, JCPenney, and Foley's), along with three "big-box" retailers (Costco, BestBuy, Linens N Things) and more than 130 other shops.[47]

Developers played a central role in the C-470 saga, and they became increasingly aggressive in their sponsorship of other highway projects in the metro area. For example, George Wallace organized a group of landowners along the I-25 corridor that volunteered to pay for enlarged interchanges, improved access roads, and more elegant landscaping, as well as a new exit to enhance access to the Denver Tech Center. Officially called the Joint Southeast Public Improvement Authority, the group spent $20 million on these improvements (augmented by matching funds from the government). The highway was already there—all they had to do to increase the value of their land was build new exits and wider access roads.[48]

These developers, and others like them across the country, were able to influence highway projects because their financial support was desperately needed, now more than ever before. Maintenance costs were sucking up ever-larger portions of highway budgets nationwide. Many of the primary routes were nearly a half-century old, and the Interstate highways were more than twenty years old. Finally, out of necessity, the 1974 Federal Highway Act added a new category of federal aid for restoration, resurfacing, and rehabilitation (the "3R" program, later expanded to "4R" when reconstruction was added). While this marked the first time that federal highway funds were used for maintenance, the matching requirements and the explosive rise in expenses meant that states were still hard-pressed to keep up.[49]

The NHUC and the AAA exacerbated the problem by continuing to fight against any attempts to collect additional revenues from motorists. As gasoline and automobile prices had risen over the years, gas taxes and registration fees had actually fallen in real terms, so that by the early 1980s all user fees put together accounted for less than 5 percent of the cost of operating a car. Motorists now paid just over half the cost of building new highways and contributed *less* than half of the cost of maintaining them.[50]

Thus, it was out of necessity that developers became key players, on an even grander scale, in the construction of the next segment of the 470 beltway, formally known as E-470. As the first portions of C-470 were approaching completion in 1984, landowners along the E-470 corridor to the east put up money for a consulting engineer's feasibility study for the new superhighway. The resulting report concluded that "if we wait for federal or state funding it will never be built," so the new fifty-mile expressway would have to be paid for by "developers and users."[51]

Fortunately, the explosive growth along the Centennial Parkway produced a surplus of real estate entrepreneurs willing to participate in the E-470 project, which held promise of even greater rewards. As a result, once the project got underway highway officials were able to entertain competing proposals from speculators willing to *give* land for rights-of-way.[52] These landowners held thousands of mostly vacant acres, and they knew that if E-470 passed through their property, they would reap a windfall. In one typical transaction, two developers donated over five miles of right-of-way for the new superhighway. Newspapers reported a steady stream of investors planning for malls, residential subdivisions, golf courses, hotels, a skating rink, a day-care center, and a twenty-four-screen multiplex theater along the route.[53]

The developers teamed up with local officials eager to oversee (and take credit for) the growth that would surely follow if the E-470 highway could be built. Together, they worked to secure construction financing. Arapahoe County put together a special bond issue to take advantage of the subsidized interest rate available for highway bonds. The technique, known as an "arbitrage deal," was prohibited after the 1986 Tax Reform Act, but the county closed the deal just before the new rules took effect. They borrowed $722 million ($1.1 billion in 2000 dollars) at low tax-exempt interest rates and reinvested the borrowed funds in a higher-yielding portfolio of U.S. Treasury bonds. After a few years, they simply liquidated the Treasury bonds and repaid their own bonds with the proceeds. The resulting profit (which was, in effect, a subsidy from the federal government since it came from the disparity between the low tax-exempt rate paid by the county and the higher interest rate earned on the Treasury portfolio) was enough to pay generous fees to the lawyers and investment houses that structured the transaction and have $63 million left over for the highway. These funds were supplemented by an unusual $30 million loan from the state highway department, which, according to one newspaper account, was arranged by a politically connected law firm that also spearheaded a campaign to unseat a county commissioner opposed to the project. The law firm was rewarded with contracts as underwriter's counsel for a large bond issue and as counsel to the E-470 general contractor, Morrison Knudsen.[54]

Simultaneously, E-470 proponents were able to institute user charges. At first, the group attempted a referendum to impose a regional five-cent gas-tax surcharge for highway projects. This measure was blocked in the state legislature by a combination of opponents that included the AAA and groups from the northeastern suburbs opposed to additional highway construction. The following year, the unsuccessful registration surcharge proposal from the C-470 taskforce was revived on a more limited basis. The revised proposal called for a levy of only ten dollars per year, would apply only in five counties (instead of the original eight), and would be supplemented by tolls collected on the new beltway segments. The plan was presented directly to voters as separate referenda in each of the individual counties. It passed in the three southern and eastern counties (Adams, Arapahoe, and Douglas), allowing E-470 to move forward, and it failed in the more densely settled Jefferson and Boulder Counties to the west and northwest, deferring the portion of the highway loop in that section, called the Northwest Parkway, or W-470.[55]

After the passage of the registration surcharge, Adams, Arapahoe, and Douglas Counties entered into an intergovernmental agreement to form the E-470 Public Highway Authority to build and operate the highway and to issue bonds secured by the surcharge, tolls, and developer impact fees. George Wallace served as chairman of the Authority's Executive Committee. After long delays from obstructive litigation and disputes over route changes, the Authority sold $588 million worth of bonds in 1995 and began construction on a forty-six-mile beltway toll road that would connect to C-470 at I-25, (near Wallace's expanding Tech Center developments) in the south, skirt the

Denver Population

	Denver	Metro Area	Aurora
1900		134	0.2
1910	213	277	0.7
1920	256	329	1.0
1930	288	385	2.3
1940	322	445	3.4
1950	416	612	11
1960	494	929	48
1970	514	1,229	75
1980	492	1,593	159
1990	467	1,777	222

furthest reaches of the metropolitan area to the east, cross I-70, and curve back around to meet I-76 to the north.[56]

Aurora, which bordered Denver on the east, was also party to the E-470 agreement, since much of the proposed route was within its boundaries, or nearby. When completed E-470 became the latest of a string of government projects that fueled Aurora's rapid transformation into a mega-suburb large enough to rival its older and more urban neighbor, Denver.

AURORA: "AMERICA'S FASTEST GROWING MIDSIZED CITY"

Aurora, located due east of Denver, was incorporated in 1891 by developer Donald Fletcher. After the 1893 panic and Fletcher's subsequent disappearance, the town declared bankruptcy, and its two hundred residents voted for annexation by Denver—but the big city rejected the petition of its suburb. Over the next quarter-century, while the metro area added more than two hundred thousand additional residents, Aurora's population remained below one thousand.[57]

In 1918, however, the U.S. Army Recuperation Camp (later renamed the Fitzsimons Army Medical Center in honor of the first official American casualty of World War I) was built in Aurora. Soon thereafter, Denver Mayor Ben Stapleton began a crusade for a municipal airport at the eastern edge of Denver, adjacent to Aurora. The site was widely criticized because it was six miles from the city. The *Denver Post* called it "Stapleton's Folly," and "Simpleton's Sand Dunes," but the mayor pushed forward, reportedly influenced by well-connected landowners. Buoyed by his two-to-one landslide electoral margin, he bought 640 acres and built four gravel runways, one hangar, and a small terminal building.[58]

The new airport, which opened one week before the 1929 stock market crash, soon hosted about thirty takeoffs and landings each day, including regular passenger service to Cheyenne, and more than a hundred instructional flights daily. Closer to Aurora's "downtown" than Denver's, the airfield and the army hospital provided jobs and commerce to support a small commercial district along U.S. 40, a federal-aid highway that became Aurora's main street and served as the primary connection to downtown Denver. Aurora's population grew to 2,295 in 1930.

The New Deal and World War II initiated the next stage of Aurora's rapid growth. During the depression, Denver foreclosed on thousands of acres of tax-delinquent land near the airport and used WPA work-relief funds to extend and pave the runways, and to build a control tower with a radio beacon. This made Denver one of the few cities equipped to accommodate the new forty-passenger commercial aircraft introduced in 1938, which needed almost five thousand feet to land and take off. United Airlines and Continental Airlines started service in Denver at this time, with the latter moving its headquarters there. In 1940, more than twelve thousand passengers used the airport. In 1942 Western Airlines began serving Denver, as did Braniff in 1943 and Frontier in 1946. By the time the field was rededicated in Stapleton's name in the mid-1940s, there were five hundred arrivals and departures each day.[59]

Military spending propelled expansion of the airport and the growth of nearby Aurora. During the war, the Army paved taxiways, built hangars,

Stapleton Airport, before the boom,
Colorado Historical Society

installed a heating plant, and constructed a cafeteria. The new buildings were meant to be temporary, but since lumber was scarce in the area during the war, they were built out of local sandstone bricks instead.[60] New defense installations were also built within Aurora's boundaries, including Lowry Field and Buckley Field. Lowry was converted to an Air Force training school after the war, was used by President Eisenhower as a summertime command center, and was temporary home to the Air Force Academy while the permanent facility at Colorado Springs was under construction. Buckley Field was at various times a Naval Air station, a bombing range, and home to the Colorado Air Guard. The Fitzsimons Medical Center was also expanded during World War II.[61] Furthermore, the Defense Highway Acts provided federal money to improve the roads and highways leading through Aurora to these installations, most notably Colfax Avenue (U.S. 40), Aurora's main thoroughfare.[62]

Aurora, ca. 1950, *Denver Public Library, Western History Collection*

These government investments accelerated Aurora's growth. Between 1947 and 1951 the school district census grew from 850 to 2706, assessed valuation nearly tripled, and the number of paved roads and streets rocketed from 22 blocks to 22.5 miles. By the 1960 census Aurora's population had grown to nearly fifty thousand, from less than four thousand in 1940.

However, Aurora's most dramatic growth was yet to come. In 1960 Aurora was one-tenth as large as Denver, but by 1990 it would grow to half the size of its neighbor. The main catalysts were the growth (and eventual relocation) of the Denver airport, the construction of I-70 across Aurora's northern edge in 1964, and the completion of I-225 right through its middle ten years later. In light of the fact that I-225 helped suburban Aurora's economy outpace Denver's, it is ironic that the BPR added it to the Interstate map in 1955 as one of the "urban" segments that secured broader congressional support.[63]

Right next to I-225, in the middle of Aurora, the Edward J. DeBartolo Corporation opened one of the largest regional malls in the United States in 1975. It cost more than $50 million to build, encompassed 1.2 million square feet of air-conditioned interior space on 130 acres, and employed 2,500 people in some 120 stores. Farther south along I-225, new apartment complexes sprouted, including one development that added almost five thousand new units to Aurora's housing stock. A second large mall opened, with 70 stores. New development activity was manifest in the 1980 census, which found that Aurora had grown by 111.5 percent since 1970, adding 84,000 new residents, while Denver's population had declined by 23,000. Aurora took on the title of "America's Fastest Growing Midsized City."[64]

Much of this development was facilitated by the creation of special "metropolitan districts" under a Colorado statute passed in 1947. Under that law, all that was needed to create a metropolitan district (for water, sewer, sanitation, police, parks, streets, or fire protection) was a *pro forma* petition with signatures from 10–15 percent of the affected taxpayers. As a practical matter, this meant that a developer could singlehandedly create such a district before selling any of his land and thereby avail himself of a broad range of municipal powers including zoning, eminent domain, levying property taxes, and—most importantly—bonding, with no debt limit. The developer could then finance his infrastructure with tax-exempt (and therefore federally subsidized) loans backed by future revenues from the as-yet-to-be-built homes, with little or no personal risk. George Wallace had used eleven of these metropolitan districts to build his Tech Center real estate empire.[65]

Other states allowed similarly aggressive use of tax-exempt bonds, most notably Texas, which joined Colorado in encouraging this practice to facilitate suburban development. However, even those states that allowed these special bonding districts did not authorize them to fund brand-new development. But in Colorado the practice was entirely unregulated; therefore developers did not have to put up any equity for capital improvements. As a result, Colorado accounted for nearly half of this type of borrowing nationwide.[66] At least six metropolitan districts sponsored by Denver-area

Stapleton Airport and Aurora, with downtown Denver in distance,
Colorado Historical Society

developers went bankrupt in a real estate downturn during the mid-1980s. As a result, the Resolution Trust Company (the federal agency created to resolve the savings-and-loan crisis) foreclosed on the defaulted loans and assumed ownership of large tracts of Douglas County. In one case, a 4.2-mile, four-lane highway called the Founders Parkway was built, but the district defaulted before anything else could be built, leaving a highway-to-nowhere replete with signs pointing to nonexistent subdivisions.[67] The developments that were successful, however, were typically annexed into nearby cities. Aurora pursued an aggressive annexation strategy so that it covered almost a hundred square miles in the mid-eighties.[68]

Meanwhile, Aurora's economy also benefited as nearby Stapleton Airport grew into the nation's fourth busiest. More than half a dozen times since the end of World War II, Denver had issued tax-exempt bonds to finance airport expansions, borrowing over $100 million. The main runways were extended on surplus federal land no longer needed for the chemical weapons installation at the Rocky Mountain Arsenal. By 1978 almost twenty million passengers used Stapleton each year (up from two million passengers a year

Aerial view of Stapleton, *Colorado Historical Society*

in the sixties). But air traffic demand was still rising, and there was not sufficient room to accommodate it at Stapleton. Old and dusty plans for a bigger facility were revived and put into motion.[69]

As early as 1943, Mayor Stapleton had proposed that the city buy farmland farther afield than the existing airport for a new aviation hub that could relieve runway congestion. The proposal never got off the ground but was often revisited. In the late sixties, airport manager Ben Bezoff wanted to use surplus revenues from Stapleton to buy land for an eventual successor airfield. However, this would have violated the covenants in the legal documents from the airport's outstanding bond issues. Finally, as Stapleton Airport was literally bursting at its seams, Mayor Federico Pena (1983–1991) spearheaded a successful campaign to begin construction of a new Denver

Denver International Airport, *Colorado Historical Society*

International Airport, financed by $4 billion worth of voter-approved, tax-exempt bonds. In a move reminiscent of Stapleton's decision to locate the first airport miles from all settlements, the new airport was placed in the middle of undeveloped farm country nearly thirty miles northeast of downtown, just beyond the borders of Aurora. "America's fastest growing midsized city" was now situated between Denver and its enormous new airport, which was slated to include nearly five thousand acres of commercial, office, hotel, and residential development.[70]

To capture the growth that would follow Denver International Airport and E-470, Aurora proposed to expand to 146 square miles. Denver covered only 111 square miles and was trying to annex another 40 square miles of its own, surrounding the new airport. The Poundstone amendment mandated that Adams County voters approve any annexation by Denver, so Aurora's leaders were able to force Mayor Pena to negotiate. After extensive haggling and litigation, the two cities agreed on new boundaries, with Denver remaining larger by a slim margin. Denver gained about 45 square miles for its multiuse development plan, dubbed "Gateway," while Adams County retained the rest of the land surrounding the new airport. When the dust settled, Denver remained larger (155 square miles to Aurora's 144 square miles), but Aurora controlled about 80 square miles of undeveloped land within fifteen minutes of the new airport. In addition, Denver agreed to restrict the number of new hotel rooms built in its new territory to one-fifth the quantity built in Adams County.[71]

At the same time that the airport project and the E-470 highway stimulated a new round of growth, Aurora continued to reap rewards from the local military investments. In 1991 Aurora began to create an 821-acre reservoir on the site of the former Lowry Air Force Base bombing range. This simultaneously freed the city from a growth-constraining water shortage (they had formerly bought water from Denver) and brought marinas, beaches, fishing, golf courses, and a bike path within easy reach. After the remainder of the base was closed, the federal government provided millions of dollars in direct grants, augmented by a $35 million tax-exempt bond issue, to replace the abandoned military buildings with parks and a new school, readying the 1,866-acre site for the development of 3,200 new homes and 1.5 million square feet of new office space. In 1999 Fitzsimons Hospital was also decommissioned and slated for federally supported redevelopment. The state announced plans to make the 577-acre Aurora campus into the new location of the University of Colorado Medical School, along with a biotech business incubator park, public swimming pools, and new recreational facilities. Nearby, on Aurora's northern boudary, the Rocky Mountain Arsenal was converted into a National Wildlife Refuge.[72]

The long-term demographic changes in Aurora and Denver over the post–World War II period were strikingly different. The 1990 census showed that Denver had dropped to 460,000 residents from a high of 514,000 in 1970. At the same time, the metropolitan area had added more than 500,000 new residents, reaching a population high of 1.8 million. Whereas before the war three-quarters of area residents lived in Denver, the 1990 census found only one-quarter of the metropolitan population still in the city. In the half century since 1940, Denver's population had grown by about 138,000, while its suburbs added 1.2 million people—nine times as many. Aurora reached a population of 222,000 in 1990 and was poised for a new round of expansion after the impending completion of DIA and E-470.

However, the area was not becoming bipolar: a twin-city metropolis with two competing downtowns. As Aurora's city manager James Gresemer acknowledged in 1987, "if the economic, social, and technological forces shaping our city today don't encourage the creation of a downtown, you'd be wasting a lot of effort to build one." Furthermore, Aurora was not the only large new megaburb to emerge along the metropolitan periphery, fostered by subsidies to decentralized growth. For example, on the other side of Denver, the newly incorporated city of Lakewood housed over one hundred thousand residents, and Arvada, Longmont, Thornton, and West-minster all grew to over fifty thousand.[73] In the face of these demographic shifts, Denver retained its central position in the metropolitan area by completely revamping its own downtown.

REINVENTING DOWNTOWN

Beginning in the 1950s, Denver's downtown shopping district lost sales (and sales-tax revenues) to new suburban shopping centers. This trend started with the Cherry Creek Shopping Center in 1953, the University Hills Center in 1955, and the Lakeside Center in 1956. It escalated in 1968 when Cinderella City, the largest mall west of the Mississippi River, opened in Englewood, and again a few years later when the Aurora Mall opened. At the same time, well-known downtown department stores closed down, one by one. Like-wise, as office parks like the Tech Center sprouted in the suburbs, propor-tionately fewer Denverites worked downtown.[74] In order to compete, central business district boosters initiated a redevelopment effort, remaking the old nineteenth-century core so that it might survive into the twenty-first century.

Downtown businessmen recognized that the planning office's designs would not help the central business district. They formed the Downtown

Cinderella City, Englewood, 1968,
Denver Public Library, Western History Collection

Denver Improvement Association ("Downtown Denver"), similar to a contemporary Business Improvement District. By 1961 they had pushed the City Council to take two initial steps: creating the Denver Urban Renewal Association and sanctioning the privately funded Downtown Denver Master Plan Committee to bypass the Denver Planning Office. In 1964, the committee formally recommended the "Skyline Urban Renewal Area," and obtained a grant from the federal Urban Renewal Administration for further planning.

"Skyline" was a twenty-seven-block urban renewal project oriented around a pedestrian mall along Sixteenth Street. It involved the demolition of old, hulking office buildings and "obsolescent residences," replacing them with glass-and-steel office towers and a new convention center. Robert

Urban renewal demolishes the Cooper Building, 1970,
Denver Public Library, Western History Collection

Cameron, the head of the Urban Renewal agency, justified the "slum clearance" component (typical of urban renewal projects in this era) with the argument that "substandard areas breed social and economic ills of the worst kind" and that "most of [the displaced residents] are skid row types." When demolition was finished, downtown looked like a wasteland, marked by the solitary profile of a single landmark clock tower.[75]

In order to finance Skyline, Downtown Denver had to be creative, and it also needed special intervention by President Lyndon Johnson. The federal urban renewal law required local government to pay for one-third of each project, but the city council was unlikely to do so. Downtown Denver first obtained voter approval for a bond issue to pay for the convention center, to be repaid from convention revenues. Then Palmer Hoyt, editor of the *Denver Post,* asked President Johnson, as a personal favor, for legislation that would allow the convention center to count toward Denver's share of the project as

Sixteenth Street after urban renewal, 1979,
Denver Public Library, Western History Collection

a "non-cash grant-in-aid." By the end of 1965, Downtown Denver had a commitment from the federal government to provide money for Skyline.[76]

In effect, Downtown Denver conceded retail business to the suburban shopping malls, for the time being, and instead developed new office buildings. Whereas in 1950 there were only 1.2 million square feet of usable office space downtown, by 1983 this had multiplied nearly tenfold. The first building, which served as an anchor, was William Zeckendorf's Mile High Center, designed by I. M. Pei and located adjacent to the new convention center. It was followed by Republic Plaza, Prudential Plaza, Sakura Square, Tabor Center, and Denver National Bank Plaza.[77] Linking these individual developments together was the new Sixteenth Street Pedestrian/Transit Mall and the proactive participation of RTD—the Regional Transportation District.

In 1969, with the Denver Tramway Company on its last legs, the state legislature had created RTD to take over the company's bus routes and formulate a mass-transit plan for the seven-county region. Ridership had dropped to 60,000 a day, fares had increased to forty cents, and there was pressure to increase wages. Therefore, DTC shareholders agreed to sell the transit operations to the city, which passed them on to RTD in 1971. Over the next three years RTD was able to acquire additional suburban bus routes, supported by a regionwide .35-mill property tax for planning and administration and an additional .5-mill levy for capital investments. The new agency then turned its attention toward rail-based mass transit and a proposed new pedestrian "transitmall."

RTD joined the Sixteenth Street Mall project in 1976. Earlier, Downtown Denver architects had designed the mall without any transit. Their plans were limited to closing the street to traffic and making cosmetic streetscape improvements, funded by special assessments on neighboring property. But with RTD involved, the project was enlarged. Using funds from a half-cent regional sales tax that had been approved after the 1973 energy crisis, RTD built new bus terminals at the foot of the mall on Market Street and at the opposite end of Sixteenth Street next to the civic center. Electric buses would link them with a free shuttle service, with stops at each cross-street. I. M. Pei was hired to design the new "transitway," and additional consultants were hired to plan the bus service.[78]

Governor Lamm, who cautioned that "Denver is in danger of becoming an endless Los Angeles in the Rockies," hoped to use new provisions in the 1973 Highway Act to divert some of the federal money earmarked for the aborted I-470 project to RTD. However, since most of the I-470 route was formally classified as "rural," most of the funds could not be transferred to mass transit, and the local highway lobby vigorously opposed the use of gas-tax revenues for mass transit. Nevertheless, after the second energy shock in 1977, a partial transfer was approved.[79]

Closed to traffic in 1980, Sixteenth Street reopened as a pedestrian transitmall in 1982. RTD commenced its free shuttle-bus service (every seventy seconds), and new office and retail development continued. The Rouse Company opened an indoor mall, Westin put up a hotel, and more than 1,500 apartment units were built nearby.[80]

The Skyline renewal effort and the Sixteenth Street Mall abated downtown's precipitous decline, so that it hit bottom by the late 1980s. By then the city was collecting a smaller share of the region's sales taxes than ever before, only a third of the area's major hotels were downtown, and 60 percent of the jobs were in the suburbs, compared to 6 percent in 1950. In 1987 Denver Dry Goods, a local department store dating back to the nineteenth century, was folded into May D & F, itself the product of earlier consolidations of landmark retailers. That same year, downtown hotel vacancy rates hit 47 percent, and office vacancy rates hit a high of 30 percent. Even though downtown added more office space between 1979 and 1983 than over the preceding three decades, the suburbs added twice as much during the same period.[81] The process of remaking downtown needed to continue.

RTD first proposed a new mass transit system for Denver in 1974. After a brief flirtation with a futuristic Disney-like system based upon small personal railpods, it joined the city in 1976 to submit an application for federal funds to build a conventional subway system. The Urban Mass Transit Administration rejected the request and instead offered $200 million for bus service improvements, citing as justification the area's dispersed population, high auto use, and low mass-transit ridership. In 1978, faced with dangerously high carbon monoxide levels and a pervasive "brown cloud" caused by auto emissions and local weather patterns, RTD began to offer free off-peak travel, supported by a matching grant from the federal government. Coming on the heels of the second energy shock, the measure temporarily increased ridership 45 percent. Much of this gain was retained when RTD reinstituted fares at a deep off-peak discount.[82]

In this new environment, with increased ridership and a new post-energy-crisis public willingness to fund mass transit, in 1980 RTD proposed a new seventy-three-mile light rail system (not referred to as a tram or trolley, because they wanted no association with the Denver Tramway Company, although it was essentially a revival of the old system). The state legislature agreed to raise RTD's regional sales tax from .5 cents to 1.25 cents, but voters rejected the measure. Nor could RTD obtain federal support for the system, despite the dedication of part of the 1982 five-cents-per-gallon federal gas-tax hike to new mass transit projects. Those limited funds were soaked up by transit projects in Los Angeles, Atlanta, and others. Nevertheless, RTD was able to leverage its existing sales tax revenues to finance the first 5.3-mile section, which opened in late 1994. Extensions to the system have since been completed, reaching C-470 in the southwest, and new lines are planned to extend southeast to the Denver Tech Center and west to Jefferson County.[83]

While RTD was planning and building its light rail system, Downtown Denver and the Denver Urban Renewal Agency (DURA) were still remaking the central business district. In a former blue-collar residential and industrial neighborhood, they condemned over four hundred separate parcels, covering 160 acres, to create a new higher education campus shared by Colorado University–Denver, Metropolitan State College, and Community College of Denver. The only building or parcel not used for the new "Auraria Campus" was the landmark Tivoli brewery, which was redeveloped as a multiplex movie theater. A new "parkway" was built to connect the new campus to downtown and to the Valley Highway.[84]

By the 1990s, professional sports had been recruited, becoming a core component of the new downtown identity. Coors Field, a stadium for the major league baseball expansion franchise, the Colorado Rockies, was built in 1994 within walking distance of Sixteenth Street. In 2000, a new downtown arena to house the NBA's Denver Nuggets and the NHL's Colorado Avalanche was completed, also within walking distance of downtown shops, hotels, and restaurants. Retail development continued, specifically oriented toward tourists and suburbanites on excursions into the city. With the help of a bond issue from the urban renwal agency, Denver Pavilions, a two-block long mall-style retail center took shape on Sixteenth Street, bringing a Barnes and Noble, Nike Town, Virgin Records, Hard Rock Cafe, two Wolfgang Puck restaurants, and a twelve-screen multiplex.[85]

Elsewhere, an abandoned warehouse district neighboring Skyline and intersecting the Sixteenth Street Mall was turned into a pedestrian-friendly collection of eateries and boutiques known as LoDo (lower downtown), intentionally reminiscent of New York City's SoHo. In 1993 DURA spent $48 million to renovate the old Denver Dry department store building, converting the upper floors to apartments and attracting new retail tenants to the street level. The Adam's Mark Hotel was overhauled and expanded, taking over the former May D & F Store (closed when the chain, the last remaining Denver-based department store company, was sold to Houston-based Foley's). As downtown's prospects brightened, about two dozen other old downtown buildings were rehabilitated and converted into loft apartments, providing 1,600 new units. In March 2000 the City broke ground on the new Commons Park, a new initiative adjacent to LoDo. The new park, with soccer fields, walking trails, and picnic areas, was part of the Denver Commons project, a 21-block neighborhood with 2,000 residences modeled after Boston's Back Bay and financed using a newly created metropolitan district.[86]

Despite all these efforts, however, downtown's fortunes remained uneven. Office vacancy rates had dropped to 9 percent by 1997, but retail vacancy rates were still as high as 30 percent in 1995, while thriving suburban retail centers sprouted in all directions. The Cherry Creek Shopping Center pursued it own makeover in 2000, retaining three premium department stores (Saks, Neiman-Marcus, and Lord and Taylor) and 140 other shops, while simultaneously expanding to add 330 new storefronts in a new pseudo-urban "Cherry Creek Village" development. Yet another new megamall, Flatiron Crossing, opened in suburban Broomfield, alongside the Denver–Boulder freeway. With three department stores, 170 shops, and a two-block long simulated streetscape, it alone makes the downtown retail complexes seem paltry, and it is not even the largest shopping complex in the metro area, a distinction still claimed—until a larger one is built elsewhere along the periphery—by the Park Meadows Mall near the Tech Center, south of the city along I-25.[87]

CONCLUSION

In the latter half of the twentieth century, Denver grew into a sprawling and decentralized metropolis, increasingly dependent on motor vehicles and a far-flung highway system. As local historian Thomas Noel has observed, it became difficult to determine where Denver stopped and suburban municipalities started, as "wheat fields, ranches, and dairies that once surrounded the Mile High City are now sprawling subdivisions, with shopping center nuclei."[88] Despite complaints about high air pollution, traffic congestion increased at twice the rate of population growth, making the battle against the "brown cloud" unwinnable. Denverites' journey-to-work time increased, carpooling declined, and bus ridership fell. Population density in the area dropped while per capita vehicle-miles traveled doubled, 84 percent of which were outside the city limits. Between 1980 and 1997, the number of cars in the metropolitan area increased by half.[89] In a poll conducted in 2000, more than three-fourths of area commuters admitted that they do not change their driving plans during air-quality advisories, even though nineteen out of twenty understood these advisories to mean that particulate pollution and carbon monoxide levels were too high and citizens should not drive. By the 1999–2000 winter, pollution had gotten so bad that one out of three days were flagged "red"—the highest advisory level. Yet, in the 2000 election, Colorado voters overwhelming rejected, by a two-to-one margin, a growth-control referendum.[90]

One local researcher observed in 1998 that when "people say 'Don't Los Angelize Denver,' they are howling at the moon."[91] Imaginative redevelopment initiatives prevented the abandonment of downtown, but the metropolis nevertheless continued to decentralize rapidly, impelled by the accumulated power of public subsidies that encouraged sprawling suburbs at the expense of the core.

These same changes occurred throughout the West, in towns and cities of all sizes, driven by efforts to accommodate automobility and by policies that funneled highway funds to rural and sparsely populated areas. By the mid-1990s, more westerners lived in urbanized areas (six out of seven) than residents of the Northeast (four out of five). As Rob Melnick, a public policy professor from Arizona State University, complained in 1996, "I've been driving from one meeting about sprawl to another for fifteen years, and the only thing that's changed is that now it takes a lot longer to get there."[92]

Automobiles and a Small Town

The relentless growth of motor vehicle use has created highway needs that constantly exceed the money available. . . . These problems resolve themselves into a simple business question of how to spend the public money so that it will give the greatest benefit to the most traffic.

—Biennial Report of the Vermont State Highway Board, 1940

BACKGROUND

Middlebury is in the Champlain Valley, next to the western slope of the Green Mountains. Permanently settled in 1783, the community depended first on farming wheat. By 1800, when local leaders started Middlebury College, the town had grown to a population of one thousand and was the Addison County seat. The state's renowned marble industry was born in Middlebury in 1802, attracting a steady flow of new settlers. By 1820 the population had doubled, and the 1830 census counted 3,468 residents, making Middlebury the largest town in the state. In 1832 the Village of Middlebury (within the larger Town of Middlebury) was incorporated, in order to provide public utilities in the more densely settled central areas. Consisting of about three hundred buildings, the village was clustered near the Otter Creek Falls, on both sides of the river.

Bridge over Otter Creek , Middlebury, ca.1860,
Henry Sheldon Museum of Vermont History

Middlebury's dominance of the marble trade was fleeting, as competing processing centers opened closer to the biggest quarries. Addison County instead became the capital of the merino wool industry, with more production than any other county in the United States. The local economy diversified, adding a pulp mill, a glass factory, furniture manufacturing, commercial apple orchards, and maple syrup production. This prosperity did not last, though. After 1850, when the wool industry was decimated by the repeal of protective tariffs and other businesses struggled to compete against firms closer to the major Atlantic markets, the population began to dwindle.

By 1870 Middlebury counted less than three thousand residents, and surrounding Addison County had about twenty-three thousand, in both cases a decline of 12 percent from earlier highs. The slide lasted one hundred years, during which time dairy farming emerged as the area's economic mainstay. By the early years of the twentieth century, there were nearly as many cows as people in Addison County.[1]

Middlebury Population

	Town	Addison County
1850	3,517	26,549
1900	3,045	21,912
1910	2,848	20,010
1920	2,914	18,666
1930	2,968	17,952
1940	3,175	17,944
1950	4,778	19,442
1960	5,305	20,076
1970	6,532	24,226
1980	7,574	29,406
1990	8,034	32,953
2000	8,183	35,924

The town's two halves, on either side of Otter Creek, were joined by a bridge across the waterway at the village center. The first bridge, built by town father Gamaliel Painter (one of the founders of Middlebury College), was a low-slung wooden structure which was replaced five times in the town's first hundred years. Finally, after a major downtown fire engulfed the sixth wooden bridge in the 1890s, the town built a permanent stone bridge, aided by a large donation from Joseph Battell, publisher of the *Middlebury Register* and one of the largest individual landowners in Vermont. Raised ten feet higher than its predecessors, the Battell bridge changed the downtown topography, requiring some Main Street merchants to move their entrances to what had previously been their second floors.[2]

In the early nineteenth century, the Middlebury bridge was the only path across the Otter for many miles in either direction, with the exception of an unstable structure three miles south. That span, built jointly with the neighboring town of Cornwall in 1801, fell into disrepair because neither town was willing to pay for upkeep. In 1815 the Middlebury town meeting voted to cease maintenance of the bridge and the connecting road. When the crossing became impassable, Cornwall sued, and in 1822 the court ordered Middlebury to rebuild it. The selectmen refused, were fined by the court, and the work was completed with the fine proceeds. Since townspeople were uninterested in contributing to regular upkeep on the Three-Mile Bridge, as it was called, and there were no private donations like those that saved the Main Street Bridge, it soon resumed its previous "precarious condition" status.[3]

Unfortunately, Otter Creek was inadequate as a waterborne travel route, even while it presented an obstacle to overland transportation. Downstream rapids and a waterfall interfered with navigation between Middlebury and Lake Champlain, making it practically unusable. Instead, the village's connections were all overland. At first, there was only a single route—a path cleared through the woods as far as the neighboring hamlets of Salisbury in the south and New Haven in the north—but this link was soon augmented by two private turnpikes.[4]

The Center Turnpike, one of the first turnpikes in the nation, crossed over the Green Mountains via the Middlebury Gap and connected to the Boston Post Road. Gamaliel Painter established the turnpike corporation in 1800, raising $2,700 for the road by selling stock. The value of the shares skyrocketed at first, topping $100 for each share by 1803, up tenfold from an initial price of $10. However, construction costs rose higher than expected, amounting to as much as $1,000 per mile in some cases, and Painter repeatedly asked his investors for additional capital. By 1815 shares had plummeted to $4 each, down 96 percent from their peak. The pike was completed in 1808, and stagecoach service to Boston was offered immediately (the trip took two days to complete). But like many other turnpike operators of the era, the company soon abandoned portions of the route, leaving Middlebury's segment to the town in 1817.[5]

Meanwhile, Painter had unsuccessfully petitioned the assembly to sanction another turnpike that would run north–south through Middlebury, covering the entire length of the state. Instead, the Waltham Turnpike Company was chartered to complete a more modest road, running north from the village center to Vergennes, on Lake Champlain. The route crossed the Otter near a paper mill at the northern edge of town, on a new bridge known as the Pulp Mill Bridge. Completed in 1807, the Waltham Turnpike was abandoned in 1828, and the bridge was jointly taken over by Middlebury and the neighboring town of Weybridge.[6]

After the turnpike companies withdrew, the new roads soon fell into disrepair. One nineteenth-century visitor, Yale president Timothy Dwight, observed that "a slight rain makes them so slippery as to be impassable with safety."[7] Another Vermonter noted that "to travel the roads with a cart loaded with six or seven hundred-weight, we had to employ half a dozen men to hang on one side or the other, to keep the cart from turning over."[8] As soon as possible, Addison County residents turned to train service for out-of-town travel.

The Rutland Railroad began service between Rutland and Burlington in 1849, with a stop in Middlebury. This was the first leg of a line that would span the state from Montreal to Bennington. At the southern terminus, there were links to New York City, and a spur from Rutland provided connection to Boston. By the end of the nineteenth century, there were more than one thousand miles of active rail tracks in the state, and eight passenger trains made scheduled stops in Middlebury each day, as well as seven freight trains.[9]

GOOD ROADS AND THE ADVENT OF THE AUTOMOBILE IN VERMONT

Of the ninety-one turnpikes that had been chartered in Vermont prior to the railroad era, only thirty ever opened, covering about five hundred miles. None was successful, driven out of business by trains and the availability of so-called "shunpike" detour paths worn around toll barriers. Most of the pikes were abandoned by 1860, and only one remained in operation in 1890. A survey done during the state's centennial, in 1891, found that the road system consisted of abandoned and dilapidated turnpikes and travel-worn paths between villages and nearby hamlets, almost thirteen thousand miles of muddy and rutted dirt roads, strewn with rocks and boulders.

Vermont's roads were in terrible condition, barely maintained by a labor tax of four days per year for each male between the ages of sixteen and sixty. Towns were divided into highway districts, each overseen by a volunteer "pathmaster," but without proper equipment or professional training, the "road gangs" were ineffective. One observer described their efforts: "A gang of men . . . proceed to break up hard settled ground, and scrape upon the surface of the road sods and other rubbish utterly unfit for road material, and call it road repairing." Mud and snow kept most roads closed for all but a few months each year, leaving most Vermonters isolated. Travel from farm to market was intermittent and unpredictable.[10]

Middlebury's Joseph Battell joined other leaders from across the state to form the Vermont League for Good Roads in 1892, "to awaken general interest in the improvement of public roads, [and to] determine the best method for building and maintaining them." The group distributed literature and appointed representatives from each county to lobby in Montpelier for legislation authorizing state-sponsored road building. Battell and the other Addison County representatives organized local committees to encourage "considerable agitation for better roads" by writing letters and appearing in person before the General Assembly.[11]

The League achieved quick success with the passage of the Vermont Highway Act of 1892, which had two main components. First, it created a state aid system for roads by imposing a special statewide property tax which was to be distributed back to townships in proportion to road mileage and spent under the supervision of town road commissioners. Second, it created a State Highway Commission, with three members appointed by the governor to study town road programs. In addition, towns were authorized to borrow money for highway projects by selling road bonds.

The Commission's lengthy report, issued in 1894, described a litany of inadequacies and recommended a stepped-up state commitment to good

Joseph Battell,
Henry Sheldon Museum of Vermont History

roads. The legislature responded by authorizing another study-only commission to reevaluate the state's involvement in road building and also renewed the 1892 state-aid program (this time restricting the expenditures to "permanent" improvements and prohibiting use of state aid for maintenance). The second report called for more centralized control of highway construction, citing the widely inconsistent results of the aid program, which was virtually unsupervised.[12] Likewise, in 1898, newly elected Governor Edward C. Smith complained in his inaugural message that the current system did not adequately ensure that public funds were spent appropriately. In a call for stronger legislation, the governor proclaimed that "civilization and good roads go hand in hand."[13] Accordingly, in 1898 the legislature created the Office of the State Highway Commissioner to administer and oversee the state aid program, authorizing the commissioner to withhold

Marble hitching posts on town green, reserved for horses,
Henry Sheldon Museum of Vermont History

funds from towns that failed to comply with state-mandated standards.
Vermonters' wariness of centralized government produced resistance to the
new state control of roads. A few towns refused to comply and unsuccessfully
petitioned the legislature in 1902 for release of "their" money. Meanwhile,
good roads advocates continued to lobby for increased funding. Battell
regularly ran editorials in his *Middlebury Register* bemoaning the inadequacy
of Vermont's dirt roads and urging a more aggressive improvement program.

Ironically, even though Battell was a good roads crusader, he was also
described by the *WPA Guide to Vermont* as "the most aggressive opponent
of automotive transportation that [Vermont] has ever known." At the same
time that he editorialized on behalf of highways, he used his newspaper to
report nationwide auto-related accidents and deaths. He reconciled these two
positions by arguing that improved roads should be reserved exclusively for

horse-drawn vehicles. He favored hard-paving downtown streets and success-fully campaigned for marble hitching posts on Main Street, while printing editorials with titles like "Should Automobiles Have Their Own Roads?" and "Let the Owners of the Highway Dragons Build Their Own Roads." His opposition to the automobile reached its zenith when he unilaterally closed the Center Turnpike road to cars where it passed through his expansive mountain-top estate on the Middlebury Gap. Nevertheless, he lost the ensuing legal battle, and his anti-auto signs and barriers were removed.[14]

Battell was not alone. At the turn of the nineteenth century, other Addison County residents echoed his complaints about cars. For example, whenever Bernice Wing, a resident of nearby Proctor, traveled across the county to visit relatives in Vergennes, she had hair-raising encounters with cruising motorists: "When a machine was spotted in the distance by its cloud of dust, with which it later enveloped us, we would aim for the nearest driveway . . . we and the horse were left panting."[15] The State Highway Commissioner recounted that "one instance was brought to our attention of a heavy automobile containing four men, running eleven miles between two Vermont villages in twenty-four minutes. Of the runaways [horses] along the route, only two proved serious." In 1904 Governor Charles J. Bell devoted part of his inaugural message to this problem, calling for speed limits and suggesting that autos be restricted to a few main trunk lines. Soon thereafter the General Assembly passed a state speed limit of fifteen miles per hour in most places and six miles per hour within all incorporated village limits.[16]

This, however, did not quell anti-auto sentiments. In 1906 Bell's successor, Fletcher T. Proctor, noted that even though "automobiles are here to stay . . . during this transition period many of the men, women, and children who are living up and down our hills and valleys are practically banished from the use of our highways." He reiterated Bell's earlier threat: "We may well consider whether for the present automobiles should not be prohibited the use of certain highways." These same concerns had already prompted mandatory vehicle registration and operator's licenses, following the precedent established by New York State in 1901. Motorists were charged two dollars when they registered their vehicle and another two dollars for a license (two 1906 dollars is equal to approximately 40 2003 dollars). Proctor called these user charges "nominal," and urged the legislature to raise them "to produce a more substantial revenue for state highway purposes." He was unable to secure legislation to raise the fees, and good roads lobbyists were able to insert a clause in the statute dedicating the existing fees exclusively to highway construction.[17]

The first motorcar in Vermont, a Stanley Steamer, had arrived in 1897, followed by a gas-powered model in 1900. By 1906 there were fewer than four hundred motor vehicles in the entire state. The community of motorists was so small that *The Vermonter*, a monthly magazine, listed the owners of all 380 registered vehicles in its July 1905 issue. There was only one Middlebury resident on the list, which is not surprising since contemporary maps indicated no passable road to Rutland, while the path to Burlington could not earn even a "good" rating from the motorists' club.[18] For half a century, most north–south movement along this corridor had been via frequent train service, but this would change over the next half century. The Rutland Railroad struggled, changed hands repeatedly (first to the New York Central in 1905, and then to the New York, New Haven and Hartford in 1911), and finally went bankrupt in 1938, halting all passenger service a few years later.[19] Instead of riding the train, Vermonters were embracing automobility, with the vigorous encouragement of the state and federal governments.

HIGHWAY FEDERALISM IN THE GREEN MOUNTAIN STATE, 1906–1940

In 1904 the Vermont Good Roads Association was formed (as the successor to the Vermont League for Good Roads) for "the improvement of the public highways of Vermont." At its first annual meeting, the group passed the following measure:

> RESOLVED: Vermont needs better and more permanently constructed main
> highways leading from the chief business and manufacturing centers of the

state to the rural communities . . . that roads which are smooth and hard at all seasons of the year make habitation along their borders more desirable, economize time and force in transporting products, reduce wear and tear on harness and vehicles and enhance the value of farm land and farm products, . . . facilitate rural mail delivery and are a potent aid to education, religion, and sociability.

They called for "more money . . . provided largely by the State or nation," controlled and administered by the State Highway Commissioner. In attendance at the meeting was future federal road Commissioner Thomas MacDonald.[20]

The drive for more state-funded road building produced a series of new laws, beginning with the Vermont Highway Act of 1906, which firmly established highways as a public good, paid for by all Vermonters, and controlled by a new Department of Highways staffed with engineers. The department was not only empowered to grant (or refuse) final approval for all state-aid projects but also charged with issuing roadway standards for width, crown height, gradient, and drainage. The Act also limited eligibility for the new dollar-for-dollar matching grants to specially designated "selected highways," or trunk lines. To supplement the state highway funds, the Act also appropriated more general revenues and boosted registration fees. In order to force townships to participate in the highway initiative, the Act also required them to make appropriations for highway repairs equivalent to 0.2 percent of their total assessed valuation. The state-aid system was further augmented two years later, with the passage of the Automobile Act of 1908, which increased the general revenue allocation by half, raised registration fees again, and required annual renewal for drivers' licenses and vehicle registration. Another measure, in 1910, doubled the annual state-aid appropriation.

A 1912 highway law raised the budget allocation again, by a third, and also introduced the Patrol Maintenance System—ten official patrol routes covering seventy miles of state-aid highways. Roving crews monitored the assigned routes, performing minor repairs and assisting stranded travelers, all free of charge. This system was soon expanded, covering almost three hundred miles along forty-four routes by 1914 and extending to over two thousand miles a decade later.[21]

As escalating highway programs produced improvements, more Vermonters purchased cars and took to the roads. Whereas in 1908 fewer than five hundred motor vehicles were registered in the state, about twelve thousand were registered in 1915, by which time more than fourteen thousand drivers held valid Vermont licenses.

In Middlebury there were fewer than a hundred registered automobiles, but motorcars and trucks drove through the village center regularly. To mitigate what the *Middlebury Register* called the "incompatibility" of automobiles, the town permanently stationed a policeman on Main Street to direct traffic in 1915, and that year's annual town meeting saw extensive discussion of anti-auto measures, including a lower speed limit and a law requiring mufflers on all vehicles passing through town. Meanwhile, propelled by state mandates, road spending by both the town and village skyrocketed.

Annual road and bridge expenditures in Middlebury had stayed level from the Civil War through the turn of the century, but they doubled by 1916 and then tripled again over the next fifteen years. This rapid rise was driven by the state's highway initiatives, which accounted for one-quarter of the state budget by 1921. But state-aid payments only provided one-fifth of the money Middlebury spent. To make matters worse, even though a portion of the state funds came from user fees, once the state imposed a gas tax in 1923, local governments were prohibited from doing likewise. Consequently, Middlebury's entire share came from local property taxes, although the vast majority of the area residents did not yet own or drive a motor vehicle.[22]

Attempts to force Vermont motorists to pay a larger share of the costs were defeated. In 1924 *The Highway Problem in Vermont* report called for registration fees of at least twenty-five dollars per year and tripling the gas tax to three cents. Likewise, in 1926, economist Henry Trumbower reported to the Rutland Chamber of Commerce that the gas tax ought to be raised to five cents, or alternatively that the state should levy a five dollar per tire annual registration surcharge.[23] In the face of stiff opposition from auto clubs and the auto industry, these proposals fell on deaf ears. At the same time, there was mounting pressure for increased highway spending.

More than four thousand miles of roads in Vermont had been graded, widened, and upgraded to gravel surfaces as a result of the Good Roads movement. However, most of the reports issued at the time turned their focus to a higher standard, bemoaning the lack of hard-paved roads. Trumbower's study found that the state had only 140 miles of hard-paved roads, and another report announced that only forty of these were outside of city or town boundaries (implying that the urban roads didn't count). Claiming that it was "an accepted fact that the gravel road was no longer sufficient," another report, the first major state-wide survey with published results, proclaimed that it was necessary for six hundred highway miles to be "superior-to-gravel."[24] In his 1926 gubernatorial campaign, candidate John E. Weeks responded to the pressure from highway advocates by pledging to build forty miles of hard roads per year. After winning the election, he delivered on this promise and won reelection in 1928, becoming the first two-term governor in half a century.[25]

As more Vermont roads became passable by automobile, Middlebury's location at a regional crossroads produced a growing downtown traffic problem, even though few residents owned cars. By the mid-1920s, close to one thousand motor vehicles per day—almost half of which were from out of state—passed through town on the north–south road (designated U.S. Route 7 in 1925). Other through-traffic used the east–west routes, which converged at the town center to use the Battell Bridge across the Otter.[26] The resultant snarl became a major concern for all. Most local residents still relied on horse-drawn vehicles, but automobiles increasingly dominated the town's streets, occasionally striking and killing horses. Starting at this time, and continuing for the balance of the twentieth century, the agenda for the annual meetings (for both the Town and the Village) included contentious discussions about traffic and congestion.[27]

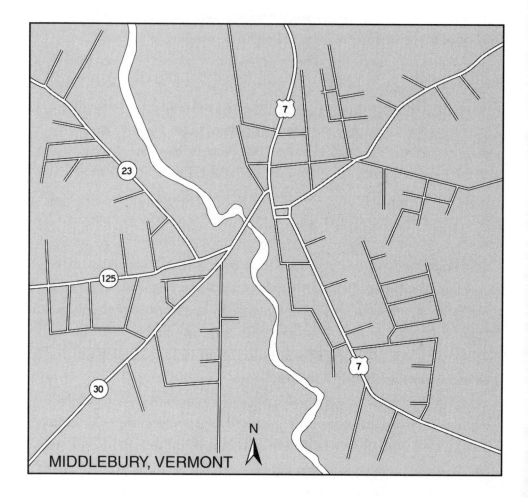

MIDDLEBURY, VERMONT

The Village implemented parking rules in 1926, soon followed by an experimental traffic light in 1929. The light, a three-color model nicknamed "the dummy," was surprisingly controversial. It intermittently malfunctioned, showing conflicting lights to different sides and thereby causing accidents, traffic jams, and frustration. Speeding through downtown soon became a problem, as some motorists would accelerate to catch the last moments of a green light. Appeals to the manufacturer for service support did not resolve the reliability problems, and the light was removed in the mid-1940s, although its pedestal was left standing in anticipation of an improved replacement.[28] The replacement never appeared because the matter was bitterly disputed at town meetings for decades thereafter, with some residents arguing that the automated traffic-control device was antithetical to Middlebury's townscape, while others were simply unwilling to pay for it.[29]

Meanwhile, Route 7 between Middlebury and Vergennes was hard-paved as part of Governor Weeks's 1927 highway initiative, which had been supported by federal aid and planned by the U.S. Bureau of Public Roads. In Middlebury, virtually the entire town turned out for a three-hundred-car celebratory motorcade and parade, followed by a baseball game and a fair, all part of a "Highway Progress Week" sponsored by the Vermont Chamber of Commerce. In the midst of such celebration, nobody seemed concerned that the federal programs that had aided the new construction would not support its maintenance. To make matters worse, the state also favored new construction over maintenance and began to assess Middlebury a per-mile fee to maintain the major highways within its boundaries. In this case, that included not only the newly paved U.S. 7, but Vermont 30 and 125 as well.[30]

State and federal mandates like these soaked up Middlebury's available resources, and the townspeople ended up with little control over how local street funds were spent. This was discussed at the 1934 Town Meeting, as the voters debated repaving Merchant's Row, one of the two main streets in the village center. Merchant's Row was not on the state highway system and therefore was not eligible for the same treatment as Main Street, the other major commercial thoroughfare in town. Main Street had been paved already,

Main Street, Middlebury, ca. 1935,
Henry Sheldon Museum of Vermont History

since it was a state highway, and also benefited from state-mandated (but underfunded) maintenance. Even though Merchant's Row was quite short, and just as important to Middlebury's street plan as Main Street, it was much more expensive to improve and maintain, because it was within the Village's incorporated boundaries but not designated as part of a trunk line.[31]

The state, however, was only following the federal lead in this regard. The previous year, the federal government had reiterated the anti-urban slant of its highway policies by mandating that most of the highway grants provided by the National Industrial Recovery Act be spent "outside of corporate limits." The Hayden-Cartwright Act also imposed the same requirements.[32]

At the same time, highway boosters used a rhetoric of crisis to press for more construction. As the completion of Governor Weeks's ten-year program approached, highway engineers announced that six hundred additional miles needed to be paved and that some of the earlier work had to be redone or repaired, even though the blueprint for the ten-year plan (as drawn up by the BPR) had promised that the state's highway needs would be satisfied "for a considerable number of years." A 1940 report complained that only 8.1 percent of the highway mileage in the state was paved, even though this represented almost ten times the 140 miles that had been paved in 1926 (the percentage figure was misleadingly low, because the highway engineers who wrote the report included thousands of miles of "unimproved dirt roads" in their estimate of statewide highway mileage). Private sector automobility advocates, too, grumbled that the state's highways were inadequate, using the self-serving statistics provided by the AAA and the state highway engineers. For example, one guidebook for motor-tourists reported that only one-eighth of the road-mileage in Vermont was usable for "touring."[33]

To further their cause, highway boosters recast the improvements made during the preceding decade as thoroughly inadequate, again using crisis-laden rhetoric. More than 1,500 road-miles outside of incorporated urban limits had been upgraded to superior-to-gravel, and none of the main roads remained unsurfaced. Only one-third were still gravel, and all but 250 miles of smaller local roads were gravel-or-better. Now, however, state highway engineers now proclaimed that gravel was no longer sufficient for secondary and tertiary rural routes, complaining that "there are 773.7 miles of the state system and 2,130 miles of [local roads] that are paved with *only* plain gravel" [emphasis added]. Not only did motorists and highway engineers declare gravel obsolete, they also demanded that roads be wider than ever before. The standard width for two-lane roads, as dictated by the federal BPR, was increased to thirty-two feet, a third wider than the twenty-four-foot roads planned (and built according to federal guidelines) in 1926. To justify these changes, state highway engineers argued in a 1940 report that "today's designs must provide a surface width to meet the requirements of wide heavy trucks and buses; alignments and grades must satisfy modern high speeds; shoulders must permit off-road parking." To meet these higher standards, they called for the reconstruction of more than half the existing state system.[34] The public cost of continuing to accommodate automobility ballooned.

In the mid-1930s the state legislature tried to close the gap between highway expenditures and revenues by experimenting with a novel return to turnpike-era practices. An act of 1933 granted rights to a private corporation to build a toll road across the Green Mountains, near the Mad River ski area. However, the venture failed to attract investors, since the toll road, to be known as the McCullough Turnpike, would face toll-free competition from state route 125 across the Middlebury Gap (formerly the Center Turnpike) and U.S. 2 to the north, along the banks of the Winooski River. In 1935 the company's turnpike rights were sold back to the state, and soon thereafter state highway 17, along the route of the failed turnpike, was added to Vermont's already overloaded road-building budget.[35]

Aside from the ever-increasing standards and expanding matching requirements from the federal highway program, another cause of the rapidly escalating financial strain was the growth of nonconstruction costs. By 1933 the state was spending $175 per road-mile on the free courtesy patrol ($2,325 per mile, in 2000 dollars), while winter sanding cost the state $32 per mile and plowing averaged $68 per mile ($425 and $903 in 2000 dollars, respectively). These costs continued to rise, as winter use of the highways rose, multiplying sixfold between 1931 and 1940 even though the economy was experiencing deflation; by 1941, winter maintenance absorbed about one-third of town highway funds, statewide. At the same time, the routine maintenance patrol system also grew considerably, employing 136 full-time "patrolmen" in 1936, cruising the entire state highway system.[36]

Highways had already been the single largest expense in the state budget since 1926, but a 1938 highway department report found that they now accounted for more than half of all state spending. While costs had skyrocketed, Vermont's population had remained stagnant: in 1910 there were 356,000 Vermonters, and in 1935 this number had increased only nominally, to 359,000—forcing each Vermonter to contribute more toward accomodating automobility. Only 27 percent of Vermont's population had drivers' licenses and even fewer owned cars (22 percent). Because there was always strong and well-organized opposition to higher user charges, available revenues could not keep up with expenditures; the annual shortfalls were made up with appropriations of general revenues (mostly raised by property taxes, although between 1931 and 1935 the state imposed an income tax, part of which funded highway projects) and by incurring debt.[37]

The state itself maintained a conservative approach to borrowing for highways, issuing debt only in the aftermath of a devastating flood in 1927 and again after a hurricane in 1938. This so-called "pay-as-you-go" approach was misleading, since the state financed it by forcing more costs onto the local governments. For example, over successive years many highway miles were reclassified from "state-aid highways" to "state highways," which meant that any municipalities these roads passed through would henceforth be assessed a charge for their maintenance. (Vermont had begun this practice in 1931, in an attempt to keep limited state funds available to match federal new-construction grants). At the same time, the Vermont Department of Highways reduced state-aid grants to towns, arguing that there were now fewer miles left in the "state-aid system." Discretionary state-aid grants to towns and villages had peaked in 1921 and steadily dwindled thereafter. Consequently, many local governments turned to the bond market, borrowing heavily to finance the increasingly burdensome state highway mandates. Highway bonds accounted for nearly one-third of the combined public debt in Vermont in 1938 (including all debt of the state and its counties, school districts, and municipalities).[38]

Middlebury suffered under these circumstances. On the one hand, the state and federal trunkline initiatives had made it easier to get to Middlebury by motor vehicle, and traffic volume at the village center rose accordingly. On the other hand, the vagaries of the highway finance mechanisms provided little assistance in adapting the local infrastructure, instead forcing the townspeople to subsidize rural trunklines, despite strong local resistance.

The statewide traffic survey completed in 1938 found that more than two thousand motor vehicles used U.S. 7 through Middlebury each day, triple the count from a decade earlier. Likewise, the number of automobiles entering town along State Route 30 nearly doubled.[39] During this same period, the number of cars and trucks registered in Vermont had increased by less than one-fifth, indicating that the increased traffic arose from out-of-state drivers and Vermonters who were choosing to use their vehicles more, in both cases attracted by government-subsidized toll-free highways. Also, by 1938 (the same year that the Rutland Railroad collapsed, unable to maintain its own infrastructure) two private bus lines served Middlebury, taking advantage of the new, heavily subsidized highway system.[40]

The increased car, truck, and bus use in Middlebury produced correspondingly higher highway maintenance needs, as well as demands for additional improvements. However, the town itself did not grow during this period, still numbering approximately three thousand residents, well below the nineteenth-century peak. Furthermore, as automotive traffic through the Middlebury area grew, so too did the wear and tear on the river crossings. Three-Mile Bridge had to be rebuilt to accommodate the heavier automotive vehicles, as did the Pulp Mill Bridge. WPA funds provided partial support to these two bridge projects in 1938, but Middlebury still had to devote scarce resources to fund the required local share of the projects.[41] At the same time, many residents objected to supporting automobility with their property taxes, especially amid the fiscal duress of the Depression.

At successive town meetings, voters cut the road tax in half. However, faced with escalating state and federal mandates, along with the increasing pressure for road building, the town manager was unable to correspondingly reduce expenditures.[42] As a result, Middlebury's debt burden increased. By the mid-thirties, the combined outstanding debt of the town and village rose to more than two-and-a-half times the 1920 level. Finally, in 1940, the populace rejected outright the town road tax, throwing the entire budget into disarray. The town manager had to transfer money from the general fund to pay for scaled-back maintenance and to fund the town's share of state-aid programs.[43] Despite the unwillingness of Middlebury voters to foot the bill, the small town was forced to accommodate automobility by the overwhelming power of state and federal policies and incentives.

THE GREEN MOUNTAIN PARKWAY

Vermonters were dissatisfied with other aspects of the expanding federal highway programs as well. For example, the Green Mountain Parkway, a scenic north–south autoroute first proposed in 1931, stirred heated public debate.[44] William J. Wilgus, the retired chief engineer for the New York Central Railroad, is generally credited with originating the idea.[45] It was taken up by the Vermont Chamber of Commerce and Governor Stanley Wilson, who asked President Franklin D. Roosevelt to fund the project. However, FDR was not yet convinced and directed the National Park Service and the BPR to conduct detailed surveys and report back.

After the resulting report was endorsed by Interior Secretary Harold Ickes, the president agreed to include the project in the National Industrial Recovery Act. This move meant that almost all of Vermont's allocation under the Act was tied to the Green Mountain Parkway, although it also authorized $2 million dollars in matching grants for thirty-two miles of concrete and macadam paving, fifty-five miles of new gravel surfacing, and repairs to seven bridges.

As details of the parkway plan became known, opposition mounted. Designed along the same lines as the Blue Ridge Parkway, the 250-mile highway's 1,000-foot-wide right-of-way would skirt lake shores and run along the spine of the Green Mountains, from Massachusetts to the Canadian border, reaching an elevation of 3,500 feet as it passed over Killington Peak: it would cut through the heart of the Green Mountain National Forest as well as many state parks. The plans called for only a nominal cash contribution by the state, but many Vermonters realized that the parkway would be costly by other measures. The Green Mountain Club spearheaded a campaign to block the project.

First, the club argued that since the federal program prohibited tolls and did not support maintenance, the parkway would "impose an impossible financial burden on the people of Vermont." In addition, it warned that the increased tourism would undermine the state's distinctiveness. Club president (and future governor) Mortimer Proctor predicted it "would attract unknown thousands . . . [an] influx of undesirable elements." Letters to the editor echoed this sentiment, cautioning that parkway users would be "just the class of people who do the state no good" and that the route would soon be littered with "noisy cheap amusements that always attract a like class of people." Another correspondent urged "people of more background, cultivation, and vision" to oppose the parkway. Conservationists warned that the Long Trail would be trampled by socially unacceptable auto-borne tourist-hikers from Boston and New York. Others cautioned that "such a road as proposed, in the hands of an invader, could dominate the state with artillery." The opposition campaign was also buttressed by editorial support in the *Rutland Herald,* one of the state's two largest dailies and published by Green Mountain Club members.

The elitist Green Mountain Club's opposition to the parkway was joined by many less wealthy Vermonters, as well. Some members of this grassroots movement did not want to pay for a parkway that was, in their opinion, not likely to help them very much. Others shared the Green Mountain Club's concerns about the parkway's impact on the scenic Vermont landscape. Art Whitney, a handyman who lived a few miles southeast of Middlebury in Goshen, Vermont, liked to take hikes in the mountains; one fall day, while the parkway debate was simmering, he announced that he would "go up to see where they are surveying for that Green Mountain Parkway." When he returned at the end of the afternoon, he was asked if he had found the survey sites. "Ayah," he said as he shed a backpack filled with surveyors stakes and red flags.[46]

On the other side of the debate, the state's other big daily, the *Burlington Free Press,* promoted the plan. Well-known author Dorothy Canfield Fisher, a larger-than-life figure in Vermont at the time, supported the parkway because she saw increased tourism as a means of reducing rural poverty. The project was endorsed by the State Planning Board twice, after separate studies, and also by the Vermont Society of Engineers. One of the parkway's leading advocates, James P. Taylor, was Secretary of the Vermont Chamber of Commerce (and, ironically, had been a founder of the Green Mountain Club). One of his arguments, which would be echoed time and again as Vermonters weighed participation in subsequent federal highway programs, was that if Vermonters turned down this project, they would effectively be declining to participate in the National Industrial Recovery Act's public works initiative and would therefore be subsidizing economic development in other states.

Furthermore, debate over the Parkway was highly partisan. Vermont was so staunchly Republican that the state's electoral votes were cast in favor of the Republican candidate at every presidential election between the formation of the GOP and 1964. In 1936, the same year that the Green Mountain parkway controversy reached its culmination, Vermont was one of only two states to vote against Roosevelt. Many anti-New Deal Vermonters saw the parkway issue as a chance to reject the expansion of the federal government into their backyards. They resented that they couldn't spend the federal funds as they saw fit on locally more popular items like flood control or the already expensive state highway program.

The Vermont House of Representatives rejected the proposal by a vote of 126 to 111 (the Middlebury representatives voted with the pro-parkway minority), but the Senate approved it 19 to 11 and the House leaders refused to allow a revote. Governor Smith asked Ickes for more time and convened a special session of the legislature to break the deadlock. Both houses bowed to Smith's pressure and agreed to submit the matter to the voters in a referendum held at the 1936 Town Meetings. It was resoundingly defeated, losing in ten of fourteen counties, by a total vote of 42,318 against and 30,897 in favor. In retrospect, one observer commented that "the sound common sense of the people came to the rescue . . . we decided to keep Vermont, as of old, Independent."

CONCLUSION

The push for more highways was not going to be denied for long, in Vermont or in any other state in the nation. Despite the financial hardships caused by the widening gap between costs and revenues, the rhetoric of crisis employed by highway boosters in the late 1930s and early 1940s succeeded in stimulating a renewed push to expand the state's highway-building program even farther. The new initiatives produced by this political pressure followed the established trend of facilitating long-distance and rural travel without aiding movement within settled cities and towns. Even small towns in agricultural areas, such as Middlebury, suffered from the skewed subsidies.

Since the advent of the Good Roads movement in Vermont, government road-building programs had specifically targeted travel through open countryside, not within municipalities. So when highway use increased, motorists experienced unencumbered long-distance travel, contrasted with lagging urban conditions. Nevertheless, despite mounting traffic congestion problems in the settled areas that had been systematically excluded from the highway subsidies, the road-building community turned its attention to new rounds of exurban long-distance highways without addressing the municipal consequences.

By the early 1940s, state and federal engineers were aware of the growing disparity between ease of movement across the countryside and mobility within urban settlements. Official reports from the Vermont highway department echoed the rhetoric emanating from the BPR, complaining that "the plugged up streets of the cities and larger villages, however, completely destroy the value of a modern highway system by creating delays and hazard. Here are the weak links." However, even though these reports indicate an awareness that the benefits of the government programs had overwhelmingly accrued to sparsely settled regions, leaving a substantial portion of Americans relatively neglected, the anti-urban emphasis remained intact in subsequent highway initiatives. Plans were underway for the Interstate Highway System, while at the same time state highway engineers recommended that Vermont cities and towns should take steps, without state or federal aid, to ease through traffic by building off-street parking and widening downtown streets.[47]

For Middlebury, these developments set the stage for important postwar changes. Traffic soon became the most significant problem faced by the small town. For the entire balance of the twentieth century, there was persistent debate about the merits of highway bypasses, new bridges across the Otter, investment in downtown traffic lights, and construction of municipal parking lots. Meanwhile, under the decentralizing influence of state and federal highway policies, sprawl took hold. Community efforts to control growth and maintain a vital downtown would be unable to stem the tide. Manufacturing jobs, once located in the downtown core, migrated to a new industrial park on the edge of town. Residences shifted from downtown apartments to detached or semidetached single family houses in new subdivisions. Shopping centers at the edge of town put traditional downtown merchants out of business, leaving an economic void filled by deliberately cultivated tourist-oriented businesses. This dispersal of population and commerce produced increased traffic congestion, prompting demands for more infrastructure improvements. However, Middlebury was constrained by, and beholden to, the government policies that fueled decentralization and sprawl.

Bridges, Bypasses, and Boulevards

THE POSTWAR HIGHWAY CRISIS IN VERMONT

After the end of World War II, highway boosters resumed their push for more government highway spending, with more crisis-laden rhetoric; at the same time towns like Middlebury struggled to adapt their infrastructure to keep up with the growing traffic on the heavily subsidized rural trunklines. Traffic congestion in densely settled areas continued to rise, while the gap between street and highway costs and the related revenues widened, at both state and local levels, precipitating a severe financial crisis in the late 1940s and early 1950s.

According to congressional testimony from 1949, highway engineers estimated that Vermont would have to spend over $150 million ($1.1 billion in 2000 dollars) on highway repairs just to maintain the prewar status quo. To put this into perspective, total federal highway grants to Vermont each year averaged less than $1.5 million between 1946 and 1950, enough to pay for 1 percent of the backlog. Construction costs per mile had doubled since 1941, and winter maintenance costs per mile (sanding and plowing) had multiplied eight times since the Depression.[1] The highway department clamored for more trunkline construction, complaining that gravel roads had not yet been eradicated and that advancing automobility had rendered prewar paving projects obsolete:

> The main trunk lines which are the backbone of the highway system and of the economic life of the state are burdened with volumes of traffic they were not designed to carry. Narrow 18-foot pavements are carrying two thousand to four thousand vehicles per day and excessive curves and grades tend to create hazardous driving conditions and congestion. Narrow and weak bridges are dangerous bottlenecks and many miles of our State Aid and Town highways need improving . . . to serve present day traffic adequately.[2]

Furthermore, the highway department complained, funding levels were woefully insufficient, given the repairs that were "needed," according to the ever-higher standards promulgated by the BPR and the AASHO. They projected that it would take thirty-three years to properly upgrade the substandard portions of the state highway system. They also cautioned that, in the meantime, currently adequate highways would fall apart under the wear and tear of statewide traffic volumes that had tripled in the preceding twenty years and were 43 percent higher than before the war.[3] The state highway engineers seemed unwilling to reassess their objectives, pledging in numerous successive *Biennial Reports* to pursue two parallel goals: a gravel road to every farm in the state; a paved road to each village with more than one hundred residents. Meanwhile, revenues from user fees were still not growing as fast as expenses.

This suited the NHUC just fine. But as the financial strains grew, the lobbying group sought to maintain the growth of the automobility subsidy by removing what they called "nonhighway" expenses from the highway department budget. In particular, they began to complain that money from the highway fund was used to pay for the state highway police. They argued that such costs would be more appropriately classified as law enforcement expenses and that motorists were being unfairly taxed, through gas taxes and registration fees, to pay for the highway patrol. This strategy was not entirely successful but nevertheless serves as an example of the relentless efforts on the part of the automobility lobbies to expand construction while keeping motorists' contributions down to a small fraction of the total funds spent accommodating automobiles.[4]

To close the gap in the highway budget, state officials deferred maintenance and forced more costs down onto cities, towns, and villages. By 1946 state maintenance appropriations had been cut so much that they were no longer "sufficient to take care of normal yearly requirements, without any regard to the accumulation of deferred maintenance." To make matters worse, current revenues could not even match federal aid for new construction, let alone pay for maintenance and nonaided projects. The gas tax was increased, but only by a penny (from 4 cents per gallon to 5 cents, in increments of .5 cents in 1947 and 1949), and registration fees were also raised, but only by 22 percent (to $22 from $18), whereas inflation since before the war amounted to 71 percent. Diesel fuel remained completely untaxed, giving diesel trucks an ever-increasing extra subsidy.[5]

Local governments were forced to absorb more and more of the maintenance costs, and incorporated cities and villages were hardest hit. A 1950 study found that state aid (including federal grants, which were administered by the state highway departments) provided less than half of the funds spent on roads in unincorporated Vermont townships and only 10 percent for incorporated Vermont municipalities, with the remaining nine-tenths derived exclusively from property taxes. Towns like Middlebury received only $25 per mile in state aid for maintenance, a rate established in 1937 and not raised until 1957, even though inflation was up 95 percent during the same period.[6]

Under these circumstances, traffic inundated Middlebury, and highway policies hamstrung the small town so that it was unable to respond to the onslaught of postwar automobility. Highways were no longer feeders and extenders for the rail system. Instead, rail traffic reached new lows, while automotive traffic hit new highs. Route 7 was now the state's busiest north–

south artery, carrying far more traffic than any other road. A 1945 report stated that "the need for relief from traffic congestion" along Route 7 was one of the state's most "troublesome problems."[7]

In addition to Route 7, other main roads to Middlebury were also paved. For example, State Route 116 was paved between 1945 and 1952, establishing another major north–south route, connecting the eastern reaches of Middlebury to Burlington. The dramatic leap in traffic volume between the new highway and the village center forced the town to spend money paving and extending adjacent local roads.

By 1953 a traffic survey counted seven thousand vehicles crossing the Battell Bridge each day and almost six thousand approaching the town center on Route 7 from the south (Court Street). This was more than two and a half times as many as before the war, in 1938. At times the hourly volume reached peaks of 840 autos over the bridge and 660 on Court Street. These volumes are striking when the local population is taken into consideration: 2,123 people lived within the two square miles of the Village of Middlebury, and another thousand resided in the surrounding unincorporated areas, making a total of 3,175 for the Town of Middlebury.[8]

Local officials struggled to keep up with the new traffic volume. Street and highway expenditures rose rapidly, first doubling the prewar level, and then tripling it. The 1955 Village *Annual Report* observed that "at the present time, many of our city and village streets, laid out for horse-drawn vehicles, are being forced to serve many times the traffic volumes for which they were designed. The result is congestion, traffic hazards and bottlenecks."[9] That same year, Main Street had to be repaved, again, and much of the removed dirt, gravel, and broken up macadam was used to build a new municipal parking lot, so that parked cars would not completely block the village streets. Meanwhile, the town manager reported that Three-Mile Bridge was "in a very serious condition and a new bridge or extensive reconstruction must be reconsidered."[10]

Local residents resisted paying the ever-escalating costs of adapting Middlebury to accommodate the traffic brought to town by subsidized trunklines. For example, three times between 1948 and 1957, voters at the annual village meeting rejected measures that would raise money for road construction by installing parking meters along Main Street and Merchant's Row.[11]

To make matters worse, the Vermont Highway Board adopted two explicit policies that exacerbated the fiscal strains in towns like Middlebury. First, under a section of the 1948 *Biennial Report* titled "Urban Traffic": "The Board hopes that cities and incorporated villages will continue their attempts to provide for a smooth flow of traffic on those streets which connect our main-line highways . . . but the correction must be undertaken by the municipality involved." Second, since state appropriations were insufficient to match all available federal grants, the Board chose not to fund the urban-extension component, instead announcing that towns were "allowed" to put up local funds to satisfy half of the state's obligated contribution, and only then would the state fund the remainder, if it approved of the project.[12]

These policies only postponed the budget crisis for a few years. The gulf between highway construction costs and corresponding appropriations from the legislature had widened to the point that it could no longer be filled with fiscal sleight-of-hand and annual transfers of general revenues. In 1953 and 1954 the state was unable to match federal highway grants and forfeited millions of dollars worth of available aid.[13] Furthermore, the pending Interstate legislation would make the crisis even more severe, raising the ante for Vermont's participation in the age of automobility, even though the state would end up with half as many Interstates as originally expected.

According to a prewar planning document put together by federal roads commissioner Thomas MacDonald and his staff at the BPR, Vermont was originally slated to have two north–south superhighways and two east–west superhighways. (This report, *Highways for the National Defense, 1941* was a follow-up to *Toll Roads and Free Roads*, as discussed in chapter 1.) The north–south roads would be based on U.S. Route 7 to the west of the mountains and U.S. Route 5 along the eastern border. One lateral route would cross the state between Burlington and Montpelier, along U.S. Route 2, while the

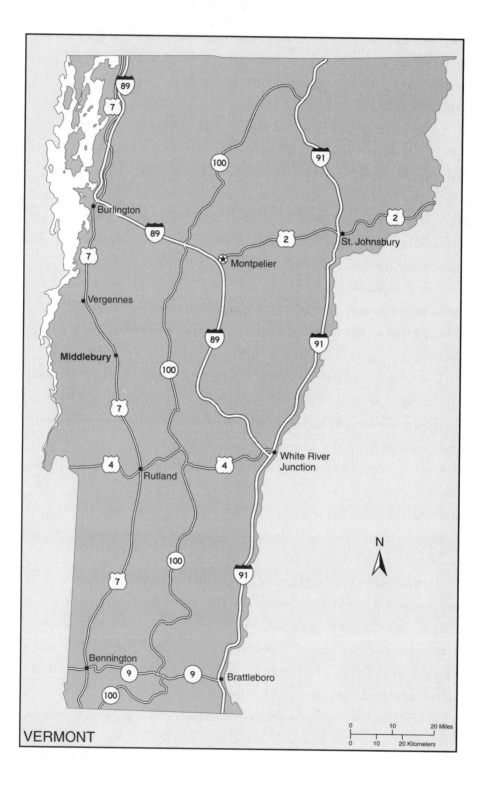

N

VERMONT

0   10   20 Miles
0   10   20 Kilometers

other would follow U.S. Route 4 through Rutland in the south.[14] However, by the time Congress passed the Interstate legislation fifteen years later, two of these four superhighways had been removed from the official maps, those based on Routes 7 and 4.

The Interstate map was laid out by Commissioner MacDonald and his engineers in coordination with their counterparts at the individual state highway departments. In these circumstances, there was a combination of factors that led to omitting the two Vermont expressways. First, MacDonald was under pressure from President Roosevelt to broaden political support and boost traffic-flow projections for the Interstate System by adding extensions reaching into the big cities, none of which was in Vermont. Second, the network that he was preparing to publish in *Interregional Highways* for inclusion in the Federal-Aid Highway Act of 1944 would encompass about one-third fewer miles than the more ambitious 1941 report. Third, Vermont already had the most federal highways per square mile of any state in the nation and was therefore vulnerable to the shift of mileage toward more densely populated areas (the state contained .48 percent of federal-aid highway mileage but housed only .27 percent of the nation's population). Also, Vermonters' refusal to support FDR at the polls may have come into play, since approval of all four of the state's designated routes would have allotted an exceedingly high proportion of highway funds to a state that had staunchly opposed each of the President's campaigns, as well as most of his legislative agenda. Last, and perhaps most important, neighboring Massachusetts flatly refused to endorse an interstate along the portion of Route 7 within its borders, while New York made no effort to connect Route 4 to the Northway (I-87), leaving Vermont to fight for these designations alone.[15]

The 1944 Act officially designated one superhighway running north–south along Route 5 in the east and a second running east–west along Route 2 from Burlington through Montpelier, discarding the other two routes (along Route 7 and Route 4). The political maneuvering and the disagreements with Massachusetts and New York were only vaguely alluded to publicly when the Vermont Highway Board reported that the final routes had been mapped "in cooperation with our neighboring states and approved by the U.S. Commissioner of Public Roads."[16]

TO BYPASS OR NOT TO BYPASS?

After it was clear that western Vermont would not have an interstate, the state highway department made plans for improvements along U.S. Routes 7 and 4 to counterbalance the uneven superhighway plan. This goal was acknowledged in official publications: "The tilt thus created by Interstate pressures pushed Vermont's highway program off balance." The legislature formally decided that all non-Interstate work would focus on the areas west of the mountains and south of Burlington, to offset this tilt.[17] For Middlebury, these plans involved two main components: a bypass highway east of town and a new bridge across the Otter, one block from the Battell Bridge.

The proposed bypass would initially be only two lanes, to save money, but configured as a limited-access divided highway to enable north–south through traffic on Route 7 to pass Middlebury without getting bogged down by local traffic. The planners' goal was to ease congestion for out-of-town motorists who were inconvenienced by the village itself, so they planned to exclude local motorists. According to the 1955 annual report of the Village of Middlebury, where the proposal was first published, local traffic "would reduce the capacity of the highway, making it unsafe, congested, and altogether unsatisfactory to the traveling public . . . therefore control-of-access is highly desirable."[18] The state was not offering to fund the project but instead seemed to be proposing it as part of a public-relations campaign to quell complaints that the Champlain valley was getting short shrift. Under these circumstances, Middlebury residents gave the bypass proposal a lukewarm response.

The downtown bridge suggested in the 1955 highway department plan got a better reception. The Battell Bridge had become the biggest bottleneck in the area's transportation flow, and the prospect of an alternative crossing was attractive, even more so after the Three-Mile Bridge was destroyed by

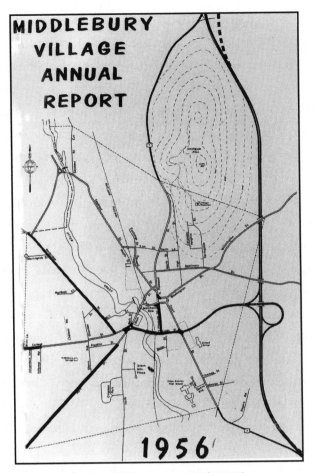

Bridge and bypass proposal, 1956,
Henry Sheldon Museum of Vermont History

fire in 1952. After discussion at town meeting, voters indicated that they were reluctant to invest in a brand new bridge as far south of town as Three-Mile Bridge, but they were much more enthusiastic about a new "in-town" crossing. The state proposal contemplated a steel-and-concrete span to the south of the existing stone structure, connecting Route 7 directly to the traffic circle where the western trunklines came together near the college, allowing both local and through-traffic to bypass the congested nexus of Main Street,

Merchant's Row, and the courthouse square. The new bridge would be more than sixty feet wide to accommodate four lanes of traffic and two sidewalks (in contrast, the roadway across the Battell Bridge was only twenty-eight feet wide, leaving room for only two lanes and one narrow parking strip). The town manager took steps to "initiate action on the possible construction" of the bridge and began to accumulate annual budget surpluses to save up enough money for the local share of the project. A sketch of the plan adorned the front cover of the Village's 1956 annual report.[19]

Neither the bridge nor the bypass received any financial support from the state or federal governments. They remained on the proverbial drawing board and were always included in the state's published plans, but they never benefited from any budget allocations. They were included in *Vermont's State Highway Needs and 12-year Construction Program* (1960) and also in the more extensive *Vermont's Arterial Highway Plan and 14-year Construction Program on the Federal Aid Primary and Interstate Systems* (1961), which purportedly placed a high priority on overhauling Route 7 by rebuilding some sections and constructing limited-access bypasses around intervening cities. The two projects were also included in subsequent publications of the Vermont Department of Highways, including three separate editions of *Vermont's 14-year Planning Program on the Federal Aid Highway Systems* (1963, 1965, and 1967), and the *Long-Range Planning Program on the Arterial Highway System* (1966).

The state was now struggling to raise enough money to fund its share of the Interstates and could not afford to back up the rhetorical commitment to other projects with any substantive financial support. In each case the bypass and the bridge were always listed in the unfunded, deferred, or postponed portions of the plans.

BORROWING FOR BOULEVARDS

One of the most popular misconceptions about the Interstate System is that since the states only had to contribute 10 percent of the funds (compared to

50 percent under previous aid programs) the highways were a bargain for state treasuries. This view does not take into account the staggering expenses of the interstates. For example, even though Vermont already had the most federal highway miles per square mile in the nation and its share of interstate miles had been halved during the planning process, the state's 10 percent share would nevertheless double the amount of money it needed to raise each year to match federal highway grants.

Costs were driven up by lofty new standards. The new superhighways required a minimum right-of-way of three hundred feet in rural locations, two hundred feet in "urban" locations. This was ten times the width of prewar federal highways, and in most cases the Interstates would follow entirely new paths: the parallel federal highways often could not practically be widened this much because they followed narrow riverside routes or were bordered by built-up business strips with established accesses and intersections.[20]

But Vermont was already overburdened by its highway obligations and had forfeited federal aid because it couldn't raise sufficient matching funds, even after forcing more and more costs onto local governments. The legislature had no choice but to reassess the state's highway finance policies.

The state's pay-as-you-go policy was already under fire. Previously, in 1949, the legislature had authorized a small bond issue for bridge construction on the state highway system, under the pretense that the borrowed money would not technically be spent on highways, just on bridges. However, such pretenses became unnecessary after the forfeiture of federal aid came to light during the 1954 gubernatorial campaign. Act 180 of the 1955 legislature authorized the state's first ever nonemergency highway bond issue. The main purpose of the loan was to raise money to match federal grants despite motorists' unwillingness to pay higher user fees, but the governor also promised to spend one-quarter of the borrowed funds on closing "gravel-gaps" on rural roads ineligible for federal aid.[21]

In the subsequent gubernatorial campaign, part of Governor Johnson's successful platform was a pledge to issue more highway bonds so that Vermont could, again, match all available federal grants and still have money available for non-interstate projects. Accordingly, the 1957 legislature authorized a borrowing that, when combined with gas-tax revenues and other user fees, would provide funds to match all Interstate, primary, secondary, and urban-extension aid, as well as pay for unaided projects, including closing gravel gaps, improving ski-access routes, and other unspecified projects along the western and southern corridors that had been left out of the federal plan. As it turned out, however, feeders to I-89 and I-91 soaked up most of the money.

Once the legislature abandoned pay-as-you-go, Vermont pursued a regular program of borrowing money for highways, rapidly taking on more debt. Over the next ten years, the state borrowed money for road construction on six separate occasions. In the eighteen-year span between 1955 and 1973, 84 percent of state highway expenditures came from bond issues.[22]

To help service this new debt, the legislature imposed nominally higher user fees on motorists. In 1957 the gas tax was boosted to 6.5 cents, and registration fees reached $32 per year in 1962. After adjusting for inflation, these charges were still lower than before the war, when they had been insufficient to fund less expensive programs. In 1959, to help close the persistent gap, the legislature authorized the collection of a sales tax on car and truck sales. Unlike sales tax on all other consumer purchases, the revenues were exclusively devoted to the highway fund, protected from so-called "diversion" by the vigilant lobbying of the NHUC and the AAA.[23]

These new revenue-raising measures, combined with the newly aggressive borrowing schedule, were still not enough. Maintenance costs continued to soar, reaching $3,000 per lane-mile by the early 1960s (about $17,000 in 2000 dollars), nearly twice the 1950 level, while inflation was up only 29 percent over the same period. In 1962 Vermont was once more unable to match all its federal aid, and the state's urban areas again bore the consequences. Half of the allotment for urban extensions was forfeit. At the same time, state highway aid to towns amounted to only $300 per mile in 1964, a pittance compared to the rising costs.[24]

As costs skyrocketed, the state was forced to devote nearly all its highway resources to the Interstate program. Money from the 1957 bond issue earmarked for the neglected western and southern corridors was instead absorbed by federal-aid projects connected to I-89 and I-91 in the east. There was not enough money left for bypass and widening projects elsewhere, so all non-Interstate undertakings were curtailed.

For example, according to the official legislative report describing the 1957 bond authorization, a substantial portion of the borrowed money was slated to be used for reconstruction of Route 7 from Salisbury (a few miles south of Middlebury) to New Haven (a few miles to the north). But by 1960 all the bond proceeds had been spent, mostly on projects tied to the Interstates, and no work had been done on this portion of Route 7, although it was still listed as a high priority in the state's twelve-year plan. The 1961 fourteen-year plan listed half of the project as unfunded, no longer pretending that it was imminent.

The 1961 report also warned that the state could not afford all the projects listed. It cautioned that expanding Route 4 to a four-lane limited-access highway between Rutland and the New York border would not leave enough money for the rest of the projects. Accordingly, the next statewide highway plan indicated that the section of Route 7 north of Middlebury, to New Haven, was indefinitely deferred. The southern segment from Salisbury up to the edge of Middlebury was scaled back to a modest repaving and improvement project, completed in bits and pieces from 1961 to 1964.[25]

The automobility programs had begun to permanently alter Middlebury. The first sign that these changes would go beyond simple downtown traffic jams had been the development of the area's first postwar, suburban-style subdivision in the mid-1950s. The small cluster of detached single-family houses was located just off Route 7 on the southern edge of town, along a short new road called Rogers Road.[26] This subdivision was soon followed by other developments on the fringes of Middlebury, marking a new decentralization of residence, industry, and commerce in the area.

In 1961 the annual report of the village boasted of the impending construction of a shopping center along Court Street (the section of Route 7 immediately south of the courthouse square). This project, which would include a supermarket, a franchised chain-hardware store, and a self-service laundry, was hailed as a form of urban renewal, since it would be built adjacent to one of the least desirable parts of the village: "It is common knowledge to most interested observers that [the area where the new shopping center would be built] currently is used rather extensively under conditions which are not the most desirable."[27] The shopping center was set back from Court Street by a large parking lot, a distinct departure from the previous pattern on the old-fashioned, tree-lined street. Another similar shopping center opened along Washington Street to the east of the square, also featuring a large parking lot and expansive one-story buildings set back from the otherwise pedestrian-friendly street. It provided another supermarket, a pizza parlor, another chain hardware store, another laundromat, and (later) a bank with a drive-through window.

Farther south of the village, as soon as the state's piecemeal effort to renovate that part of Route 7 was completed, the town manager announced that the Standard Register Company would build a new factory along the highway. As incentive to attract the company, the town paid three-fourths of the land costs, borrowing the necessary money with a tax-exempt bond issue, and offered a ten-year tax break—guaranteeing the company that property taxes on the $1.2 million plant would not exceed $2,000 per year. The factory, located in an area that had previously been entirely agricultural, would be surrounded by acres of asphalt to accommodate eighteen-wheel tractor-trailer trucks and workers' automobiles. It was too far away for employees to reach by foot from the village.[28]

As the built-up portion of Middlebury began to sprawl beyond the Village boundaries, the distinction between the Town and the Village became less clear-cut. Whereas the Village had formerly encompassed almost all of the built-up areas in Middlebury, this was no longer the case. In 1966 the voters decided to consolidate the Village and Town, merging them back together. The consolidation eliminated many bureaucratic redundancies but did not resolve the underlying fiscal strains that had bedeviled the two governments over the preceding years.[29]

The town manager's annual budget requests during this period always included a request to pay down some of the accumulated road debt. However, each end-of-year financial report showed repeated annual deficits and, therefore, increases in road debt. At the road-tax rates that voters were willing to approve at town meetings, it was impossible to carry out the roadwork mandated by the state. For example, in 1966 the Town had to issue a ten-year, tax-exempt bond to raise enough money to rebuild Weybridge Street, the in-town portion of State Route 23. Likewise, the Village spent about ten times as much on routine road maintenance and street cleaning as it received in related state aid. Even though local taxes also had to support schools, courts, police, fire, municipal utilities, and general administration, streets absorbed more than 15 percent of every Village tax dollar.[30]

The new auto-oriented developments, far removed from the traditional commercial and industrial center of Middlebury, exacerbated the area's growing traffic problems. 1968 traffic surveys counted twice as many vehicles at Courthouse Square during peak hours as in 1955. Likewise, more than seven thousand vehicles a day traveled along Route 7 south of town, up two-thirds between 1960 and 1968. Along Court Street (the portion of Route 7 south closest to the square) this figure exceeded ten thousand, according to a 1970 survey, which also found almost ten thousand vehicles crossing the Battell Bridge each day.[31]

While the physical footprint of the town expanded rapidly and the traffic volume skyrocketed, the population of the area grew at a much more modest pace. In 1950 Middlebury's population finally matched its nineteenth-century levels, partially because that year's census included Middlebury College students for the first time. Between 1950 and 1960 (the last census that counted the Village separately from the Town), the Village population remained flat, while the county population matched the modest statewide increase of 3.25 percent, and the Town (reflecting the new peripheral development tendencies) grew 11 percent.[32]

Even the state and federally funded trunklines that had initially boosted automobility and facilitated Middlebury's deconcentration were now suffering from neglect, as all the government highway money was absorbed by Interstate-related projects on the other side of the state. According to the highway engineers' rapidly inflating standards, Routes 125 and 30 were both rated as "poor," and the unrebuilt sections of Route 7 north of town were "bad." Nevertheless, while these roads were included in *Vermont's 1965 14-Year Planning Program on the Federal Aid Highway Systems*, they were not allocated any funds.[33]

To make matters worse, the railroad had long since given up on passenger service. Since emerging from bankruptcy—temporarily strengthened by war-related traffic—the railroad limped along but could not compete with automotive transport. It was finally crippled by a strike in 1961, then taken over by the state in 1963. A 1968 guide to Middlebury for newly arrived college students reported that one train passed through town headed north in the morning, another headed south in the evening, but they were reserved for freight only. Passenger service had stopped in 1954, although the guide advised adventurous students to "make friends with the cabooseman before hopping freight." Before long, even freight service for Middlebury (and all other stops in Addison County) was limited to a "whole-car" basis, meaning that individual shipments were not accepted—only entire railcars full of freight. Bus service to Burlington and Rutland provided a limited replacement for the declining railroad, but this too was ineffective, serving only thirty passengers a day.[34]

In an attempt to resolve the tangle of auto-related problems, Middlebury turned to professional planners. Over the next twenty-five years, residents would consider half a dozen different comprehensive town plans. Each of them made reference to the two permanent planning controversies in Middlebury, a Route 7 highway-bypass and a new bridge across the Otter, neither of which would reach fruition in the twentieth century.

NO BYPASS, NO BRIDGE

In the early 1960s the Town and the Village each created planning commissions, which together hired the private firm of Sargent, Webster, Crenshaw, and Foley to draft a master plan for Middlebury, including a capital improvement program and a zoning ordinance. The consultants' reports, released in 1963 and 1964, made sweeping recommendations. First to be published was the *Master Plan*, which voters formally adopted at a town meeting.[35] However, almost none of it was ever implemented.

The 1963 plan revived the east-of-town bypass suggested in 1955 and likewise repeated the earlier bridge proposal, in both cases with only minor alterations. The new plan also went much farther: It proposed extending Route 125 to the former site of Three-Mile Bridge, building a brand new span there in addition to the in-town bridge. Furthermore, it proposed the erection of a third new river crossing adjacent to the Pulp Mill Bridge, the rarely used covered bridge on the northern edge of town. As for the village center, Sargent-Webster proposed an urban renewal scheme that left almost no part of Middlebury untouched. In particular, the consultants suggested that the Battell Block, a distinctive stone building at the corner of Main Street and Merchant's Row, be torn down and replaced with a modern multistory office and commercial building. The remainder of Merchant's Row would also be razed to make room for a large parking lot and a tiled plaza.[36]

The far-reaching 1963 plan was stillborn. The only part of the plan that Middlebury residents agreed upon was the premise that their town was swamped by automotive traffic and that they needed help to cope with it. Beyond that, in the absence of state funding for the infrastructure projects and the unwillingness or inability of the local taxpayers to raise the funds themselves, the plan turned out to be little more than thought provoking. In unstated recognition of this economic reality, the *Capital Improvement* schedule published by Sargent-Webster the following year was stark, calling for capital expenditures of only a few thousand dollars per year.[37]

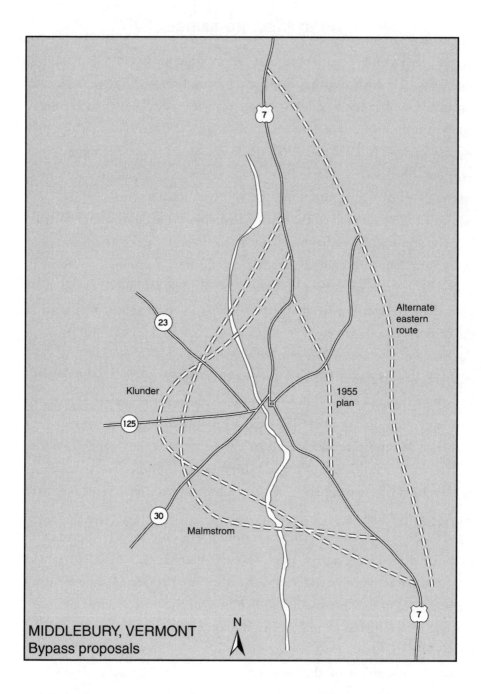

MIDDLEBURY, VERMONT
Bypass proposals

N

David Crawford, the town manager hired after the 1966 Town-Village consolidation, served until 1983, presiding over more than fifteen years of acrimonious planning debates. Almost immediately after Crawford took office, the Town Planning Commission was revived, this time under the guidance of chairman Vincent Malmstrom, a professor at Middlebury College. Focusing on plans for a bypass, a new bridge, and an "improved traffic plan for downtown," Malmstrom discarded the more radical urban-renewal elements of the 1963 plan. His plans were published in the local newspaper, the *Addison Independent,* in an attempt to build popular support. Meanwhile, the county created its own planning body, the Addison County Regional Planning Commission, which retained the firm of Hans Klunder Associates to draft an alternative comprehensive plan.

As the number of alternative plans grew, so too did the difficulty in gaining adequate support for any one of them. The most divisive debates concerned the placement of the bypass (east of town, or west?) and of the bridge (downtown, south of town, north of town, or some combination?). The two projects were obviously related, so the debates could not be resolved independently. The Klunder firm ran into resistance before it could even publish a plan, perhaps because it advocated a west-of-town location for the bypass, which Middlebury College staunchly opposed. The 1969 *Annual Report* for the town indicated that the Town Planning Commission was willing to adopt the "basic concepts" of the first-draft Klunder Plan but stopped short of endorsing any details of the plan itself. By the time the final version was released to the public in 1970, it was already stalled. The town meeting held in March of that year was marked by extensive discussion about the bypass, the bridge, and the need for more parking. The only transportation matter put to a vote, though, was the perennial question about reinstalling traffic lights downtown. The question was defeated (albeit narrowly), as it had been at successive town meetings for years.[38]

State officials tried to keep their distance from the increasingly intractable local planning debates in Middlebury. This was not only politically prudent but also convenient, in light of the tight highway budget. Having decided, in 1966, to devote the limited noninterstate funds to the four-lane expansion of Route 4 between Rutland and the New York border as a first priority and Route 7 south of Rutland as a second priority, the engineers in the highway department were content to let the Middlebury controversies remain unresolved.[39]

However, other state planners knew that Middlebury needed help to adapt to auto-dominated transport, as one 1969 report noted:

> [In Middlebury,] problems of highway circulation are particularly troublesome for both through traffic and local traffic . . . a north–south relocation of U.S. Route 7 has long been recognized as essential, but there are no plans for carrying this out . . . [the town also needs] a new bridge over Otter Creek, but funding for these projects in the near future is uncertain even with matching assistance . . . development of downtown municipal parking areas, combined with the elimination of parking on Main Street would also be helpful.[40]

The easiest of these suggestions to implement was the construction of more parking space and, accordingly, a new municipal parking lot was constructed near Main Street in 1971.[41] However, parking facilities like these, which Middlebury continued to build over the years, attracted more traffic and exacerbated the other problems.

The Vermont highway department was unable to avoid the controversy for long. In 1971 the town Board of Selectmen formally requested a state study of four different bridge locations. The resulting report, *Middlebury Inner Belt Location Report,* was completed rapidly and published before the year's end. However, the state officials assigned to the project orally reported that the state could not allocate funds to any bypasses for at least a decade because of obligations related to completing the Interstates and their feeders. Furthermore, they reminded town leaders, when state-aid funds became available, the bridge or bypass project would require a 25 percent contribution from the local government since they would fall under the urban-extension program.[42]

Meanwhile, sprawling development in the area continued. About a mile south of Courthouse Square, a new shopping center went up along Route 7, flanked by a gas station and a car wash. Set behind an enormous parking lot, the shopping center housed an A&P supermarket more than twice the size of the existing building on Court Street, a drug store that dwarfed the pharmacy on Main Street, a clothing store, a liquor store, a bank, and an Ames department store many times larger than the family owned dry-goods store downtown.[43] East of town, on formerly undeveloped open land, another suburban-style subdivision took shape. Consisting of detached and semidetached single family homes on suburban-style tracts, the development was called Buttolph Acres. It had a single main road access, dumping additional rush-hour traffic onto the already crowded Court Street.

A new industrial area north of town, covering one hundred and thirty acres, was developed in 1973. Formally known as the Middlebury Industrial Park, the new industrial zone was initially anchored by a Kraft swiss cheese processing plant. The sixty-thousand-square-foot factory was located on a thirty-four-acre site, and a milk company announced plans to build a receiving, storage, and shipping station on an adjacent six-acre site. In order to accommodate these two facilities—and for the convenience of company suppliers, employees, and truckers—the state highway department agreed to build a short street (Exchange Street) connecting the industrial park directly to both downtown and Route 7 north, and to build a "betterment" project along Route 7 at the new intersection. State officials approved this expenditure because the Kraft plant was expected to be one of the state's largest milk purchasers (it turned out to be *the* largest). Since the park was outside of the old village boundaries, municipal utilities had to be extended to reach the plants. The milk company and Kraft Foods made nominal contributions to help pay for these services, but the balance of the costs were born by the Town government.[44]

Traffic congestion reached crisis proportions at this time. Newspaper articles reported that "all last week traffic was bumper to bumper on Main Street for several hours daily," and that "traffic in Middlebury's streets has become so chaotic lately that many citizens have been disturbed. Afternoon traffic on Main Street has been virtually bumper to bumper." Between 1970 and 1976, traffic counts all over Middlebury jumped 23 percent on average. A 1974 study found over one thousand cars crossing Courthouse Square at peak hours, up more than a quarter from just six years earlier. Furthermore, through traffic made up a dwindling portion of the congestion problem, to the point where more than three-fourths of the vehicles crossing the Battell Bridge were going to or from local destinations. On Route 7, through traffic still accounted for about half of the traffic, but this, too, was lower than earlier levels. Clearly, the latest growth in traffic congestion had been mainly driven by the decentralization of the local economy. Growth in through traffic was now limited by the area's well-known traffic jams.[45]

To make matters worse, Vermont's neglect of the area's major roads in favor of Interstates and isolated projects in the southern portion of the state had produced deteriorating local road conditions. Since the Interstate legislation had passed in 1956, Addison County's share of federal and state highway funds plummeted to nearly the least of all the counties in Vermont. Accordingly, all roads into Middlebury suffered from persistent undermaintenance and were now rated as "bad" by the state highway department. Despite rhetoric recognizing the "urgent need for improvements to Route 7 north of Rutland," a 1973 long-range plan for the department indicated that they were not expecting to allocate any money for such work for at least six years. Even then, while a Middlebury-area Route 7 project was listed as a "priority primary" project, a budget of less than one million dollars was planned, and spending would be limited to preliminary work on planning, engineering, landscaping, and design. Actual construction was postponed even farther into the future.[46]

There were very few options open, especially after voters rejected a traffic consultant's recommendation for installing three linked traffic lights downtown. A Downtown Task Force convened to formulate a counterproposal. They suggested that Main Street and Merchant's Row be converted to one-way traffic, thereby turning the town green into a traffic circle. A similar effort, involving the restriction of Merchant's Row to one-way traffic, had failed a few years earlier because storekeepers complained that Main Street would not be similarly regulated. Now, both streets were included in the proposal. This too was rejected, mainly because it was feared that the town center would loose its small-town feeling if it adopted these big-city traffic control techniques, especially when combined with recently implemented parking restrictions on parts of Main Street.[47]

The 1975 town Annual Report listed "transportation issues" as the most serious long-term problem for Middlebury. It specifically cited the bypass deadlock and the lack of support for a downtown bridge. In an attempt to break the impasse, leaders from various groups agreed to form a "Route 7 Task Force" to formulate a plan that could be presented to the state for funding with the unified support of as much of the local community as possible. The task force included representatives from the town and county planning commissions, the Chamber of Commerce, the Downtown Business Bureau, the college, the selectmen, the school district, the highway commission, the Middlebury Garden Club, and the League of Women Voters.

The final recommendation of the task force, released late in 1976, called for a westerly bypass, including two new out-of-town bridges across Otter Creek. They expected that this would relieve Route 7 through traffic by providing a detour around downtown, while simultaneously relieving congestion on the Battell Bridge by providing alternative routes for east–west traffic that otherwise had to go through the heart of downtown. But two important groups dissented from the recommendation. The Town Planning Commission simultaneously endorsed an easterly bypass route, published in the 1976 Town Report. The college, which wielded considerable influence over local political and economic affairs, also lobbied against the task force's western route because they were concerned that it would pass too close to their scenic main campus. On the other hand, many elected officials opposed the alternate eastern route because it would pass through prime developable residential land and would not relieve congestion on the Battell Bridge. Consensus was unattainable.[48]

In any case, there had been no signs of any state financial support for either the bypass or the bridge for many years. Middlebury residents were unwilling to approve the expenditure of $20,000 for traffic lights (which they said were too expensive), let alone devote much larger sums to more ambitious projects. To make matters worse, the state highway budget, already strained to the point of breaking, was whipsawed by changing American economic conditions. The combination of the energy crisis and high inflation in the 1970s dealt a double whammy to Vermont's highway program: Projects like the Middlebury bypass, reconstruction of Route 7, or erecting new bridges across the Otter became flights of fantasy. At this point, even if the townspeople could have agreed upon a traffic-relief plan, nobody was willing to pay for it.

THE ENERGY CRISIS AND
ITS EFFECT ON HIGHWAY FINANCE IN VERMONT

Even before the 1970s, the state's highway program had been in trouble. It seemed impossible to raise funds for projects unrelated to the Interstate Highways. Each time that the legislature authorized increased highway budgets, federally mandated projects absorbed the additional funds.

In 1965, available state revenues were unable to keep up with the rising Interstate burden, so grants-in-aid to local governments were frozen, allowing all subsequent increases in gas-tax revenues to go toward federal projects. Then, in 1967 and 1968, the legislature authorized the highway department to borrow almost $100 million dollars ($500 million in 2000 dollars) by issuing tax-exempt bonds to match federal grants for finishing Vermont's portion of the Interstate system.[49]

At the time, the legislature expected that the federally sponsored superhighway initiative would be finished as projected, in 1970, freeing up millions of highway dollars each year thereafter. Accordingly, they directed that some of these borrowed funds also be used for the Route 4 expansion (between Rutland and the New York border) and overhauling Route 7 in the south of the state (between Manchester and Bennington). Official reports indicated that the highway department planned to finish these projects with money freed up after the completion of the interstates.

Almost immediately, legislators found that all the bond proceeds had been spent, and the two southern projects were not even close to completion. After investigation, a 1968 legislative inquiry found that the highway department had not only underestimated the state's Interstate costs but also drastically understated the costs of the two southern projects in order to obtain approval of the bond issues. Furthermore, the projects themselves were surreptitiously changed to four-lane limited-access boulevards, built almost to the same standards as Interstate highways. Consequently, these projects used up the vast majority of non-Interstate government aid for years and even needed a supplemental bond in 1971 before they could be opened.[50]

Numerous official reports indicated that the highway department erroneously expected, after the completion of the Interstates, to have enough money to rectify the accumulated decay on the state's other roads. For example, a 1966 survey by private consulting engineers commissioned by the governor optimistically predicted that "the completion of the Interstate as projected in 1970 should permit an annual increase in the number of miles that can be brought up to standard" on primary and secondary routes statewide. A total of 764 miles of highways originally built with federal aid had fallen into "critical condition," and 14 percent of the state's bridges needed to be replaced, while another 37 percent required widening. Until Vermont's Interstates could be finished, the state's fourteen-year construction plan could only tentatively include provisions to cure less than half of the deficiencies along the trunklines, let alone the secondary and urban roads: Phase one of the plan covered only forty-two miles of primary highways out of 214 that needed work. The consultants also explained that one source of Vermont's problems was its history of "trying to spread its assistance over too many sparsely settled miles, to supply service to citizens who are widely separated."[51]

In retrospect, the rosy post-Interstate prognostications turned out to be unrealistic in three respects. First, completion of the Interstates was far from imminent. By 1970, when the system was supposed to be finished, the deadline had been pushed back to 1977. It would actually be 1982 before Vermont's portion would be completed, and by then the earlier stretches needed repairs, repaving, and replacement. Second, the mid-1960s predictions grossly underestimated the combined costs of accumulated undermaintenance and the lofty automobility expectations of American motorists. Third, they failed to reckon with the persistent unwillingness of motorists and auto manufacturers to bear the costs of automobility.

Catching up with the accumulated maintenance deficit would be a herculean task. According to one 1968 study, Vermont would have to spend $1.1 billion by 1985 ($5.45 billion in 2000 dollars) to this end. In particular, the report said, funds would need to be funneled toward the southwestern and central sections that had not benefited from the focus on the Interstates and their feeders, and had in fact suffered from that focus. Numerous reports echoed this latter point. A 1970 publication of the state highway department agreed that "the emphasis which Vermont has necessarily placed on the construction of the Interstate System and its linkage to other parts of the Vermont State Highway System has expanded the backlog of construction needs." Likewise, a 1972 survey reported that the focus on the Interstates "has led to deferment of much-needed projects in the remainder of the state system," causing 37 percent of Vermont's arterial and collector system to deteriorate into "critical condition" (rated as either "bad" or "poor").[52]

Even though the Interstates were an overwhelming burden for Vermont, it was never a realistic option to voluntarily "opt-out," as it had with the Green Mountain Parkway. As difficult as it was to participate, choosing not to participate in the new dominant transportation network would have meant refusing billions of dollars of federal money over thirty years and putting the local economy at a permanent disadvantage. So, on the one hand, there was little choice in the matter. On the other hand, Vermonters repeatedly resisted legislative measures to raise adequate revenues to pay their mandated share of the costs. But it was not the Interstate programs that suffered from these tight purse strings but streets and roads elsewhere in the state, most particularly within urban areas.

Prior to the energy crisis, rising auto use generated increased revenues each year, even while accelerating the highway system's decay. Between 1963 and 1973 the number of registered vehicles increased 74 percent, while the population increased by a much lower proportion, 16 percent. Estimates of the number of highway miles traveled within the state rose by 80 percent, from five million miles per day to nine million.[53] To augment the rise in highway revenues, the legislature also occasionally increased the state gas tax, to eight cents in 1968 and to nine cents in 1972. Even with these increases, however, the levy remained below its 1930 level, adjusted for inflation.

Furthermore, because of the high inflation of the 1970s, the state gas tax continued to drop, when measured in real terms. A call for a phased-in boost of ten cents per gallon issued by the Governor's office in 1973 was rejected by the legislature.[54] Between 1970 and 1980 the Consumer Price Index doubled, but motorists' user fees stayed virtually flat in Vermont. The annual registration fee stayed at the level set in 1961, while prices had nearly tripled since then. License fees, which had started at $2 in 1906, were now $4, or only 22 percent of the original charge after adjusting for inflation. The state gas tax remained at nine cents, which in 1980 amounted to only 8 percent of the retail price, about one-third of the proportion the state had collected in 1970.

The result was disastrous for the state budget, made all the worse by the energy crunch. As motorists were forced to conserve gasoline (through increased fuel-efficiency, lower speed limits, and scaled-back pleasure driving), gas-tax revenues fell, even before accounting for inflation. At the same time, highway construction costs multiplied, rising a remarkable 53 percent in one two-year period between 1978 and 1980.[55]

All along, highway boosters continued to complain about existing conditions and push for higher standards:

> The highways and bridges of our state are deteriorating faster than present available revenues allow for repair and reconstruction. Deferred maintenance

operations in recent years have accelerated the rate of deterioration of road surfaces . . . [and] our present system will require reconstruction to improve alignment and sight distance, widening of roads and bridges to meet increased traffic volumes, and bypasses of towns and villages to adapt to changing traffic patterns and alleviate congestion in thickly settled areas.[56]

Successive capital budgets consistently devoted more money to new construction than to maintenance, exacerbating the problem, even while the state accumulated "more than a billion dollars of backlogged improvements needed to restore Vermont's state and local roads to minimum tolerable conditions.[57]

There were not many options open to state officials charged with resolving this intractable situation. They issued more tax-exempt debt and transferred general revenues to the highway fund. Also, they continued to force costs down on local governments by threatening to forfeit federal urban-extension aid unless the affected town or city agreed to pay half of the state's share. In some years, the legislature or the highway commissioners did not even approve state contributions to make up the remaining portion. Instead, they convened a new advisory board to "review and analyze the present methods of funding transportation." The resulting report recommended a new policy of accepting "federal funding *selectively* rather than attempting to match all available funds" and "to secure only those funds which can be used to serve the state's priorities."[58]

In practice this meant that urban grants were passed over. It also stimulated a legislative moratorium on any further construction of new "major segments of four-lane highways" unless "proven unavoidable." A joint resolution of the state legislature instead directed the highway department to finish the Interstates and focus on improving existing roads with any remaining funds.[59]

The formal adoption of these new state policies meant that the Middlebury bypass and bridge proposals had no chance of obtaining state or federal support. Accordingly, beginning in the mid-1970s, state planning documents no longer even mentioned either of the two projects, except in occasional wish lists of deferred and unfunded ventures.[60] Instead, the funds that the highway department had hoped to spend on extensions to the four-lane projects near Rutland and Bennington, and on other major highways and bypasses, were reallocated to smaller projects around the state.

Middlebury officials tried, unsuccessfully, to obtain some of these reallocated funds for a drastically scaled-back Three-Mile Bridge reconstruction, ostensibly unconnected to the grander bridge–bypass plans. Three-Mile Bridge appeared in the Town's 1974 *Annual Report* as a $200,000 project, with 20 percent local funding. But the 1975 report listed it as "after 1980," the 1977 report described it as beginning in 1982, the 1978 report categorized it as "not included in any definite year," and subsequent reports made no mention of it whatsoever.[61] Instead, state highway engineers announced plans for widening Court Street, a move that surprised many people in Middlebury and immediately sparked controversy.

Court Street had been twenty feet wide (not counting sidewalks) since it was initially paved, before World War II. In contrast, the connecting portion of Route 7 to the south had been expanded to forty-four feet when it was rebuilt in 1963, although it still only carried two lanes of traffic. The extra width was taken up by broad shoulders and wider lanes. The engineers in the state highway department considered the narrow portion along Court Street and around the courthouse square a nuisance for motorists passing through Middlebury on Route 7. Many townspeople had a different perspective. For them, Court Street was a charming tree-lined and grass-embanked approach to their small New England town. The engineers' plan would have allowed four lanes of traffic along this congested stretch but at the cost of all the trees along the street. In their place, the edge of the new street would be marked by city-style cement curbs. Furthermore, because the project was classified as an urban-extension, state policy required the town to pay half of the state's share of the costs.

Opponents moved quickly. They tried to start a landmarking process to designate the entire village (including Court Street) as an historic district, as a means to limit reconstruction efforts. At the same time, they filed a petition

Court Street, before widening,
Henry Sheldon Museum of Vermont History

with the selectmen, suggesting a less disruptive reconstruction plan. In response, the town manager and the selectmen called for a nonbinding vote on the matter at the 1976 town meeting. The community was deeply divided on the issue, and after all the ballots were tallied, there were 632 (50.6 percent) votes for the project and 617 (49.4 percent) against.

A compromise was put forth, calling for a narrower roadway with one lane in each direction and a center turning lane for strategic intersections (in front of the shopping center built in the early 1960s, and in front of the entrance to the Buttolph Acres housing development, for example). As a part of this compromise, no parking would be permitted on either side of the new roadway (previously, local residents had routinely parked on the dirt-and-grass shoulders that would be replaced by the cement curbs). Frustrated by this narrower compromise proposal, the highway engineers threatened to withdraw the federal funds unless the full forty-four-foot version went through.

Court Street, after widening, with traffic,
Trent Campbell

In the end, after many months of litigation and negotiations that involved additional protagonists in Montpelier and Washington, the tiny endeavor was finally approved. Construction took just five months—in the spring and summer of 1979—and even though the three-lane plan prevailed, the grand old street trees still had to be taken down, sacrificed to ease traffic flow. In its final form, the project also included the installation of traffic lights along the new thoroughfare, even though residents remained steadfast in their opposition to a similar device at the intersection of Merchant's Row and Main Street (it had been inserted into the 1977 capital plan, but at town meeting voters refused to approve the budget until an amendment excluded the offending device).[62] The Court Street renovation symbolically marked changes in Middlebury. Overrun by cars and sprawling in all directions, the town was being transformed, refashioned by the now-overwhelming influence of automobility, whether inhabitants liked it or not.

SMALL TOWN SPRAWL

In 1977, the Addison County Regional Planning and Development Commission warned local residents that their town would continue to change:
"It's going to happen, so let's choose how." The plan cited the continued
development of suburban-style, single-family-housing subdivisions along the
edges of town as especially problematic.[63] This call to action produced scant
results. Antigrowth sentiment occasionally gave rise to community activism,
but Middlebury nevertheless continued along its established trajectory. For
the next twenty-five years, spread-out residential and commercial development continued. Longtime resident and community leader Harold Curtiss
recollected: "There has, of course, been some sprawl, but there is a fight
against it. In many cases, victory has been won."[64] But these victories were
vastly outweighed by successful new development on the periphery.

On the north side of town, new tenants moved into the industrial park:
a circuit-board manufacturer, Simmonds Precision Products; a plastics
plant, Continental Precision Company; and a clothing distribution warehouse, Geiger of Austria. The Middlebury Development Commission,
with the help of the Vermont Industrial Development Agency, offered an
array of incentives to attract employers to the site, including discounted
land prices ($10,000 per acre), low-interest construction financing (at a 4-
percent interest rate, financed by tax-exempt bonds), and credit guarantees
to insure bank loans. Soon, across Exchange Street from these industrial
concerns, new commercial buildings went up, housing a wide range of
businesses including small offices, a health spa, a microbrewery, and
doctors' offices, all taking advantage of the easy access to Route 7 and
avoiding the downtown traffic snarl.[65]

A large expansion of the Buttolph Acres subdivision, called "Valley
View," was approved in 1983; in 1984 the town invested in new municipal
parking lots; between 1985 and 1990 Middlebury issued building permits
for 547 new housing units, virtually all of which were on previously
undeveloped open land. In addition to new tract-style subdivisions, other

new homes went up along the government-funded roads that reached out into the surrounding countryside like spokes on a wheel. To the south, the shopping center on Route 7 south expanded to make room for a McDonald's restaurant, complete with drive-through window.

Farther south along Route 7, car dealers built expansive new showrooms. Before long, another large health spa opened, operators of "big-box" stores began to make plans for the "Route 7 South" corridor, including Rite-Aid drugstores and Stop 'n' Shop supermarkets, and hoteliers planned to build two new eighty-room hotels along the growing strip.[66] All of this new construction was exclusively auto-oriented, as it was too far from town to be linked by pedestrian sidewalks and all were therefore accompanied by large parking lots.

Between 1970 and 1990 Addison County added nearly six times as many residents as Middlebury (8,687 versus 1,502). In contrast, for the twenty-year period a half century earlier, between 1920 and 1940, before the cumulative effects of automobility policies had begun to decentralize American towns, the county had lost two and a half times as much population as the town had gained. The 2000 census revealed that this trend toward peripheral growth continues unabated—between 1990 and 2000 the town grew 3 percent while the expansion rate for the surrounding area was 11 percent.[67]

But even while the population was expanding and new employers were coming to the area, downtown Middlebury businesses closed down. The old-fashioned pharmacy on Main Street could not compete with the strip-mall drugstores on the edge of town. A self-proclaimed "department store" in an old building downtown shut its doors, having lost the routine sales of dungarees, winter coats, boots, and back-to-school clothing to other outlets. The Western Auto franchise couldn't keep up with competitors with more parking and faster highway access. Ruby's Ice Cream Shop closed, as did the diner-style Cannon Restaurant.

Local leaders were aware that downtown was in trouble but seemed unable to stem the tide. When the Town Planning Commission approved one of the large new hotels planned for the Route 7 South corridor in 1999, one member acknowledged that "it would have a potentially adverse impact upon the economic vitality of downtown." Similarly, when a major local hardware store got approval to move to a new site farther from the town center, another commission member commented on the trend: "Cumulatively, it is bad news." The merchants along this burgeoning strip were aware that they constituted a new commerical hub for the area, with divergent interests from downtown. They formed a new, competing chamber of commerce called the "Route 7 Business and Property Owners Association."[68] Downtown Middlebury, like many larger cities, had to adapt to these new trends or face obsolescence.

In place of the defunct small-town shops, downtown redevelopment featured tourist-oriented stores. A bike shop to service summer bike-tours opened. A photo shop took the place formerly occupied by the auto parts store, and a gift shop replaced the pharmacy. A former tavern near the base of the falls (on the site of one of the nineteenth-century mills) was redeveloped to house half a dozen small retail stores: a computer consultant, a camping equipment store, a Ben & Jerry's scoop shop, a clothing boutique, and a purveyor of gourmet cooking supplies, sandwiches, and prepared foods. Another nearby mill building was rebuilt as the new State Crafts Center—a retail showroom featuring the work of Vermont artists and craftspeople. Other crafts shops moved in next door, displacing another bar-restaurant. Skihaus, a recreational clothing and outdoor equipment store, expanded, eventually taking over almost one entire block on Main Street. Swift House, former home of one of the town's oldest families, was renovated and expanded as a country inn. At Courthouse Square, the Middlebury Inn built a new annex, and a small apartment house nearby was converted to The Inn on the Green. A major redevelopment of the abandoned downtown marble works was initiated in 1988, involving a pedestrian bridge with a view of the falls and the conversion of old workshop buildings into a warren of boutique-sized retail shops and small offices.[69]

The influx of tourism, dispersed population growth, and sprawling commercial development produced further increases in traffic. Traffic counts conducted in 1982 found that the number of daily crossings on the Battell Bridge had risen to over sixteen thousand, more than 50 percent higher than the levels found only eight years earlier. Route 7 South carried more traffic than any other non-Interstate in Vermont, with the exception of a handful of roads in much bigger cities like Burlington and Rutland.[70]

Renewed discussion of bypasses and bridges went hand in hand with the continuing traffic problems, prompting vitriolic public debates. Polls showed that the town was still "sharply divided on bypass choices," although there was "considerable support for the reconstruction of Three-Mile Bridge." However, these polls understated the costs of the Three-Mile Bridge project, which planners cautioned would require "extensive improvement" to access roads, including a linkup with Route 125 near East Middlebury.[71] State and federal highway engineers, unconcerned with easing traffic *within* Middlebury and much more concerned with making it easier to get *around* the town, would not consider any bridge aid, however, without first resolving the bypass deadlock.

The state and federal highway engineers jointly conducted a preliminary environmental impact review of both bypass routes, selected the east-of-town version, and made a one-time offer to the town of a multimillion-dollar grant to build the new highway. The state's Interstates were finally nearing completion, and the highway department was planning to fund some of the long-neglected projects. They assumed that some highway money would be raised through continued issuance of tax-exempt bonds backed by general revenues, since that had become a standard financing practice. Accordingly, Middlebury voters were given the opportunity to consider the state's bypass proposal at a special 1981 town meeting. Leaders of the Route 7 Task Force opposed the measure, restating their support for a westerly bypass. Middlebury College adamantly opposed the westerly route and strategically bought land along the state's proposed easterly route and offered to make it available. Many noncollege residents were concerned that the easterly route would disrupt the extensive residential areas on that side of town. Some farmers spoke in favor of the state plan, pleased that it would save the fertile Champlain Valley land to the west and instead would take the prime residential land to the east. Others argued that an in-town bridge was more important than a bypass, and the town could not afford the state-mandated local contributions for both. When the vote was counted, the controversial measure was rejected by nearly a two-to-one margin.[72]

In reporting the results, Town Manager David Crawford wrote, "The Middlebury Bypass is not any longer under active consideration [by the state] . . . there will be a very dramatic increase in traffic. . . . We can expect more congestion and the problems that go with it."[73] Despite a subsequent re-vote in 1988, this time rescinding the previous decision, and a report that same year from a "Bypass Committee" of the town selectmen endorsing an east-of-town bypass, the state and federal engineers avoided further involvement in the debate and declined to take up the matter again.[74]

Immediately after the bypass rejection in 1981, Crawford turned to the bridge proposal. The following year, with the endorsement of the selectmen and the Town Planning Commission, voters authorized preliminary engineering work by a 60–40 electoral margin. The timing was perfect, since the state almost immediately thereafter received an infusion of highway funds from a 1982 increase in the federal gas tax. A token $28,000 was allocated to Middlebury for the bridge project, but that was enough to complete the engineering study and conduct a right-of-way survey.[75] Soon thereafter, when the "unified support" for the project appeared to remain intact, the state transportation board officially re-included the Middlebury bridge in the state's long-term plan. The 1986 town report noted that "with traffic congestion in the downtown reaching critical proportions this summer, this has come none too soon." A new bridge was now the town's top priority, since delays crossing the Otter were now obstructing hospital access and slowing police and fire response times. Minor adjustments to parking and one-way designations of key parts of downtown streets in 1981 had produced only marginal effects, quickly offset by continuing sprawl, so construction of the new bridge was eagerly awaited by many.

But, while the state put the bridge back in the long-range plan, it did not provide any funds, instead scheduling it for construction at some undetermined time, largely because the state's borrowing practices had been in a state of flux ever since interest rates had risen to unprecedented highs in the 1970s.[76] After repeatedly borrowing for the Interstates over the past twenty years, highway debt now accounted for nearly half of Vermont's outstanding debt, and one-seventh of all state revenues were devoted to debt service. The state's highway debt per capita was the fifth highest in the nation, as a percentage of income per capita. Therefore, when interest rates climbed, the highway budget was buffeted by rising interest payments and a virtual moratorium on additional borrowing for highways.[77]

When the Federal Reserve Board reined in inflation in the early 1980s, a part of Chairman Paul Volcker's strategy was to keep interest rates high. For Vermont, this meant that as older bond issues came due, the same interest payments could only support diminished replacement borrowings. Accordingly, much to the consternation of highway officials, the transportation department was not permitted to use borrowed funds again until 1991, when interest rates had fallen considerably and stayed lower.[78]

Fortunately for the Middlebury bridge project, this new round of borrowing was expected to focus on replacing or expanding bridges across the state, many of which had been originally built with proceeds of the state's first highway borrowing, in the aftermath of the 1927 flood. Still, the Middlebury project proceeded slowly and suffered from repeated postponements. Voters didn't get a chance to formally approve the fully engineered plans until 1992 (the measure passed by a vote of 1,987 to 1,632), at which point construction was not slated by the state to begin at least until 1997, when a bond issue was expected to raise matching funds. Once again, the closeness of the vote and ongoing bickering about the exact design and location of the bridge led state planners to defer the project, returning it to the proverbial backburner.[79]

Traffic along Main Street, 2002,
Trent Campbell

CONCLUSION

Whether a bridge or bypass will ever be built in Middlebury is uncertain. Town selectmen continue to complain that "gridlock has been plaguing the gateways to town," and yet another governor recently declared the Route 7 corridor a "highest priority construction project."[80] Town meetings continue to spend more time on traffic matters than any other issues, debating new traffic lights, proposing new traffic islands, arguing over bypass routes, re-proposing the new downtown bridge, and appropriating small sums to repair the existing bridges. But in the meantime, Middlebury continues to sprawl, under the influence of century-long automobility policies that foster decentralization. As in the past, Middlebury remains "a college town, a farm town, and Addison County's regional service center and industrial hub," but it has changed shape and continues to do so, mutating to accommodate automotive transportation.[81]

Traffic backup waiting to enter Middlebury from west, 2002,
Trent Campbell

Other cities across Vermont also sprawled during the latter half of the twentieth century—some as much as Middlebury, some even more so. Decentralized growth patterns were most apparent along the interstates. Recent reports have proclaimed that "the economic revival that turned Vermont's income graph upwards arrived on the Interstate Highway System," and some Vermont economists have hailed the Interstates as the best thing to happen to Vermont in its entire history.[82] But the growth fueled by the Interstates came at a price. Despite the oft-repeated Vermonter ethos of preserving open space, allowing farmers to work the land, and maintaining historic villages, and despite high profile growth-control measures like Act 250 (one of the toughest land-use statutes in the country), the state has still literally lost ground to sprawl.

Chittenden County can serve as an example. Between 1940 and 1995, the population of its urban centers grew by 55 percent, while the surrounding areas grew at ten times that rate (530 percent), capturing more than two-thirds of the region's postwar growth. In 1948, 90 percent of the county's retail and wholesale trade had been in its three largest incorporated municipalities (Burlington, Winooski, and Essex Junction), but in 1992 those same areas claimed only 40 percent of retail business and only 35 percent of wholesalers. This figure has deteriorated since that time, as big-box retailers like Wal-Mart, Circuit City, and Home Depot have opened new outlets in sparsely settled areas. Similarly, in 1948, three-fourths of the county's service businesses were in Burlington, compared to one-third in 1992; in 1947 two-thirds of the county's industry was located in Burlington, while the corresponding statistic for 1992 was only 27 percent.[83]

Transportation policy debate in the state remains virtually unchanged, following the precedents established early in the twentieth century. A recent report on the topic repeated many of the same old refrains, proclaiming that "the most significant current highway problems are deterioration and deferred maintenance." Highway boosters complained about "archaic stretches," "a patchwork of thoroughfares . . . [and] a lack of funds to improve them." At the same time, motorist groups pushed for renewal of measures to protect the Highway Fund from so-called diversion, so as to "avoid the emotionally charged issue of comparing paving projects with, say, the needs of widows and orphans; in other words, transportation would not have to compete in the state budget with welfare or educational programs." Meanwhile the state gas tax continues to fall farther behind inflation. It was nominally increased: By 1990 it reached sixteen cents per gallon, a 78 percent increase from the nine-cent level set in 1972, but inflation was 213 percent over the same period. Instead, the gap continued to widen when, for example, Governor Howard Dean pushed an initiative to increase the state's paving budget by half in 1999, with no rise in user fees.[84]

Likewise, a recent report from the Vermont Economic Progress Council repeated comments about Route 7 heard for half a century: "In our view, first priority should be given to projects which create better north-south access on the western side of the state." But, since the bulk of state's economic growth has been along the Interstates, and the superhighways themselves need expensive maintenance, there are still insufficient funds to make good on these statements. Meanwhile, the easiest solution to looming shortages of highway funds is penalizing the state's cities, postponing state aid for urban projects in favor of less-expensive work in the open countryside between cities.[85]

Motorists have been persistently undercharged. This has produced more demand for automobility than supply. In response, the state has poured enormous sums of money into new construction (at the expense of maintenance), trying to help the supply catch up to the demand. The result is a highway system that the government can not afford to maintain and an economy that is now predicated on artificially cheap, subsidized automotive transport. Small towns like Middlebury, as much as big cities like Denver, have been remade by this dynamic, rapidly spreading out across the countryside and simultaneously reinventing their downtowns in order to survive in the automobile age.

AutoCity: Smyrna, Tennessee

Driving south on I-24, through a scenic landscape of rolling Tennessee hills twenty-three miles beyond Nashville, a road sign indicates that the next major city is Chattanooga, more than one hundred miles away. On the side of the highway, in addition to a peppering of roadside billboards, rests an occasional crumbling shack. Suddenly, in the middle of nowhere, an exit ramp connects to Tennessee State Route 102, a striking combination of two different highway standards: In one direction a two-lane country road, but in the other a four-lane limited-access divided highway, complete with a wide grassy median and grade-separated intersections. Here, incongruously enormous trucks lumber along, slicing through verdant farmland; cows graze next to the road, in the shadow of "For Sale" signs and wooden placards hawking new subdivisions. Then, around a bend, it looms–the largest auto assembly plant in North America, by itself constituting a landscape like that of a small industrial city. With production capacity of half a million cars a year, staffed by more than five thousand workers and hundreds of robots, the plant occupies over five million square feet, or if you include parking lots and satellite buildings, 782 acres.

At the beginning of the twentieth century, Smyrna, Tennessee, was an insignificant town. No more than a hamlet, it housed only a few hundred people. By the late twentieth century, seemingly by accident of location,

Smyrna had become a booming industrial settlement, attracting a steady flow of new employers and new residents. The movement of people and businesses to Smyrna was far from accidental, nor can it be solely attributed to natural features of the region. Instead, Smyrna's remarkable growth can be directly traced to a series of government programs, each of which involved subsidized rural infrastructure construction.

The late-century prosperity of Smyrna is the product of a *de facto* industrial relocation initiative, a web of government policies—both implicit and explicit—that have reconstructed the American landscape. In Smyrna's case, this web included the pre-Interstate federal-aid highway program, New Deal construction projects, federal defense spending, subsidies embedded in the tax code, and the construction of the toll-free Interstate Highway System.

BACKGROUND

Smyrna is in the heart of the central basin of Middle Tennessee. The Nashville and Chattanooga Railroad first established the town in 1851, as a whistle-stop midway between Nashville and Murfreesboro. A post office opened the following year, and the railroad soon attempted to develop a town at the site, mapping streets and offering lots for sale at public auction. However, there was no demand for the land, the auction failed, and the new town grew slowly. The railroad could not sell its first lot until 1859, and it took an entire decade to complete the sale of the first group of sixty-four lots, at an average lot price of about one hundred dollars.[1]

The timing was not good for new cities in Tennessee. Although more than two dozen businesses were established in Smyrna during the town's first few years, only six survived the Civil War and Reconstruction. For decades afterward, the local economy showed no signs of recovery. The population of the surrounding county (Rutherford County) peaked in 1880 at 36,741 and did not reach this level again until the 1950 census.[2] Smyrna remained quiescent and stagnant until World War II. But important changes to the physical infrastructure took place in Smyrna during the 1920s and 1930s, when the population was only 464.[3]

First, and perhaps most important, the main road through Smyrna was incorporated into the emerging network of major autoroutes. Known locally as the Nashville-Murfreesboro Road or the Nashville Pike, the rambling dirt road became one component of the new Dixie Highway, a pioneering interregional highway promoted by Carl Fisher, an auto-parts manufacturer and the primary real estate investor-booster in Miami Beach. Fisher had been involved in the formation of the Lincoln Highway–the first of the modern interregional highways efforts, meant to connect New York, Philadelphia, Pittsburgh, Chicago, Omaha, Salt Lake City, Sacramento, and Oakland–and he recognized that it would be good business for him to promote additional similar roads to foster cross-country driving, especially those with a final destination near his holdings in south Florida. The first meeting of his Dixie Highway association was in nearby Chattanooga, in 1915. This route, which connected Chicago (where it intersected the Lincoln Highway), Indianapolis, Louisville, Nashville, Atlanta, and Miami, was paid for by a haphazard patchwork of state and county funds from ten states and more than fifty counties—often financed by tax-exempt bond issues—augmented by contributions from merchants along the route who were involved in tourism or other auto-related businesses.[4]

Smyrna was now on a new transportation corridor. The route was designated a primary state highway, and was officially known as State Route 1 and U.S. Highway 41, after it was incorporated into the nationwide network of trunk lines created by the 1921 Federal-Aid Highway Act. These designations brought money for improvements to the road.[5] Had Smyrna been a bigger town, with more than 2,500 residents, the local portion of road would not have been eligible for federal aid. But because Smyrna was not considered an "urban area," federal funds paved the highway. As a byproduct of this government aid, some nearby connecting streets and sidewalks in Smyrna were hard-paved in 1928 with state-aid funds, as part of an effort to make secondary improvements along the routes of the new primary federal highways. Many of these roads in Smyrna had previously been little more than rough and unsurfaced dirt paths, although some of the busier streets had been occasionally covered with gravel or cinders discarded by locomotives passing through on the nearby railroad.[6]

Thus, the Federal-Aid Act had endowed Smyrna with a modern road system. Similarly, funds from the Tennessee Valley Authority financed a new electrical distribution system and a connection to the TVA power grid. In 1937 the town's first water system was built by the Works Progress Administration; by 1940 Smyrna could boast of a modern highway, and new water and electric systems, all federally subsidized. Nevertheless, despite these government outlays, the population of the town was still minuscule and was actually dwindling at the time, from 531 in 1930, down to 483 in 1940.[7]

SEWART AIR BASE

In 1941, Washington came to Smyrna on an even larger scale, changing the town dramatically and setting the stage for transformations that would occur decades later. In the weeks following Pearl Harbor, Tennessee spent almost $400,000 on behalf of the U.S. Army, buying farmland in the Smyrna area to assemble a 3,300-acre bomber training base. The state spent additional funds improving the local infrastructure, paving access roads (only a tiny portion of the town's streets were paved at the time) and strengthening or replacing nearby bridges in anticipation of the much heavier car and truck traffic that would accompany the opening of the air base.[8] The location of the installation, requiring the construction of an entire airport from scratch, can be partially attributed to the policy of the military to encourage "dispersal" of defense facilities. This federal policy, initiated during World War II and continued through the Cold War, constituted a drain of resources from urban areas and a corresponding subsidy for the emerging "Sunbelt."[9]

Within a few months the Army completed several terminal buildings in Smyrna, along with three runways, numerous hangars, and enough barracks to house nearly four thousand enlisted men and one thousand officers, as well as fifty-four additional support buildings and a complete hospital with over two hundred beds. The Army also installed water filtration equipment and a sewage treatment facility for the base and added eleven more buildings before the end of the war.[10] After almost a century of stagnation, Smyrna's population grew by a factor of ten, practically overnight.

After the war, Sewart Air Force Base became the home to the 314th Troop Carrier Wing. During the 1950s the Air Force used Sewart as a training base and in 1958 invested in a new round of capital improvements, making it the sole base for the well-known C-130 Hercules aircraft.[11]

Meanwhile, using funds appropriated in special wartime "Defense Highway Acts," the state began to rebuild U.S. Route 41. The section northward, in the direction of Nashville, was completed in 1943, and the section southward from Smyrna toward Murfreesboro was done two years after. These wartime appropriations allowed the BPR to bypass the state-by-state aid allocation formulae and instead disburse extra money (on a three-to-one ratio to state expenditures, instead of the regular one-to-one matching ratio) to state highway departments for projects that would correct "critical deficiencies in the strategic system of highways having military importance," which generally meant primary routes leading to rural and suburban military installations.[12] By 1951 the entire stretch from Nashville to Murfeesboro had been widened to four lanes, because of base-related automotive traffic.[13] This aggressive expansion of the local trans-portation network in the Smyrna area is particularly noteworthy when juxtaposed with the woeful condition of those components of the local infrastructure that did not benefit from the same generous federal subsidies. At about this same time, in 1950, there was considerable local debate about whether Rutherford County could afford to install indoor toilets in nearby white schools.[14]

The federal commitment to Smyrna increased even more during the fifties and sixties. By 1965 the base population had swelled to over thirteen thousand. The total payroll was about $28 million annually, including a civilian payroll of over $3 million.[15]

As a result of this increasing federal presence, additional money was available for local infrastructure improvements. For example, the Air Force paid a fee to the local school system for each dependent child of base employees. These revenues, amounting to approximately $2.3 million per year in the mid-1960s, were used to finance expansions.[16] In addition, the town received "bonus" payments every few years from a special federally financed housing project connected to the base. Built as an FHA project, with the town as the nominal "owner," the project was structured so that the rents provided slightly more revenue than was needed to repay the FHA mortgage. The surplus moneys accumulated over time and were periodically distributed to the town as a dividend; the town used these funds in 1959 to pave streets. A new park and playground were built in 1961 with another dividend from the housing project, as was another major paving initiative in 1968. The final dividend was used in 1970 for a brand-new public library.[17] Separately, the TVA finished a new hydropower project in 1967 that created the J. Percy Priest Reservoir adjacent to Smyrna, providing substantial new recreation facilities.[18]

In addition to direct federal largesse, the base also provided indirect benefits to Smyrna. Washington's commitment to Smyrna made it more creditworthy, so that the town could borrow money for local improvements by issuing tax-exempt bonds. In 1955 Smyrna borrowed money to build new sewers and borrowed again in 1957 for a gas distribution system. In 1961 the town added almost half a million dollars in debt to build a water treatment plant at Stones River, with an integrated wastewater treatment plant. Funds from another bond issue, this time for $1.2 million, paid for further expansion to the waterworks in 1967, and a bond-financed municipal hospital was also erected at this time. Thus, within a little over ten years, the town had used its federally supported (and subsidized, either through the tax-exemption or through low-interest loans from the Farmers Home Administration) borrowing capacity to expand its physical infrastructure.[19]

Not surprisingly, the population grew, but in 1950 the county's population was only four times the base's population, and the base accounted for a similar percentage of the available jobs in the county (about one-fourth). Ninety-two percent of county land was still used for farming, and the value of all the real estate in the county added together was only $20.8 million. The population of the town (not counting the base) had grown from 483 in 1940 to about 2,300 in 1950, and to 3,619 in 1960.[20] By the mid-sixties, the town was spending more money on debt service in a single year than the entire budget from a decade earlier, even though debt-service requirements were still low as a percentage of the entire budget (16 percent). By 1970 the budget had grown to nearly twenty times the amount spent fifteen years earlier.[21]

Abruptly, the federally financed party in Smyrna seemed to come to an end in 1965, when Defense Secretary Robert MacNamara announced that Sewart Air Force Base would be decommissioned. There was widespread belief that the town would stagnate and wither, reverting to its former state. Indeed, within a few months of the base closure in 1970, the population of the town (not counting the base itself) had dropped by 50 percent.[22]

In retrospect, Sewart's effect on Smyrna over thirty years had been dramatic, but not universally positive. The local economy remained monolithic, since no other significant employer had located in the area. Furthermore, no retail economy had developed, because no private merchants could compete against the base exchange and the commissary. In fact, the local economy had not grown beyond a handful of businesses, the largest of which was a car dealership, owned by longtime mayor Sam Ridley. It seemed that Smyrna's moment of prosperity had come and gone, leaving a half-abandoned town with an anemic economy, a contracting tax base, and an almost nonexistent business community.

Fortunately, the facilities that the Air Force turned over to local authorities constituted a considerable arsenal for the town's impending battle for survival. The 635 units of family housing had central air conditioning, and about one hundred other permanent buildings contained 730,000 square feet of space suitable for commercial or industrial use. There were twenty-nine miles of paved roads within the base grounds and four miles of rail tracks that connected to the main trunk line. Sewart's water treatment plant had a rated capacity of over 800,000 gallons per day, and the sewage treatment plant had a rated capacity of 675,000 gallons per day.[23] Similarly, the schools now had excess capacity. With the student census reduced to ninety-two, and the teaching staff cut back to ten, that still left a nine-to-one student-teacher ratio.[24]

Sam Ridley—mayor, state legislator, utilities commissioner, local car dealer, and irrepressable booster—may have been the only observer to recognize that Smyrna was not near death, as many supposed, but instead was well-equipped for growth. Ridley believed that the abundance of developable land and the excess infrastructure capacity would attract new businesses to Smyrna. He proclaimed that Smyrna had "the brightest future of any town in Tennessee. . . . We are at the crossroads of rail, interstate highways and airline service. We are a prime site for industry. We have the most modern school system, hospital, library, churches, and public buildings. We have ample water and superb recreation facilities."[25]

Although many people dismissed these comments as the desperately over-optimistic talk of a small town politician, Sam Ridley sincerely believed in this vision of Smyrna as a mecca of corporate relocation. In the years following the base closure, which he has since hailed as "the best thing that ever happened to Smyrna," he expanded his business interests well beyond his Chevrolet franchise. Ridley and his twin brother, Knox, purchased parcels from many of the fleeing landowners after Sewart's closing was announced. "It was like rats leaving a sinking ship," he recalled. "People were selling their houses for $250, just so they could get out." The Ridleys bought wide swaths of land for $1,000 an acre. By 1979 Ridley also owned "considerable" portions of the First National Bank of Smyrna, the Murfreesboro Bank and Trust Company, and the Citizens Central Bank of Murfreesboro. He boasted that it was "hard to run into something in Smyrna that Sam Ridley is not involved in."[26]

In this run-down and nearly abandoned middle-American small town, Ridley, a short and unimposing man who never finished college, became a larger-than-life personality, almost single-handedly dominating the business and political scenes for years to come. When asked to describe his role in Smyrna's rebirth, he boasted that "Everything you see in Smyrna, we built. I had complete control. I ran everything, truthfully. You know, the dictator form of government is the best in the world, if he's benevolent." Ridley's tenure as mayor lasted forty-six years, ending only when he was forced from office in 1987 by a conflict-of-interest ruling stemming from the town's dealings with his car dealership for the purchase, service, and repair of town vehicles. Even then, he was succeeded in office by his twin brother and long-time business partner, and later by younger politicians that he "put up to be mayor."[27]

Sam Ridley was not the only person to recognize Smyrna's competitive advantages; he was, instead, the only person to stake his life's savings on the town's future in its darkest hour. A study conducted by a Vanderbilt University business-school student in 1967 had concluded that "it was already evident" that the growth in Rutherford County would be along the soon-to-be-completed I-24 corridor and that Smyrna was ripe for residential and industrial development.[28] These predictions, both the academic analysis and Ridley's gutsy optimism, turned out to be surprisingly accurate, despite the contradictory material conditions in Smyrna at the time. In retrospect, the turning point that marked the emergence of a proverbial Smyrna-phoenix from the ashes of military abandonment was the opening of the Interstate Highway.

INTERSTATE 24

The Interstate was, ultimately, the most powerful weapon in Smyrna's economic development arsenal. In 1970, the same year Sewart Air Force Base was finally closed, the new superhighway I-24 was completed from Murfreesboro to Nashville, roughly parallel to the old U.S. 41. At first, this was devastating. "You could cross the street (U.S. 41) blindfolded and be safe," once the through traffic shifted to the new road, remembers Sam Ridley. But the new highway actually initiated the next era of Smyrna's growth, which would be fueled by the availability of a distribution network paid for by the

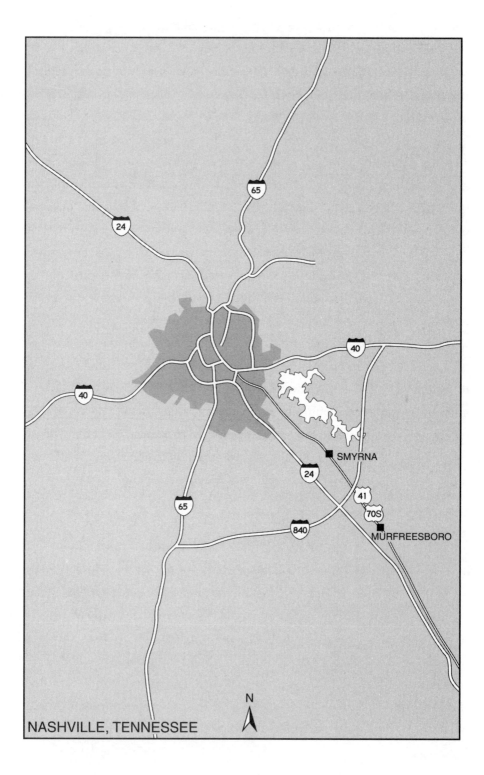

NASHVILLE, TENNESSEE

N

federal government.[29] This transportation advantage enabled little Smyrna, Tennessee, to compete with much bigger and better-known municipalities for new business and residential investment.

On the Interstate Highway System, Smyrna was roughly equidistant (400–500 toll-free miles) from New York, Detroit, Milwaukee, Dallas, Houston, and Tampa. Closer still, between 200 and 400 miles away, were Chicago, Washington, D.C., Baltimore, Cleveland, Pittsburgh, and Kansas City. Atlanta, St. Louis, Cincinnati, Richmond, Louisville, Raleigh-Durham, and Indianapolis were all less than 200 miles away. At the outer reaches of a circle delineating a long day's truck trip from Smyrna, 600 miles away, were Boston and Minneapolis/St.Paul.[30] The system was particularly efficient in Smyrna's case because nearby Nashville was one of only six metropolitan areas in the nation with Interstates extending in six different directions, instead of the more typical two or four.[31] Without the federal highways, Smyrna would be in the boondocks, but with them a large portion of the American economy was within reach.

On the initial plans for I-24, there was only one Smyrna exit, which provided access to the south end of town via a short stretch of winding country road unsuitable for commercial truck traffic. Ridley and other county leaders wanted another exit at the northern end of town, to provide a straighter and more direct connection from the highway to the abandoned air base, so as to maximize its redevelopment potential. The federal government had sold the base to the county for $2 million in 1971 in a complicated arrangement that left the aviation facilities and many major buildings under the control of a newly created town-county agency called the Rutherford County–Smyrna Airport Development Authority and the nonaviation property, including the water and sewer systems and most of the land, in the sole possession of the town.[32] The town also was given title to the eighteen-hole golf course of the former officers' club.[33] Knowing that these discarded resources from Sewart could be valuable economic development assets, town and county leaders recognized that linking them more directly to the interstate with a second exit would enhance their value even more.

In 1974, just three years after the initial opening of I-24, final plans were approved and contracts let for the second, more northerly, Smyrna exit on I-24, with a brand new state highway that would go straight from the interstate to the abandoned base, where there would also be a new interchange built to connect the new route (State Route 266) to U.S. 41, at the northern edge of town. The I-24 interchange would be 90 percent paid for by the federal government (with the 10 percent balance coming from the state), the U.S. 41 interchange would be funded as a federal-aid highway project and as such would get 50 percent federal funding (again, with the balance coming from the state). The actual connecting road (later renamed the "Sam Ridley Parkway") would be funded as a state-aid highway, with financing responsibilities split evenly between the state and the county.[34]

Within a few years of the completion of this second connection to the interstate, the local economy began to stabilize and show signs of moderate growth. This change occurred gradually, in fits and starts, and the economy was not fully transformed for another ten years. In the mid-1970s, for example, almost three-quarters of the land in Rutherford County was still used for farming.[35]

Not surprisingly, almost all of the new economic activity in Smyrna took place on the abandoned Air Force property. By 1978, twenty-nine different businesses employed nearly two thousand people on the nonaviation portion of the base, while an additional sixteen businesses with about 750 employees were on the aviation section, which had been renamed Smyrna Airport. Some of these businesses were small local and regional ventures, while others were large companies with national visibility. Capital Air (a charter airline) moved into part of the airport facilities, making Smyrna the headquarters for operations that had formerly been split between higher-cost airports in Nashville and Wilmington, Delaware. BetterBilt Aluminum, a door-and-window manufacturer, became the area's largest single employer, with a payroll of about five hundred. In 1977 the region's first shopping center opened, with a Winn-Dixie supermarket and a Treasury drugstore, along

U.S. 41 on a parcel of land bought from Sam and Knox Ridley. This was the first time since the base exchange and commissary had closed that Smyrna residents could do their grocery shopping without driving all the way to Nashville or Murfreesboro.[36]

In 1979 and 1980 the FAA installed instrument-landing capabilities, which induced the overnight delivery arm of Emery Air Freight to establish a hub at Smyrna, flying to as many as eighty-six different cities each night.[37] The Square-D corporation, a leading manufacturer of specialized electrical components, built a plant at the airport, employing 150 workers per shift.[38] These employers were attracted to Smyrna for many reasons, but a major factor was the transportation infrastructure available in the area, at little or no marginal cost to new users.

Meanwhile, throughout the 1970s, Mayor Ridley and his fellow boosters continued to pursue a program of civic investment. "We tried to stay ten to fifteen years ahead of our growth," he later recalled.[39] A $1.1 million bond issue was sold to finance a hospital expansion and modernization effort.[40] In 1980, Ridley announced a multimillion dollar water and sewer expansion, planned in stages to accommodate prospective growth that he optimistically predicted would boost the town to a population of 25,000 by 1990, about three times the 1980 count.[41] These investments were modest, but they had the effect of complementing the large accumulation of federal subsidies. In conjunction with the town's relatively low level of previously outstanding debt, they increased the town's prospects for economic growth.

Before Sam Ridley began to use federally subsidized debt financing to beef up municipal services, Smyrna had combined outstanding debt of less than $2 million and annual debt service requirements (interest and principal) of less than $150,000. This encompassed all the previously issued bonds for streets, the water system, the gas system, the sewer system, and the hospital. Of course, the federal government had paid for the lion's share of the development of those systems, either as New Deal projects or as part of its commitment to Sewart (which had, after all, been virtually synonymous with Smyrna for more than twenty years).

To prospective employers considering relocating in Smyrna (or employees moving to Smyrna, to follow employers), the low debt level meant that property taxes did not have to support debt burdens attributable to an aging infrastructure. Instead, prospective corporate citizens could be confident that their property taxes would support relatively new infrastructure. Since Smyrna was little more than a well-located repository of excess capacity for delivery of municipal services—much of which had been already paid for by the federal government—new taxpayers could be confident that they would not have to shoulder the expense of shoring up a financially strained urban government. The entire consolidated budget for the town at this time, including the hospital, the water system, the sewer system, and the gas system, was only $1 million a year.[42] Smyrna was ready for its next big step.

NISSAN

On October 20, 1980, Smyrna was transformed into a late twentieth-century boomtown when Nissan, the Japanese automobile manufacturer, announced plans for an enormous new factory. The plant would cost $450 million to build, with an annual construction payroll of $25 million, and would have an initial production capacity of over 100,000 vehicles, starting in 1983. Once it began operations, the plant would directly employ more than two thousand workers, at an annual cost of $44 million. This announcement marked the conclusion of a three-year selection process that had involved proposals from thirty states.

Nissan had retained the management consulting firm of Booz-Allen, Hamilton to aid in the selection process and had visited and evaluated potential sites late in 1978. Company officials had specifically stated that they wanted a minimum of four hundred acres of flat land (this requirement was later expanded to six hundred acres) closely connected to the Interstate Highway System and near an international aviation facility (more than half of the assembly components were expected to be imported). In addition, Nissan's site selection process also took into account the costs of land, water, electricity, and sewage treatment. Although it was not directly stated by Nissan officials, there is little doubt that Tennessee's "right-to-work" law was also an important factor, since it afforded the company reassurance that the plant would probably not become unionized. (The UAW has since mounted several unsuccessful attempts to organize the Nissan workers in Smyrna.) However, the President of Nissan, Takashi Ishihara, cited highway access and distribution location as the key factors that led to the selection of Smyrna from a short list that included sites in Georgia and Ohio, and two other sites in Tennessee (one near Knoxville and the other near Memphis).[43]

When Ishihara referred to Smyrna's "good access to highways," he was oversimplifying the situation.[44] To be sure, Smyrna was situated just a few miles from the Interstate system, but highway officials had also promised to spend public money on custom highway modifications that would further enhance accessibility. As a part of the negotiations with the company, extensive plans had been arranged, involving state and federal funding for major new highway initiatives. These specially designed projects capitalized on the extensive transportation facilities already in place.

Although there were already two Smyrna exits along I-24, only the northernmost such exit provided a direct, highway-style connection between the town and the Interstate. The older exit near the south end of town was a short stretch of meandering back road unsuitable for the heavy truck traffic that would go to and from the Nissan plant. Thus, the agreement with the company required the state to construct a new four-lane connector road that would provide a direct and uninterrupted connection from the Interstate to the plant's main entrance, with grade-separated interchanges for all cross-routes in between, including an enormous cloverleaf interchange with U.S. Route 41.[45] In addition, the old town road that fronted on the plant, which had been known as J. S. Young Road in honor of Mayor Ridley's grandfather, would be rebuilt into a five-lane highway that would lead from the new I-24 connector around to the airport and meet up with the other, more northerly, I-24 connector (the Sam Ridley Parkway). This new "beltway," connecting the new factory to the airport and to both of the Interstate 24 access roads

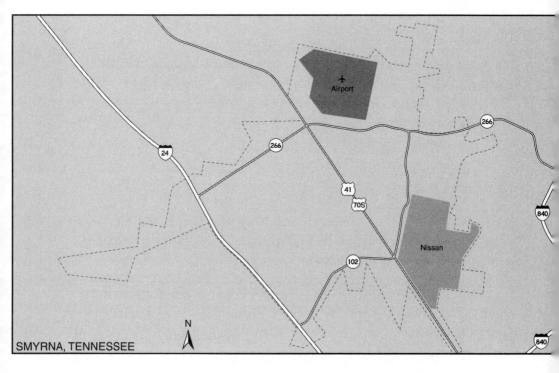

SMYRNA, TENNESSEE

would be called Nissan Drive. The funding for these improvements would come almost entirely from federal-aid programs, since all but a very small portion could be described as reconstruction or improvement of existing federal and state highways. In all, the agreement with Nissan mandated more than $40 million worth of externally funded highway improvements in Smyrna.[46]

The tract of land assembled for the plant consisted of two working farms, a church, a campground, a motel, and a stock-car racetrack. Not surprisingly, Sam Ridley was part owner in some of the purchased land. The largest plot, a dairy farm, was owned by a retired school teacher who, according to a newspaper account, refused to sell until Governor Lamar Alexander personally visited her home to persuade her. Some of the assembled land was turned over to the state as highway rights-of-way for new interchanges, some was given to the Louisville & Nashville Railroad for plant-related spur lines and sidings, and the remaining 782 acres was sold to Nissan at a cost of under $6 million (only about $7,500 per acre).[47] The entire tract, as well as almost six hundred acres of surrounding land, was formally annexed by the town and zoned for industrial and light industrial use, with commercial use specifically prohibited, at Nissan's request, to "keep restaurants and beer halls out of the vicinity." Nissan had asked for the annexation so that the town could provide gas, water, sewer, fire, and police.[48]

The terms under which Smyrna provided these municipal services were part of the complex financial package worked out between the company, the town, Rutherford County, and the state of Tennessee. In general, the town was obligated to maintain a specified minimum service level, and Nissan was obligated to pay pre-negotiated rates. In many instances, Nissan paid for system expansions, as well as the cost of servicing outstanding debt that had been issued to finance the existing systems. In addition, the federal government paid for a substantial portion of the capital costs of upgrading Smyrna's municipal services.

For example, the company agreed to pay all of the costs of a $3.2 million water system expansion, plus 65 percent of a $4 million second-phase expansion to accommodate growth in the local economy. The company also agreed to pay rates that would cover ongoing operating costs and existing debt-service requirements. The town, however, already had excess water capacity. Existing demand was running about two million gallons per day, only half of official capacity. Furthermore, the federal government had promised Economic Development Administration grants to whichever town won the site-selection contest. These grants, combined with the Nissan water charges, enabled Mayor Ridley to expand the water system (doubling it, to an eight-million-gallons-per-day capability) in order to accommodate future growth at virtually no out-of-pocket cost to the city.[49]

Similar arrangements were negotiated for other infrastructure systems. The sewer treatment arrangement was almost identical to the water deal, involving a fivefold increase in capacity, paid for by contributions from the company ($3.2 million), supplemented by federal EPA grants ($3 million), with the town responsible for the balance ($2.5 million). The company agreed to buy natural gas through the town distribution system, at prevailing rates, and to pay all of the costs of new rainwater drainage systems. Low-cost TVA power would be delivered by the local electric co-op.

The cumulative effect of these contracts was that Nissan financed almost the entire infrastructure of the town—including forward-looking expansions—with federal assistance. In addition, the company agreed to pre-negotiated tax payments capped at half a million dollars per year for ten years, to be split between the town and the county. If Smyrna had a sprawling or aging infrastructure and a heavy accumulated debt burden, like many other American communities, Nissan undoubtedly would have taken a more limited approach. They could afford to be expansive because they knew that they would benefit, either directly or indirectly, from the community-wide services supported by these rates, fees, and taxes. All the beneficiaries would be employees, suppliers, vendors, and local service industries economically tied to Nissan. There was nothing else in Smyrna for the company to be concerned about.[50]

Needless to say, the public investments related to the arrival of Nissan required substantial borrowing by the town and county governments. A large portion of the utility improvements were financed through the issuance of municipal bonds, indirectly supported by the company's strong credit rating. Furthermore, the county acted as a conduit for a $25 million pollution-control loan to Nissan, also funded by tax-exempt (and therefore federally subsidized) bonds.[51]

The overall picture can be readily summarized. The town itself had few financial resources. Nevertheless, by virtue of externally funded projects, the most significant of which were highways, a multinational corporation decided to make a half-billion dollar investment. In its initial production phase, the plant was projected to have an annual payroll of more than $40 million, would generate over $60 million in increased retail sales and about $15 million in annual state and local taxes.[52] At the same time, in other parts of the country, many local economies were facing crippling plant closings. This suggests that a *de facto* industrial relocation policy was at work, driven by the complex web of subsidies that supported some types of privileged infrastructure, in certain types of locales, while neglecting others.

THE NEW SMYRNA

Seven months before the first automobile rolled off the line in 1983, there were already over one hundred thousand applications for the first jobs at the plant. The projected payroll for the first year of operation had grown to over $90 million, representing over 2,600 new jobs.[53] Since there were not enough available workers in the local area, applications had been accepted from all across the nation. As part of the agreement with Nissan, the state of Tennessee established a special office to screen the applications and also contributed $9 million toward training the new workforce.[54]

Within a few years Nissan expanded its manufacturing operations in Smyrna. In 1986, just three years after the plant opened, the company added an assembly line for the new Sentra, alongside the existing line producing the quick-selling Datsun small pickup truck. The total capital investment in the plant had risen to $848 million, as more than 3,200 employees—assisted by more than 350 robots—worked inside a facility that covered the equivalent of 70 football fields, turning out 250,000 vehicles each year. Then, in 1989 the company announced plans to spend another half billion dollars to accommodate production of Altima sedans. This new round of expansion, completed in 1992, increased the payroll by another 2,000 workers, bringing the total annual payroll to an astonishing $176 million.[55] Within the plant's first decade, its footprint had grown to over 5 million square feet, its work force had swelled to almost 6,000 jobs, and its annual production capacity was almost 500,000 vehicles.[56]

Of course, Nissan's effect on the local economy was not just limited to its direct payroll, which was by itself larger than the entire 1970 population of Smyrna. Since Nissan utilized the Japanese practice of "just-in-time" inventory control, in which the company maintained no more than thirty-six hours' worth of parts inventory, many of the domestic content components of Nissan vehicles were purchased from local suppliers. As a result, many other manufacturing concerns relocated to the Smyrna area.

Hoover Universal, a car-seat manufacturer, built a new $5 million plant in neighboring Murfreesboro, with a built-in computer link to the Nissan inventory control system. This factory employed sixty workers when the Nissan plant was producing only two-seat pickup trucks, and it expanded when the Sentra and Altima sedans went into production. Similar arrangements were made with a windshield-wiper plant in Smyrna, while the windows themselves came from a nearby Ford glass plant that had previously been on the brink of closure. The Firestone tire company soon employed 1,200 workers in neighboring Lavergne and was making plans to expand the facility (in Interchange City, the burgeoning industrial park at the next exit north on the highway). These are just a few examples of the myriad new industrial employers that set up shop in the area during the 1980s. In 1987 Nissan was using millions of dollars worth of parts every day, purchased from forty-six Tennessee companies, fourteen of which had established operations in the area solely to be near the big Nissan facility.[57] The far-reaching and beneficent effects of the Nissan plant on the local economy led one historian to conclude that when Nissan started its first assembly line at the Smyrna plant, it opened "a new chapter in Tennessee's economic history."[58]

Parts not manufactured locally came to Smyrna by three different modes of transportation. There was a continuous cavalcade of trucks arriving via I-24, Nissan Drive, Sam Ridley Parkway, and State Route 102 to deliver just-in-time parts—and to pick up fully assembled cars and trucks for delivery to dealers nationwide. Other parts shipments arrived on the rail line, which had custom-built spur-lines leading directly into the belly of the factory. Additional components arrived by air, at the old air base, now known as Smyrna Airport, which soon ranked among the busiest freight-only airports in the nation. With over three thousand employees, the airport generated an annual operating surplus for Smyrna and for Rutherford County, the joint owners. They, in turn, expanded the airport facilities by using their federally subsidized borrowing capacity to raise money for new land purchases and new construction. Projections called for a work force of over five thousand workers to be employed at the airport by the end of the decade.[59]

In addition to the direct and indirect jobs brought to Smyrna by Nissan, there was also the "multiplier effect," involving the creation of new service jobs in the area to meet the needs of the thousands of people living on paychecks from Nissan and its local suppliers. As a result, there was an explosive growth in demand for retail shops, restaurants, and professional services.

But even as Smyrna transformed into a postmodern industrial city, it still retained some unpleasant hangovers from pre-industrial Southern culture. In 1980 the local newspaper, the *Rutherford County Courier*, casually reported that a Ku Klux Klan rally was held at Smyrna "without incident, and could almost be called a family outing." Estimated attendance was 350, with 70 decked out in robes. Another telling moment came when a prominent citizen, a retired Air Force colonel, objected to the name "Nissan Drive," and instead suggested that the new road be named "Pearl Harbor Boulevard." While this suggestion did not gain much support, the town's leadership

Smyrna Population

	Smyrna	Rutherford County
1880		36,741
	———	
1930	531	32,286
1940	483	33,604
1950	2,300	40,696
1960	3,612	52,386
1970	5,698	59,428
1980	8,839	84,058
1990	13,647	118,570
2000	25,569	182,023

certainly appeared willing to indulge in some Old South bigotries. In an interview, Sam Ridley boasted that there were no synagogues in the entire county and that "we have only 7 or 8 percent minorities, and when they're dispersed around they're not a problem."[60] Some aspects of Smyrna were changing faster than others.

Needless to say, the physical appearance of Smyrna changed dramatically during this period. From the moment that the Nissan plans were announced in 1980, the community began a rapid expansion and reconstruction. Formerly, the town had been clustered either near the railway station and the adjacent Main Street, or on and near the air base. However, the spectacular new growth of the local economy was mirrored by a similarly rapid transformation of the physical landscape. Almost overnight, Smyrna was remade into a sprawling neo-city.

Just two weeks after the groundbreaking ceremony at the Nissan factory, Wal-Mart announced plans to build a store on the Old Nashville Pike.[61]

Others followed Wal-Mart's lead, and by January 1984, there were already nearly two hundred more business permits outstanding than in 1980. Soon Smyrna had a considerable retail and commercial community, where there had been none before. One resident wrote that "At one time residents had to travel fifteen miles north or south to grocery shop or to eat out. . . . In just three years, two department stores, two drug stores, two supermarkets, one steak house, and about ten fast-food restaurants have moved to Smyrna . . . [and] three bank branches have opened."[62]

By 1989 there were three new shopping centers planned.[63] Wal-Mart built a bigger store directly across Nissan Drive from the factory, abandoning its "old" store and leaving it vacant. The town soon had a McDonald's, a Burger King, a Taco Bell, a Shoney's, a Ponderosa, a Day's Inn, four grocery stores—two Krogers (one with a new post office inside) and two Winn-Dixies—a Wendy's, a Hardee's, a K-Mart, an Eckerd Drugs, and a sushi bar, all lined up in sprawling strip malls and shopping centers along U.S. 41. This type of strip-mall development had proliferated nationwide during the postwar era, partially fueled by the accelerated depreciation provisions of the income-tax code, which favored investment in new construction at new locations and discouraged renovation or reconstruction of existing structures.[64]

Housing construction in Smyrna also skyrocketed, so that town revenue from building permits in 1983 was twenty times that of 1980. Rental occupancy rates remained above 95 percent.[65] The vast majority of the new housing, however, was owner-occupied. As such, it was subsidized by the mortgage tax deduction and by bond-financed state programs offering low-interest mortgage loans to first-time home buyers, as well as other more subtle forms of government support.[66] Housing prices remained relatively low because there was still abundant land, and the new residents were predominantly blue-collar workers.[67]

Most of the new housing construction occurred outside the town limits and was then annexed. Since the town had maintained excess capacity in its water treatment, wastewater treatment, and gas systems (by virtue of the facilities from the abandoned air base, the agreements with Nissan, and federal grants), the hook-up fees charged to residents of annexed subdivisions could be combined with building-permit fees and increased property-tax revenues to maintain excess capacity in the town's infrastructure systems.[68] In 1995 the town awarded contracts for yet another addition to its wastewater treatment network.

According to the 1990 Census, Smyrna grew to almost 15,000 residents within the first few years of Nissan's operations, and it continued to grow rapidly. The county unemployment rate was well under the statewide rate and less than half the national rate. New business permits were being issued at a countywide rate of one thousand per year, which was extraordinary for a county with a total population of only 123,000. The 2000 federal census indicated that the town grew by 75 percent in the 1990s, reaching a total of almost 26,000.[69]

As the town grew, so did the demand for roads, streets, fire protection, police patrols, street lights, and recreation. By 1984 the town boundaries encompassed eighteen square miles, up from only eight square miles in 1980. Furthermore, annexation continued apace, so that Smyrna grew southward all the way to Murfreesboro, which was itself expanding to encompass some of the new regional growth. Not surprisingly, the sprawling new auto-dependent subdivisions required extensive new road and street networks. Also, a new hospital emergency room was opened in Smyrna, marking the first time such a service was available between Nashville and Murfreesboro.[70] Two new fire stations were built (and two new fire trucks purchased) at a cost of over half a million dollars.[71] The empty building that had formerly housed the old municipal hospital was renovated at a cost of over $2.5 million, and the resulting 55,000-square-foot facility was rededicated as a new city hall, replacing the tiny and dilapidated town assembly hall that sat on the now nearly abandoned old Main Street.[72] As a sign of the times—an indicator of the auto-centered landscape of the United States—the new town hall was located on the U.S. 41 strip and included a drive-through window for paying taxes, fines, utility bills, and municipal service fees.

A state-of-the-art recreation center was built on town-owned land from the old air base. In addition to conference facilities, the new building included a pool, exercise room, community center, and numerous meeting rooms, all of which were made available to the public free of charge.[73] Also in the early 1990s, work started on a new seventeen-field, thirty-acre soccer complex intended to accommodate the fifty soccer teams in the growing local leagues.

Some of the funding for these improvements came from a fiscal maneuver that represented yet another federal subsidy for Smyrna. Despite the fact that the town treasury was flush with surplus cash, Mayor Ridley continued to borrow money by floating tax-exempt bonds. So, even though the city banked a budget surplus of $3.7 million in 1982 and an estimated $6 million in 1983, it floated over $5 million in tax-exempt bonds during the same period. These funds were borrowed at a federally subsidized interest rate of under 9 percent and then immediately reinvested at rates as high as 16 percent, netting the town a handy arbitrage profit for a few years, until tax regulations required the town to retire the bonds.[74]

This "free" money was only one component of a financial outlook that enhanced Smyrna's attractiveness. City leaders kept outstanding debt down so that it was lower in 1992 ($7.5 million), ten years after the Nissan factory opened, than it was in 1983 ($8.75 million), having reached a peak of $12 million in 1988. In 1991 the ratio of outstanding debt to combined annual municipal budgets, a statistic used by many fiscal experts to measure the financial health of a community, dropped below one—an unusually low figure.[75] Despite the fact that the budget grew fivefold between 1981 and 1991, the town was able to cut property-tax rates repeatedly, from 75 cents to 62 cents in 1986, and then to 55 cents in 1989, and again to 48 cents in 1995. Similarly, county taxes were cut to under three dollars for the first time in decades.[76] These tax cuts provided additional stimulation to the local economy. New employers, some of them unrelated to the automotive business, began to relocate in the area, attracted by the same transportation and financial advantages that had attracted Nissan.

Smyrna Chronology

1851	Whistle stop established
1852	Post office opened
1855	64 lots platted, offered for sale
1859	First lot sold
1868	Sale of lots completed
1869	Incorporated
1881	Charter repealed
1915	Reincorporated as "Town of Smyrna" (legally a city)
	Street improvement taxes fund first non-mud streets (gravel/cinders)
1922	Smyrna Light & Power Company formed
1927	Dixie Highway (US Rt-41) built through town, connecting Chicago and Miami
1928	First hard-paved streets
1935	Stones River Electric Membership Corp. formed as a TVA-supplied co-op, absorbs Smyrna Light & Power (renamed Middle Tennessee Electric Membership Corp. in 1936)
1937	Water system built, funded by WPA loan
1942	Sewart Air Force Base constructed
1951	Major expansion/renovation at Sewart
	New Nashville Pike/Murfreesboro Road completed (US 41-70S)
1955	Town sewer system built
1957	Town gas system built
1961	Water/Sewer treatment plants built at Stones River
1965	New hospital built
1967	Major waterworks expansion
1970	New library completed
	Sewart Air Force Base closed, permanently
1971	Base property sold to Rutherford County
	Interstate-24 completed, Nashville-Murfreesboro
1975	Sam Ridley Parkway (State Route 266) built
1977	First shopping center opens
1980	Nissan chooses Smyrna as site of huge new facility
1983	Nissan plant opens–production of pickup trucks begins
1986	Nissan adds second assembly line–Sentra production begins
1992	Nissan adds third assembly line–Altima production begins
1999	Interstate-840 completed

Rutherford County was soon home to the world's largest book and video distribution center, operated by the Ingram Book Group.[77] Carrier, the major manufacturer of air-conditioning equipment, built a 250,000-square-foot warehouse and distribution center in Smyrna, right next to the Square-D factory, which had been built at the airport earlier.[78] The strength of the local economy also attracted new residents. Between 1980 and 1990, the population of Rutherford county grew by 46 percent, and Smyrna itself grew by 54 percent.[79]

Soon, the U.S. 41 strip was not big enough to contain Smryna's sprawling growth. Strip-style development expanded along the Sam Ridley Parkway—which was widened to four lanes in 1998—so that by the turn of the century the new corridor housed a new shopping center (anchored by yet another grocery store), another bank, a business park, and an assortment of restaurants, doctors' offices, car dealers, gas stations, and drug stores. Plans were announced for a second Smyrna hospital to be built on the parkway, and a new convention center went up, containing two large meeting rooms and a 120,000-square-foot exhibition hall, officially named the "I-24 EXPOsition Center."[80] The Interstate had become a central aspect of the booming city's identity.

Smyrna's transformation from a run-down village buried in the countryside to a burgeoning economic magnet was seemingly complete. But the government programs that had formed the foundation for Smyrna's profound economic makeover were still underway, still funneling investment away from older urbanized areas and toward newer communities. Accordingly, only ten years after the Nissan plant opened, Smyrna was poised for yet another round of economic growth fueled by yet another federally funded highway project.

POSTSCRIPT: INTERSTATE-840

The industrial and residential development in Smyrna was not only fueled by automobile production, it was also based upon the exclusive use of cars to transport goods and people around town. New housing was dispersed in sprawling subdivisions, filling up open farmland on the periphery. At the same time, commercial development spread out along the U.S. 41 and Sam Ridley Parkway corridors, while all of the industrial development in the region was predicated on the availability of the nearby Interstate Highway network. Accordingly, the area witnessed a sharp increase in traffic and vehicular congestion.

A surprisingly large portion of the traffic on nearby I-24 was going to or from Smyrna. As early as 1986, just three years after Nissan began production, the average traffic volume on the southern connector to I-24 had climbed to about 8,000 trips daily, accounting for an astonishing 27 percent of the total I-24 traffic volume. These figures continued to climb, and a few years later the traffic count on *each* of the two Smyrna connectors was over 16,000 trips per day, on average, compared to a total traffic count on I-24 itself of 53,660. In addition, the traffic volume along the U.S. 41 strip through Smyrna was measured at 27,730 vehicles per day, on average.[81] As this traffic volume grew, so did the pressure for new highway construction. Finally, in February, 1994, the Tennessee Highways Department announced plans to widen I-24 to six lanes, from Nashville to Smyrna.[82] This marked a significant initiative and another enormous expenditure of federal funds that would boost the Smyrna economy, but nonetheless it paled next to another project launched just beyond Smyrna's southern border at about the same time: the construction of an entirely new Interstate Highway.

The "Memorandum of Understanding" with Nissan in 1980 had specifically contemplated the eventual construction of a new highway (financed three-quarters by federal funds and one-quarter by state funds) to connect I-24 near Smyrna with I-40, which extends eastward from Nashville. As the economic activity in the area accelerated and traffic on the nearby Interstates continued to increase, the need for this additional route seemed to grow. In 1986 the state highway department formally announced the new route, a seventy-five mile southern loop that would serve as an outer beltway for the extended Nashville region.

One of the stated purposes of the new route, which was formally designated I-840, was to relieve the growing "major league traffic problems" on the Nashville inner loop that were directly attributed to new economic growth in exurban areas like Smyrna. The new beltway would connect I-65, I-24, and I-40 to divert trucks traveling to and from major industrial sites like the Nissan plant and the new General Motors plant in Spring Hill, Tennessee. This plant, built as the manufacturing headquarters for GM's new Saturn division, was located to the west of Smyrna. General Motors had been attracted to the site by many of the same transportation incentives that had previously brought Nissan to Tennessee, including the construction of a special "Saturn Parkway" to connect the new plant to nearby I-65, funded by government highway grants.[83] As traffic along the region's Interstate highways grew, state highway engineers made plans for the new I-840 beltway, to ensure continued traffic-free trucking access for the new big businesses in the area, providing a high-speed bypass around Nashville proper.

Land acquisition for the new superhighway began in 1990, and construction started soon thereafter. Plans called for three interchanges within a few miles of Smyrna town limits, a mere three and a half miles from the Nissan parking lot. In 1992, to capture the expected growth associated with this new project, Smyrna extended its official borders by annexation to the south and east, in order to meet up with the new superhighway and thereby encompass some of the inevitable economic development that would follow its completion. Soon after the completion of the sections of the highway nearest Smyrna, Nissan committed to invest another $1 billion in further expansions, adding a thousand new jobs and boosting production capacity by a third. At the same time, the airport announced that the runways would be extended to accommodate even larger freight planes (747s and 767s).[84]

CONCLUSION

The transformation of Smyrna over the past sixty years from a tiny village into a dynamic and burgeoning industrial magnet was the result of a *de facto* industrial relocation policy. At the core of this policy were government interventions that revolved around infrastructure. Smyrna serves as one example of how the cumulative effect of government programs had a profound effect on the American landscape. Powerful support was provided for certain investments at the expense of others, fueling the dispersal and deconcentration of jobs and people across the United States.

During the interwar years, the federal highway program provided Smyrna with a modern road system. Soon thereafter, the New Deal provided a modern water treatment system and low-cost hydroelectric power. Later, while Sewart Air Base was open, the federal government built and paid for a full-size airport, more highways, and new streets, as well as bigger schools, new gas and sewer systems, a hospital, and a new library. All of these projects were externally funded—in effect, they were *given* to Smyrna.

Then, blessed with the ultimate attraction for economic development— ready access to the toll-free Interstate Highway System—Smyrna achieved national prominence as an important new manufacturing center. It may seem that the Nissan company played a major role in the reversal of Smyrna's prospects, but this is not really the case. Prior to Nissan's decision to locate in Smyrna, other employers had already been attracted to the town, drawn in by the same factors that won over Nissan. If Nissan had not arrived during the 1980s, a different major employer or employers certainly would have, responding to the abundant benefits of locating a business in the Smyrna area, most of which were the direct result of extensive, powerful, and multifaceted government subsidies.

Conclusion

At the end of the nineteenth century, the Good Roads movement worked to define highways as a "public good." Bicyclists were soon joined in this effort by auto manufacturers, dealers, oil companies, civil engineers, road-building contractors, planners, and the car-using public. The resulting system of highway finance, as it evolved over successive iterations of federal legislation, had the effect of institutionalizing subsidies for automobility and encouraging decentralized development. Complementary housing policies aided investment in suburban real estate while simultaneously impeding urban investments, and the federal income-tax code created yet another layer of incentives. Thus, a series of separate decisions had the aggregate effect of changing where and how Americans lived and worked, amounting to a de facto national urban (suburban?) policy.

The high-stakes campaign in support of automobility not only affected government programs but also propagated cultural beliefs that were soon embedded in Americans' expectations. In particular, it fostered the notion that a gas tax of a few pennies per gallon and registration fees of a few dollars per year entitled Americans to roads that led wherever one desired. Expectations continued to rise, so that motorists (through self-appointed spokesmen) soon demanded wider and more expensive roads to accommodate larger, heavier vehicles traveling at faster speeds. They insisted on longer sight distances, higher safety standards, and better integration of routes until, eventually, Americans came to expect that they should be able to travel anywhere in the country by automobile, near or far and as frequently as desired, without paying additional tolls and without the inconvenience of too many other people doing the same thing at the same time.

This was not possible, though, because the consistent underpricing of auto use produced an imbalance between supply and demand. Demand far exceeded supply for the economic commodity at hand: properly maintained toll-free and traffic-free roads. Public response to this disparity, under the influence of Good Roads movement rhetoric, was to build more roads to satisfy the excess demand, without addressing the underlying disparity between the costs of automobility and the charges passed on to motorists. Furthermore, a consistent emphasis on new construction to help the supply of road-miles catch up to the demand exacerbated the pricing problem, creating a highway system that governments could not afford to maintain. The economy was increasingly predicated on artificially cheap, subsidized automotive transport.

There was never any sustained effort to offer a differing perspective. Highway policy discussions were generally framed as questions of efficient service delivery and were initially dominated almost exclusively by engineers. The narrowly conceived public debates obscured the powerful effect of the resultant subsidies on American communities of all shapes and sizes. The terms of the discourse and the main policy precedents were firmly established by mid-century, at which point they were set in concrete, literally, by the Interstate Highway legislation.

The Denver case provides an example of how these decisions underwrote growth on the periphery and redirected economic resources toward suburban development. In the first half of the twentieth century, the anti-urban slant of state and federal policies, the collapse of mass transit, and civic initiatives meant to accommodate cars undermined the sustainability of the city itself, fundamentally altering settlement patterns. These trends continued, and even accelerated, later in the century, transforming Denver.

Seemingly separate decisions concerning toll roads, airport construction, real estate speculation, and suburban highway planning collectively transformed the compact city into a sprawling and decentralized metropolis, increasingly dependent on motor vehicles and a far-flung highway system. The old urban downtown, formerly the undisputed hub of the region, was barely able to survive this new auto-oriented framework and had to be converted into an office and entertainment node, struggling to compete with suburban counterparts scattered throughout the surrounding area.

Smyrna, on the other hand, highlights the de facto industrial relocation policy of the United States, which has encouraged investments in rural locations by providing numerous incentives, not least among them a massively subsidized transportation network. Between 1940 and 1990, Smyrna changed from a stagnant village into a burgeoning industrial magnet. After federal aid provided Smyrna with a modern road system, New Deal programs added water treatment facilities and low-cost hydroelectric power. The federal government even paid for a full-size airport, sewers, schools, a gas system, a hospital, a library, and more highways. Then, with the construction of the Interstate Highway System as the keystone, endowed by skewed financing mechanisms, Smyrna entered a new era.

When Nissan Motors invested a billion dollars in Smyrna to build the continent's largest auto assembly plant, the company was responding to the power of extensive and multifaceted subsidies. The cumulative inducement of many decades worth of government policies favoring deconcentration had become overwhelming. Not surprisingly, within a few years of Nissan's decision, other auto manufacturers made similar choices, including BMW and Mercedes-Benz, as well as General Motors, which built its brand new Saturn facility in rural Tennessee even as it closed down factories in urban locations. Everywhere across the nation, for similar reasons, other corporate operations moved away from their urban sites, sometimes to suburban locations within the same metropolitan area, and sometimes to entirely new spots like Smyrna.

As the third case, Middlebury demonstrates that these transforming effects have been both pervasive and ubiquitous. Even though Vermont is physically and culturally distant from big cities and newer growth areas in the Sunbelt, there are parallels between Middlebury and these other areas. Vermont's highway-building program, shaped first by the Good Roads movement and later by highway boosters' crisis-laden rhetoric, emphasized long-distance and rural travel without aiding movement within settled cities and towns. Also, each time the state expanded its automobility programs, the gap between highway costs and user-fee revenues widened. Middlebury suffered from both these trends.

Manufacturing jobs migrated from the downtown core to an industrial park on the edge of town. The population moved from homes in or near downtown to detached or semidetached single family houses in new auto-oriented subdivisions. Shopping centers at the edge of town put traditional downtown merchants out of business, leaving an economic void filled by deliberately cultivated tourist-oriented businesses. This dispersal of population and commerce produced increased congestion, so that traffic became the most significant problem faced by the small town. For the entire balance of the twentieth century, there was persistent debate about road taxes, express bypasses, new river crossings, investments in downtown traffic lights, and construction of municipal parking lots. While these debates raged, usually unresolved, the small town continued to spread, covering more and more of the surrounding countryside. Traffic complaints mounted, prompting renewed demands for infrastructure improvements. The small town was indeed hamstrung by highway federalism, unable to alter course and break the cycle.

Taken collectively, these three case studies and the supporting material demonstrate the complexity and enormity of the changes wrought on the American landscape over the course of the twentieth century, as a direct result of overlapping programs and interventions implemented at all levels of government. The changes cannot be explained as a straightforward consequence of either immutable cultural preferences or technological developments. Instead, culture and technology were channeled and focused by the cumulative effect of subsidies that skewed personal and corporate decision making, underwriting sprawl while undermining urban density. The manner in which Americans adapted the national infrastructure to accommodate the automobile encouraged the dispersal of jobs and people across the continent and fueled a nationwide need for capital expenditures unmitigated by considerations of equity, efficiency, or affordability.

Disparate communities adjusted to the transportation revolution at different times and in different ways, but there has been, nevertheless, an essential continuity in the American system. Small towns like Middlebury, as much as big cities like Denver and boomtowns like Smyrna, have been remade by this dynamic, rapidly spreading out across the land while simultaneously reinventing their downtowns in order to survive in the automobile age. The drive to accommodate automobility, as the United States built far more pavement per capita than any other nation on earth, transformed all American communities, big and small, east and west, north and south.

Notes

CHAPTER ONE

1. *Oxford Dictionary of Quotations* (New York: Oxford University Press, 1999); and *Cassell Dictionary of Contemporary Quotations* (New York, 1996). Charles Wilson's words are often misquoted, and at least one other popular guide to familiar quotations contains an incorrect version of Wilson's statement and incorrectly places it in 1952.

2. National Transportation Committee, *The American Transportation Problem* (Washington, D.C.: Brookings Institution, 1933), 526–29; John McCarty, *Highway Financing by the Toll System* (Berkeley: University of California, 1951); National Council on Public Works Improvement, *Fragile Foundations: A Report on America's Public Works* (Washington, D.C.: Government Printing Office, 1988), 33; Federal Highway Administration, *America on the Move: The Story of the Federal-Aid Highway Program* (Washington, D.C., September 1984).

3. George Chatburn, *Highways and Highway Transportation* (New York: Thomas Y. Crowell, 1923) 128–142; Gregory C. Lisa, "Bicyclists and Bureaucrats: The League of American Wheelmen and Public Choice Theory Applied," *The Georgetown Law Journal* 84 (1995): 385, 394; James Flink, *The Automobile Age* (Cambridge: MIT Press, 1990), 4–5; Phil Patton, *Open Road: A Celebration of the American Highway* (Simon & Schuster, 1986), 56.

4. Howard Preston, *Dirt Roads to Dixie: Accessibility and Modernization in the South, 1885–1935* (Knoxville: University of Tennessee Press, 1991), 171; American Public Works Association, *History of Public Works in the United States, 1776–1976*, Ellis Armstrong, ed. (Kansas City: American Public Works Association, 1976), 72.

5. The Massachusetts and New Jersey laws were first suggested in 1887 and 1888, respectively. The Massachusetts law contained more generous aid provisions, wherein the state provided three dollars for each locally appropriated dollar, while the New Jersey statute only provided fifty cents per local dollar; Chatburn, 150; American Public Works Association, 70; Poyntz Tyler, ed., *American Highways Today* (New York: H.W. Wilson, 1957), 15.

6. Bruce Seely, *Building the American Highway System: Engineers as Policy Makers* (Philadelphia: Temple University Press, 1987), 15–36; Lisa, 375–81.

7. The LAW claimed over 100,000 members by 1898 and may have had more were it not for restrictive membership rules, which required new members be nominated by a current member, with notice in the *Bulletin* to give the membership an opportunity

to comment (i.e. "blackball") any of the prospects. Lisa, 375–93; Chatburn, 128–42; and Seely, *Building the American Highway System*, 15–36.

8. American Automobile Association, *Why Federal Aid in Roads*, 1916. (Colorado State Archives); William Richter, *Transportation in America* (ABC-CLIO, 1995), 571.

9. Ibid., 5, 169.

10. Vermont Good Roads Association, *Proceedings of the First Annual Meeting of the Vermont Good Roads Association, May 5, 1904*, 46.

11. American Automobile Association, *Why Federal Aid in Roads*; Ballard C. Campbell, "Pope, Albert Augustus," *American National Biography Online* (Oxford University Press, February 2000), http://www.anb.org/articles/10/10–01332.html. The decline of the LAW's influence has been attributed to three main factors: (1) as bicycle use became more widespread, the elitism and clubiness of the League's membership procedures became a liability; (2) the narrower, roads-only focus of other groups made them more effective standard-bearers; and (3) Albert Pope, the pioneering bicycle manufacturer who had provided substantial subsidy funds to the league turned his entrepreneurial energies away from bicycles and increasingly toward automobile manufacturing. (Lisa, 394). See also Flink, 170.

12. The Office of Road Inquiry was briefly known as the Office of Public Roads and Rural Engineering, and also as the Office of Public Roads, before it was renamed the Bureau of Public Roads. During the Roosevelt administration it was renamed again, as the Public Roads Administration. To avoid confusion, I use "Bureau of Public Roads" or "BPR" to refer to the agency throughout the remainder of the text.

13. Seely, *Building the American Highway System*, 9; Bruce Seely, "A Republic Bound Together," *Wilson Quarterly* 17, no. 1 (Winter 1993): 30.

14. Surprisingly, the railroads supported highway projects through the 1920s. An official of the Erie Railroad wrote "Function of the Motor Truck in Reducing Cost and Preventing Congestion of Freight in Railroad Terminals" for the 1924 *Annals of the American Academy of Political and Social Science*.

15. American Public Works Association, 75; Preston, 171.

16. Wayne Fuller, "Good Roads and Rural Free Delivery of Mail," in *Mississippi Valley Historical Review* 42, no. 1 (June 1955): 79; Stephen Goddard, *Getting There: The Epic Struggle Between Road and Rail in the American Century* (Chicago: University of Chicago Press 1994), 48. American Public Works Association, 75.

17. Fuller, "Good Roads and Rural Free Delivery of Mail," 81.

18. Postcard from Cal Dowling to Mrs. Dowling, ca. 1912, author's collection.

19. Mark Wolfe, "How the Lincoln Highway Snubbed Colorado," *Colorado Heritage* (Autumn 1999): 3–21.

20. For further information on the Dixie Highway, see Chapter 6.

21. Preston, various pages, including maps.

22. Ibid., 5.

23. American Farm Bureau Federation, "A Few Country Boulevards and Mud Roads vs. Development of a Great Road System," undated typewritten press release, 1919 or 1920, Colorado State Archives.

24. There were previous attempts at securing federal-aid legislation. In 1912 a Joint Congressional Committee on Federal-Aid in the Construction of Post Roads held hearings,

conducted surveys, and researched the road-aid practices of all the states and many foreign countries. The resulting proposal (which was not well received in Congress) was ambitious, complicated, and aggressive, based upon the issuance of $1 billion in fifty-year federal bonds, the proceeds from which would be lent to the states for rural highway construction. This proposal was unpopular for numerous reasons, not the least of which was that the "aid" would have to be repaid by the states, and that the federal government would get away without making any contribution other than the use of its borrowing capacity. U.S. Congress, Joint Committee on Federal-Aid in the Construction of Post Roads, *Good Roads: Hearings Held on January 21, February 10, 11, 18, 1913* (Government Printing Office, 1913); *Public Road Systems of Foreign Countries and of the Several States* (1913); *Federal Aid to Good Roads: Suggested Plan for Intelligent and Practical Expenditure of Three Billions of Dollars During a Period of Fifty Years by the States and The Federal Government in the Construction, Improvement, and Maintenance of Good Roads* (Government Printing Office, 1913).

25. Patton, *Open Road*, 45.
26. Seely, *Building the American Highway System*, 38; Goddard, 60.
27. *The Federal Aid Road Act and the Rules and Regulations Thereunder*, September 1, 1916. Sixty-fourth Congress, 1st Session, document no. 548 (Government Printing Office, 1916).
28. Seely, *Building the American Highway System*, 48.
29. Ibid., 43.
30. There was precedent for using this type of provision for ensuring that road aid would not be used within, or very near, any cities. The 1913 Maine road-aid statute also contained the 2,500 population cutoff and specified a minimum project length of seven miles. ("Maine Legislature Believes It Has Model Motor Law," *Motor Age*, June 26, 1913). While these provisions seemed to make the grant programs more efficient, helping to fund more road-miles by excluding the most expensive projects, this was misleading. Even though each mile of urban highway costs about three times as much as a mile of rural highway, because the urban road is used so much more, the cost per vehicle-mile is actually less than on rural routes. (*Transportation Economics: A Conference of the Universities-National Bureau Committee for Economic Research*, [New York: Columbia University Press, 1965, 143]). Herbert Farrington, *History of the Agency of Transportation*, Vermont State Archives.
31. This same formula was used to distribute surplus war machinery valued at $139 million, much of which ended up in state highway departments, after World War I. (Chatburn, 156)
32. 1918 scrapbook, no name, containing undated newspaper clippings, Colorado State Archives.
33. Department of Highway correspondence files, Colorado State Archives; American Public Works Association, 79.
34. American Public Works Association, 80; Charles Dearing and Wilfred Owen, *National Transportation Policy* (Washington, D.C.: Brookings Institution, 1949), 419.
35. Ann and Albert Manchester, "From D.C. to the Golden Gate: The First Transcontinental Military Motor Convoy" *American History* 32, no. 5 (December 1997): 38–42, 68–69.

36. Seely, *Building the American Highway System*, various pages; American Public Works Association, 81; Bruce Seely, "Page, Logan Waller," *American National Biography Online* (Oxford University Press, February 2000) http://www.anb.org/articles/05/05–00929.html

37. Alan A. Altshuler, "The Intercity Freeway" in *Introduction to Planning History in the United States*, Donald A. Krueckeberg, ed. (New Brunswick, N.J.: Center for Urban Policy Research, 1983); Goddard, 196.

38. Frank Sheets, *The Development of Primary Roads During the Next Quarter Century: An Address Delivered at the 25th Anniversary Meeting of the AASHO, October 9–13, 1939*, 139.

39. Goddard, 110–14.

40. Bruce Seely has found that, while the Act authorized the highway departments to designate the federal-aid highways, the heavy hand of the BPR (which had veto power over the state-proposed maps) tended to produce final maps that conformed to those that had already been internally developed by BPR staff, under MacDonald's supervision. (Seely, *Building the American Highway System*, 75).

41. Dearing and Owen, 106; American Public Works Association, 81; American Association of State Highway Officials, *Digest of Federal Highway Act, 1–1072, As Approved by Conference Committee of Congress, October 8, 1921*; National Automobile Chamber of Commerce, *Highway Bulletin H-134*, 1921.

42. Kenneth T. Jackson, *Crabgrass Frontier: The Suburbanization of the United States* (New York: Oxford University Press, 1985).

43. National Transportation Committee, *The American Transportation Problem* (1933), 529; Joel Tarr, "The Evolution of Urban Infrastructure in the Nineteenth and Twentieth Centuries," *Perspectives in Urban Infrastructure*, Royce Hanson, ed., (Washington, D.C.: National Academy Press, 1984), 35; Mark Rose, *Interstate: Express Highway Politics, 1939–1989* (Lawrence: University Press of Kansas, 1979), 2; American Public Works Association, 83.

44. John C. Burnham, "The Gasoline Tax and the Automobile Revolution," *Mississippi Valley Historical Review*, 48 (December 1961): 443.

45. William H. Connell, "The Highway Business," *Annals of the American Academy of Political and Social Science* 116, no. 205 (1924): 115; Dearing and Owen, 128; *Financing Highways: Symposium Conducted by the Tax Institute, 1956* (Princeton, 1957), 42.

46. Roy D. Chapin, vice-president, National Automobile Chamber of Commerce, *Annals of the American Academy of Political & Social Science* 116, no. 205 (1924): 8.

47. David St. Clair, *The Motorization of American Cities* (New York: Praeger, 1986), 159–60; Frank Coffey, *America on Wheels* (Los Angeles: General Publishing Group, 1966), 64.

48. Highway Research Board, Special Report 83, *Law of Turnpikes and Toll Bridges* (Washington, D.C.: National Research Council, 1964), 7.

49. Burnham, 438, 444; National Transportation Committee, 544; C.S. Duncan, *A National Transportation Policy* (New York: Appleton-Century Company, 1936), 296.

50. *Financing of State Highways* (New York: H.W. Wilson, 1929), 93. A one cent increase in the gas tax works out to $6.66 per year for the average motorist of this period, based

on 10,000 miles driven per year, and an average fuel economy of fifteen miles per gallon; Sheets, 39. Urban extensions became eligible for aid in 1928 but only if houses were more than 200 feet apart, on average, for the segment of road in question. George Smerk, *Urban Transportation: The Federal Role* (Bloomington: Indiana University Press, 1965), 123.

51. Duncan, 296; Tarr, 37–38; Vermont Motor Vehicle Department, *Wheels: Vermont Highway and Motor Transport Economics, 1940,* 25; Philip H. Burch Jr., *Highway Revenue and Expenditure Policy in the United States* (New Brunswick: Rutgers University Press, 1962), 37; Mark Foster, "The Automobile and the City," *Michigan Quarterly Review* (F/W 1991): 468. One survey decried the condition of rural roads, pointing out that only 13 percent of nonurban highways had any surface (gravel, oil, etc.) in 1920, and that this had only increased to 23 percent by 1930. The remaining 87 percent of nonurban roads were untreated dirt roads or overgrown two-tracks; National Transportation Committee, 531.

52. *Annals of the American Academy of Political and Social Science,* "Planning for City Traffic," vol. 133, no. 222 (September 1927).

53. *Financing Public Improvements: A Discussion of Public Revenue Bonds* (New York: Van Ingen & Co., 1939), 134. This study was based on research by Charles Breed, MIT professor of Highway Transportation; W.D. Downs, a University of West Virginia engineering professor; and Clifford Older, a consulting engineer.

54. Dearing and Owen, 106, 110; Seely, *Building the American Highway System,* 142; Seely, "A Republic Bound Together," 32.

55. Dearing and Owen, 106; Seely, *Building the American Highway System,* 144; Seely, "A Republic Bound Together," 31; Owen D. Gutfreund, "Strangled: New York City Traffic Conditions in the 1920s," *Seaport: New York City's History Magazine* 24, no. 2 (Fall 1990).

56. The Automobile Safety Foundation was organized and financed under the aegis of the Automobile Manufacturers Association, which had been formed in 1914 as the National Automobile Chamber of Commerce. St. Clair, 136–40.

57. Seely, *Building the American Highway System,* 144, 159.

58. Twenty states imposed a sales tax by 1933. Morton Keller, *Regulating a New Economy: Public Policy and Economic Change in America, 1900–1933* (Cambridge: Harvard University Press, 1990), 226–27.

59. *Published Proceedings of the Highway Conference Held in Knoxville, 1941* (Knoxville: University of Tennessee Press, 1941), 12.

60. Highway Research Board, Special Report 83, *Law of Turnpikes and Toll Bridges* (Washington, D.C.: National Research Council, 1964), 8; Burnham, 456.Diesel fuel was exempt from this federal tax until 1951 (Highway Research Board, 7–8).

61. National Highway Users Conference, various publications; St. Clair, 136–40. Sloan ran the NHUC until 1948, after which it was dominated by other GM executives (Flink, 19).

62. The Act allowed previous "diversions" to continue at the same level, unpunished. *Published Proceedings of the Highway Conference Held in Knoxville, 1941,* 12. More complete text of the Hayden-Cartwright Act (U.S. Code Title 23, heading "Highways," Section 126, subheading "Diversion"): "(a) Since it is unfair and unjust to

tax motor-vehicle transportation unless the proceeds of such taxation are applied to the construction, improvement, or maintenance of highways, after June 30, 1935, Federal aid for highway construction shall be extended only to those states that use at least the amounts provided by law on June 18, 1934, for such purposes in each State from State motor vehicle registration fees, licenses, gasoline taxes, and other special taxes on motor-vehicle owners and operators of all kinds for the construction of, improvement, and maintenance of highways and administrative expenses in connection therewith, including the retirement of bonds for the payment of which such revenues have been pledged, and for no other purposes, under such regulations as the Secretary shall promulgate from time to time." Federal Highway Administration, *The Evolution of the Highway-User Charge Principle* (N. Kent Bramlett, Highway Users and Finance Branch, Highway Statistics Division, 1982), appendix A, 36.

63.   National Highway Users Conference, *Vermont Highway Facts: State Statistics on Highway Mileage, Use, Finance* (1947), 31. For example, the Colorado antidiversion amendment was approved by referendum on November 6, 1934, and was later cited by the NHUC as a model for subsequent amendments to other states: "On and after July 1, 1935, the proceeds from the imposition of any license, registration fee or other charge with respect to the operation of any motor vehicle upon any public highway in this state and the proceeds from the imposition of any excise tax on gasoline of other liquid motor fuel shall, except costs of administration, be used exclusively for the construction, maintenance, and supervision of the public highways of this state." National Highway Users Conference, *Dedication of Special Highway Revenues to Highway Purposes: An Analysis of the Desirability of Protecting Highway Revenues Through Amendments to State Constitutions* (Washington, 1941).

64.   Goddard, 110.

65.   *Published Proceedings of the Highway Conference Held in Knoxville, March 14–15, 1940* (Knoxville: University of Tennessee, 1940), 12; Burnham, 443; National Transportation Committee, xix and xxxiv.

66.   Bureau of Business and Social Research, "Financing Highways in Colorado," *University of Denver Reports* 16, no. 1 (March 1940). (Colorado State Archives). For examples of the "general benefit" rationale, and its use by lobbying groups, see various publications of the National Highway Users Conference. (See Harry Stocker *Transportation and the Public Welfare in War and Peace* (Washington, D.C.: National Highway Users Conference, 1943.)

67.   Adam Smith, *The Wealth of Nations*, Book V, Chapter 1, Part III, Article 1.

68.   *Published Proceedings of the Highway Conference Held in Knoxville, March 14–15, 1940,* 11; Chatburn, 151.

69.   Thomas MacDonald, "The Financing of Highways," *Annals of the American Academy of Political and Social Science* 116, no. 205 (1924): 164; *Financing of State Highways* (New York: H.W. Wilson, 1929), 52; National Transportation Committee, 540; Duncan, 294–95; Chatburn, 151. In 1940, the face value of outstanding state and local highway debt reached $4.7 billion, more than half of which was issued by local governments (Tyler, 49).

70. This tax exemption has repeatedly been challenged. Calvin Coolidge unsuccessfully urged its abolition in his first presidential message to Congress. During the New Deal, the Senate version of the National Industrial Recovery Act abolished it, but this provision was killed in conference committee. The Supreme Court has heard arguments about it numerous times, most recently in 1988, when the court ruled that the exemption had no constitutional basis but was instead enjoyed at the discretion of Congress (*South Carolina v. Baker*). See Alberta Sbragia, *Debt Wish: Entrepreneurial Cities, U.S. Federalism, and Economic Development* (Pittsburgh: University of Pittsburgh Press, 1996).

71. National Transportation Committee, 540–43.

72. Patton, 79; Gates Rubber Co., "Building America's First Super-Highway," *Industrial News* 10, no. 7 (July 1940); E.L. Schmidt, "Does Additional Federal Aid Solve the Highway Problem?" (paper delivered at the Annual Convention of the North Atlantic States Highway Officials, February 21, 1950), 5.

73. Seely, *Building the American Highway System*, 163, 176.

74. Brian D. Taylor, "When Finance Leads Planning: The Influence of Public Finance on Transportation Planning and Policy in California" (Ph.D. diss., UCLA, 1992); St. Clair, 145. President Roosevelt's proposal never garnered very much political support. In part, this may have been because he coupled it with an ambitious program of government-sponsored real estate development. He suggested that the government acquire a two-mile wide right-of-way for the toll roads, and then later resell the extra land alongside the completed thoroughfares at a substantial profit that would reflect the higher, posthighway land values. This technique, called "excess takings," was considered by many people to be too socialistic and big-government, even for the New Deal era. In the 1920s, many states had specifically forbidden this use of eminent domain. Goddard, 159.

75. Ibid., 205; John McCarty, 19–21.

76. McCarty, 23; Taylor, "When Finance Leads Planning."

77. National Interregional Highway Committee, *Interregional Highways: Report and Recommendations* (Washington, D.C.: Government Printing Office, 1944), appendix II, 13–140; Taylor, "When Finance Leads Planning"; American Association of State Highway Officials, *American Highways* 20, no. 1, 7; Goddard, 159; Seely, *Building the American Highway System*, 170.

78. National Interregional Highway Committee, *Interregional Highways*; St. Clair, 145; For an illustration of the extensive planning activities during this period, see the voluminous correspondence between the Colorado State Highway Department and the BPR (Colorado State Archives). As a specific example, see letter from Charles Vail, state highway engineer to Public Roads Administration, October 17, 1940.

79. Flink, 371.

80. *Federal Aid for Post-War Highway Construction: Hearings Before the Committee on Roads, U.S. House of Representatives* (Washington, D.C.: Government Printing Office, 1944), 1083.

81. Ibid., 1084. This reference to "other modes of transportation" echoed an equally specious argument made by the NHUC a few years earlier, suggesting that the railroads pay for part of the new highways because "the benefits railroads receive from highway transportation bring with them a special responsibility for financing the cost of roads."

(National Highway Users Conference, *Dedication of Special Highway Revenues to Highway Purposes*, 5).

82. Interregional Highway Committee, iii and viii.
83. Ibid., 3.
84. Ibid., ix and x.
85. National Interregional Highway Committee, *Interregional Highways*.
86. Rose, 27.
87. Dearing and Owen, 110; *Proceedings of Conference on Highways of the Future, April 1947* (Knoxville, 1947), 75; Armstrong, 85.
88. Dearing and Owen, 110; Vermont State Highway Department, *Biennial Reports, 1946*, 22.
89. Wilbur Smith and Norman Hebden, *State-City Relationships in Highway Affairs* (New Haven: Yale University Press, 1950), 86.
90. Pennsylvania Economy League, *Public Capital Improvements Planning and Finance by Major Governments in the Principal Metropolitan Areas* (Pittsburgh, 1956), 76.
91. Hebden and Smith, 86.
92. Seely, *Building the American Highway System*, 205–6; Pennsylvania Economy League, 74; Goddard, 177; McCarty, various pages; Patton, 74–75.
93. *Proceedings of Conference on New Frontiers for Highways* (Knoxville: University of Tennessee, 1952), 21.
94. Angus Gillespie and Michael Rockland, *Looking for America on the New Jersey Turnpike* (New Brunswick: Rutgers University Press, 1989), 28.
95. Western Businessmen's Highway Conference: Denver, Colorado - December 6, 1955; *Facts and Figures* (Chamber of Commerce of the United States: 1956), (Colorado State Archives), 17; *Financing Highways: Symposium Conducted by the Tax Institute* (Princeton: 1957), 132; Tyler, 106.
96. R. S. Wilson, *Wanted—Another Bong from the Liberty Bell: A Call to the Citizenry to Get into the Fight for Adequate Roads* (Goodyear Tire and Rubber Company: 1952), Colorado State Archives; Burch, *Highway Revenue*.
97. Colorado Petroleum Industries Committee, *P.I.C. News* 16, no. 10 (October 1955).
98. National Highway Users Conference, *Dedication of Special Highway Revenues to Highway Purposes*, 2–6.
99. Charles P. White, *Report on Financing an Expanded Highway Program in Tennessee* (Knoxville: University of Tennessee, 1956), 27, 42.
100. *Proceedings of Conference on Highways of the Future, 1947* (Knoxville: University of Tennessee, 1947), 84–85.
101. For examples of the rhetoric of crisis and the use of "sufficiency ratings," see White, *Report on Financing an Expanded Highway Program*, and Vermont Highway Department, *1954 Report*, 43.
102. Edward J. Konkol, vice president, National Good Roads Association to Ike Ashburn, National Good Roads Association, October 10, 1955. (Colorado State Archives)
103. *Public Roads* 26, no. 8 (June 1951).
104. Rose, 38, 43, 79; Burch, 235; Armstrong, 92.
105. Tyler, 49; Pennsylvania Economy League, 73, 81; *Proceedings of Conference on New Frontiers for Highways*, 21, 29.

106. Goddard, 178, 183.

107. Coffey, 172.

108. National Highway Users Conference, *The Highway Transportation Story, In Facts,* 4th ed., 1961; These autoless families were *not* all city-dwellers. Many lived in rural and suburban settings. As late as 1960, one of five rural households and one of six suburban households did not have an automobile. (U.S. Dept. of Transportation, *A Statement on National Transportation Policy,* 1971, appendices, Fig. 2).

109. Details concerning the political process leading up to the passage of the 1956 Act and the intermediary 1954 legislation is beyond the scope of this book. See Mark Rose, *Interstate: Express Highway Politics, 1939–1989.* Nevertheless, it is interesting to consider how the administration forced the entrenched elements of the highway community to reach an accommodation, most notably the NHUC. Only a few months after the President announced his commitment to the interstates in 1954, the NHUC and its member organizations were jarred from their rigid antitax stance by a White House press release supporting toll-road construction and urging a doubling of total toll-road mileage. (Department of Commerce, Undersecretary for Transportation, press release, October 8, 1954). The NHUC responded to this threat to the long-established status quo subsidy system by tacitly agreeing to increased gas taxes, the least obtrusive method of charging motorists.

110. Federal Highway Administration, *America on the Move.*

111. Taylor, 136.

112. Taylor, 41. This was after the legislation failed once, in 1955, without the support of urban Congressional delegations.

113. *Financing Highways,* 67; Vermont Department of Highways, *1956 Biennial Report,* 49.

114. *Financing Highways,* 139. The Indiana experience is fairly typical in many regards. Most states had been unable to raise their gas taxes for decades because of effective lobbying by the NHUC and its members. However, it was not typical for states to forfeit their federal aid, as did Indiana.

115. Tyler, 47.

116. Taylor, 41, 59; Vermont State Highway Board, *The Highway Fund in Perspective* (1970), 9.

117. John Pucher and Ira Hirschman, *Path to Balanced Transportation* (New Brunswick: Rutgers University Press, 1993), 35.

118. Even after 1992, when transit costs for commuters were granted limited tax deductibility, up to $65 per month, the limit for deductibility of parking expenses was set at a much higher level, $175 per month. (*Wall Street Journal,* November 8, 2000, 1.)

CHAPTER TWO

1. Raymond Mohl, *The New City: Urban America in the Industrial Age, 1860–1920* (Arlington Heights, IL: Harlan Davidson, 1985), 72; *Encyclopedia Britannica, eleventh edition* (1910); U.S. Census Data.

2. David Halaas, "The Legacy of Boom and Bust," *Colorado Heritage* (Winter 2000): 3.

3. Special Committee on Public Improvements, *Public Improvements* (1892); Denver History Museum, *The Interactive Videodisc: Facts and Figures.*

4. Denver History Museum, *The Interactive Videodisc: Tale of a City, Facts and Figures.*

5. Leroy Hafen, "The Coming of the Automobile and Improved Roads to Colorado," *Colorado Magazine* (January 1931): 12; Erin Christensen, "Lifelines: The Story of Colorado's Public Road System," *Colorado Heritage* 3 (1987): 5; David Hill, *Colorado Urbanization and Planning Context* (Denver: Colorado Historical Society, 1984), 160.

6. Christensen, 5; Clark Secrest, "Colorado Fritchie Electric Auto: Cross-Country in 1908," *Colorado Heritage* (Winter 1999): 39–44; Denver History Museum, *Facts and Figures*; Colorado State History Museum, *Timeline.*

7. Denver Planning Commission, *Denver Planning Primer*, 13; Charles A. Johnson, *Denver's Mayor Speer: The Forgotten Story of Robert W. Speer, the Political Boss with a Rather Unsavory Machine Who Transformed Denver into One of the World's Most Beautiful Cities* (Denver: Green Mountain Press, 1969), xiii; Denver Planning Office, *Denver Tomorrow* (1957); Denver History Museum, *Tale of a City.*

8. DeBoer Papers, box 17, folder 8.

9. Don Etter, *The Denver Park and Parkway System* (Denver: Colorado Historical Society, 1986), 5, 27; Denver Planning Office, "The Parkway Plan," *Comprehensive Plan Bulletin* 10, no. 3: 18; Thomas Noel, "Denver Boosters and Their 'Great Braggart City,'" *Colorado Heritage* 3 (1995): 15; Denver History Museum, *Tale of a City*; Denver Planning Commission, *Denver Planning Primer*, 20; City and County of Denver, City Service Bureau, *Denver the Distinctive* (ca. 1917).

10. City and County of Denver, City Service Bureau, *Denver the Distinctive* (ca. 1917).

11. *WPA Guide*, 134; Denver History Museum, *Tale of a City*; City and County of Denver, City Service Bureau, *Denver the Distinctive*. The consolidated debt when Denver was formed in 1904 was just over $1 million, and it was $6.5 million when Speer left office, including $2.1 million for parks and $3.7 million for local improvements.

12. Denver History Museum, *Facts and Figures.*

13. Colorado Good Roads Association, *Resolutions Adopted and Papers Read at the Fourth Annual Convention of the Colorado Good Roads Association, Colorado Springs, January 15–16, 1914*; Hafen, 12; Lawrence Marshall, *Road Development in Colorado, 1830–1930* (unpublished typewritten manuscript, January 17, 1931 [at Hart Library, Colorado Historical Society]), 15.

14. Colorado Department of Highways, *Paths of Progress*; Hafen, 12; *Rocky Mountain News*, January 9, 1919, 1; *Financing of State Highways*, 52; *WPA Guide to Colorado*, xi.

15. *Denver Post*, February 8, 1925, sec. 3, 1; *Rocky Mountain News*, April 5, 1927, 5; April 22, 1927, 2.

16. Colorado Deptartment of Highways, *A Report on Colorado's Highway Needs and Highway Finances*, 8; *WPA Guide*, xxxv–xxxvi, 73; Colorado Department of Highways, *Annual Report*, 1954.

17. *Rocky Mountain News*, March 26, 1921, 1; September 29, 1924, 14.

18. Bureau of Business and Social Research, "Financing Highways in Colorado," 19–20.

19. Most state legislatures were unfairly dominated by rural interests and structurally anti-urban, until the *Baker v. Carr* Supreme Court decision in 1962, which forced more

equal representation. For further reference, see Robert B. McKay, *Reapportionment: The Law and Politics of Equal Representation* (New York: 20th Century Fund, 1965).

20. Colorado Highway Planning Survey, *Estimated Cost of Bringing Colorado Roads Up to Desirable Standards Required by Vehicle Use in 1950* (1941).

21. Colorado Department of Highways, *A Report on Colorado's Highway Needs and Highway Finances* (1945).

22. Stephen J. Leonard, "Bloody August: The Denver Tramway Strike of 1920," *Colorado Heritage* (Summer 1995): 19; Denver History Museum, *Tale of a City: Facts and Figures*; Stephen J. Leonard and Thomas J. Noel, *Denver: Mining Camp to Metropolis* (Niwot, Colo.: University Press of Colorado, 1990), 53–54.

23. Denver Tramway Company files, Colorado State Archives; Federal Writer's Program, *Denver's Streetcars*; Richard Thomas, *Regional Transportation District: The Roots, The Ride* (Denver: Regional Transportation District, 1979); Leonard, "Bloody August"; Denver History Museum, *Tale of a City: Facts and Figures*.

24. Denver Tramway Corporation, *The Denver Tramway System: Its Past, Present, and Future* (1948); Leonard, "Bloody August"; Federal Writer's Program, *Denver's Streetcars*; Thomas, *RTD*.

25. Denver Planning Commission, *The Denver Plan*, vol. 3; *Denver Planning Primer*, 33; *Denver Planning*, 4, no. 3.

26. City and County of Denver, Mayor's Office. Highways and Transportation Scrapbook, 1918–1919; David Hill, *Colorado Urbanization and Planning Context*, 273.

27. Map dated December 1921 in the DeBoer papers, box 9, folder 4; *Encyclopedia Britannica* (eleventh edition, 1910); McCrary, Culley, and Carhart, "A City Plan for Half-a-Million Population: Report to City Planning Association, 1924," *Municipal Facts* (May–June, 1924).

28. Carl Abbott, *The Metropolitan Frontier: Cities in the Modern American West*, (Tuscan: University of Arizona Press, 1993), 24, 80; Stephen J. Leonard, "Denver's Post-War Awakening," *Colorado Heritage* (Spring 1997).

29. Colorado Highway Planning Survey, correspondence files; Denver History Museum, *Facts and Figures*.

30. S.R. DeBoer papers; Denver Planning Commission, *The Denver Plan, Vols. 1–8, 1929–1938*; Denver History Museum, *Tale of a City*; Etter, *The Denver Park and Parkway System*, 5.

31. William Jones and Kenton Forrest, *Denver: A Pictorial History* (Golden: Colorado Railroad Museum, 1993), 30; Denver History Museum, *Tale of a City*; DeBoer papers.

32. Bureau of Business and Social Research, "Financing Highways in Colorado," 18–19; Leonard and Noel, 257, 260.

33. Clem Collins, city manager of revenue, *Taxes and the Taxpayer: How Serious Is the Tax Situation in Denver and the State* (1931), 100; various correspondence in Department of Highways files, Colorado State Archives.

34. Robert Autobee, *If You Stick with Barnum: A History of a Denver Neighborhood* (Monograph 8, Colorado Historical Society, 1992), 43.

35. George Cranmer, oral histories at Hart Library, Colorado Historical Society; George Cranmer, scrapbook, Denver Public Library.

36. Denver Planning Commission, 1941 report, quoted in *Tale of a City*.

37. Leonard, "Denver's Post-War Awakening."
38. Steven Mehls, et al., *Aurora: Gateway to the Rockies* (Aurora: Cordillera Press, 1985), 94.
39. Works Projects Administration, *Guide to Colorado* (Lawrence: University Press of Kansas, 1967), 135; Denver History Museum, *Facts and Figures.*
40. Jones and Forrest, 149; Phil Goodstein, *Denver Streets: Names, Numbers, Locations, Logic* (Denver: New Social Publications, 1994) 30; Denver History Museum, *Facts and Figures.*
41. Leonard and Noel, 351–53; Denver History Museum, *Facts and Figures.*
42. Jones and Forrest, 140; Noel, "Denver Boosters and Their 'Great Braggart City,'" 21. The spread-out placement of these military sites may have been part of an intentional effort to "disperse" strategic facilities. See Kermit Parsons, *"Shaping the Regional City: 1950–1990: The Plans of Tracy Augur and Clarence Stein for Dispersing Federal Workers from Washington, D.C.,"* Proceedings of the Third National Conference on American Planning History *(Cincinnati, November 30–December 2, 1989),* abstracted by Wendy Plotkin on H-Urban, June 1995, www.h-net.msu.edu.
43. Oral history interview with Maxine Kurtz, Director of City Planning Commission (Denver Public Library, Western History Department).
44. For more on government support for suburban home ownership, see Kenneth T. Jackson, *Crabgrass Frontier.*
45. Hill, 273.

CHAPTER THREE

1. Denver Planning Commission, *Planetoid* 6, no. 7 (1946).
2. Scrapbooks and miscellaneous documents, George Cranmer papers; Leonard and Noel, 269–70; Stephen Leonard, "Denver's Post-War Awakening."
3. *Brodhead v. City and County of Denver,* Supreme Court of the State of Colorado, docket no. 16870; *Rocky Mountain News,* October 20, 1949.
4. Maxine Kurtz, oral history interview, Denver Public Library.
5. Denver Planning Office, *Denver Tomorrow.*
6. Denver Planning Office, *General Street Plan, Denver Metropolitan Area (Preliminary),* introduction.
7. Denver Planning Office, *General Street Plan.* In 1960, Denver tried to raise revenue for streets with a registration surcharge. However, opposition forced legislators to limit the surcharge to $1.50, limiting the measure's effectiveness. *Rocky Mountain News,* February 5, 1960, 8.
8. Downtown Denver Master Plan Committee, *Central Area Transportation Study.*
9. Denver Planning Office, *Comprehensive Plan Bulletin,* no. 2–2 (1966); Denver Planning Office, *Denver 1985: A Comprehensive Plan for Community Excellence* (1967).
10. Colorado Department of Highways, *Denver Metropolitan Area Transportation Study: Land Use Report, Summary Edition* (Denver, 1961).
11. Denver Planning Office, *Denver Tomorrow* (1957).

12. DeBoer papers, Denver Public Library. In particular, see two manuscripts from the Denver Planning Office, *Tentative Annexation Policy* and *Urbanized Denver and the Metropolitan Area*.

13. Regional Transportation District, *A Public Transportation Plan: Summary Report* (1973), 3.

14. *Keyes v. School District 1, Denver, Colorado*, 413 U.S. 189 (1973); Paul Lewis, *Shaping Suburbia: How Political Institutions Organize Urban Development* (Pittsburgh: University of Pittsburgh Press, 1996), 86–89.

15. E.W. Carr, oral history interview, Denver Public Library; Pennsylvania Economy League, *Public Capital Improvements Planning and Finance by Major Governments in the Principal Metropolitan Areas*.

16. Colorado Highway Planning Committee, *Recommendations of the Highway Planning Committee*, 8; *Rocky Mountain News*, June 5, 1979, 8.

17. Ben Bezoff, oral history interview (Denver Public Library). Bezoff, a former state senator, went on to serve as a top Stapleton Airport executive (1966–1971) and was Denver's Executive Officer (1971–1977).

18. Colorado Municipal League, *The Facts Are Crystal Clear: Town and City Streets Are Highways . . . Vital Links in Colorado's Highway System* (Boulder, 1950); *Rocky Mountain News*, June 28, 1962, 40; Colorado Department of Highways, *The Facts of the Matter: 1953 Annual Report*; Letter from R.E. Livingston to Mark Watrous, August 20, 1951.

19. City Clerk's Office, ordinance records; *Colorado Magazine* (September 1972): 5.

20. Crocker and Ryan, Consulting Engineers, *The Valley Highway: A Preliminary Report on a North-South Limited-Access Highway Through Denver, December 9, 1944*, 4.

21. Colorado Department of Highways, *Your Highways: What Does the Future Hold*.

22. Crocker and Ryan, 29, 38, 71. The exclusion of buses echoes the policies of Robert Moses in the New York area. See Robert Caro, *The Power Broker: Robert Moses and the Fall of New York* (New York: Random House, 1975).

23. Goodstein, 30.

24. Clark Secrest, "The Valley Highway: The Road That Colorado Loves to Hate," *Colorado Heritage* (Summer 1995), 41; *Denver Post*, August 9, 1951, 35.

25. *Rocky Mountain News*, November 20, 1988, 8; Leonard and Noel, 272; Secrest, "The Valley Highway," 38–41; Colorado Department of Highways, *Paths of Progress*, 42; *Commemorating the Opening of the Denver Valley Highway*, November 23, 1958, 1.

26. *Denver Post*, August 9, 1962, 1; *Denver Post Magazine*, Special Issue for Twenty-fifth Anniversary of Valley Highway, November 6, 1983.

27. *Rocky Mountain Business Journal* (May 12, 1988): 1; Lewis, 147–48; *Denver Business Journal* (January 18, 1988): quoted in Lewis, 147.

28. George Wallace papers, Western History Collection, Denver Public Library.

29. Mehls, et al., 173.

30. Secrest, "The Valley Highway," 37, 42.

31. Roderick L. Downing, "Highway Economics" in *Papers Presented at the Highway Conference Held at the University of Colorado on January 18–19, 1940* (Boulder: University of Colorado, 1940); Clark Secrest, "A Promise Kept: The Denver–Boulder Toll Road," *Colorado Heritage* (Winter 1996): 13.

32. *Denver Post*, September 10, 1967, 12.

33. Colorado Department of Highways *Denver–Boulder Turnpike: Engineering Report*, July 1949; *Rocky Mountain News*, April 15, 1948, 8.

34. Colorado Department of Highways *Denver–Boulder Turnpike: Report on Economic Feasibility, Denver Post*, July 25, 1950, 2; *Rocky Mountain News*, September 30, 1950, 15.

35. Sinclair Weeks, Secretary of Commerce, *Progress and Feasibility of Toll Roads and Their Relation to the Federal-Aid Program* (Washington D.C.: Government Printing Office, 1955), 9.

36. Colorado Department of Highways, *Denver–Boulder Turnpike: Final Engineering Report* (1954); *Paths of Progress*, 42.

37. Secrest, "A Promise Kept," 15; *Denver Post*, March 7, 1965, 22.

38. *Denver Post*, May 14, 1972, 51; January 30, 1989, 1. Similarly, tolls on the Saw Mill and Hutchinson River Parkways in Westchester County, New York, were removed in 1994, and local newspapers soon reported public dissatisfaction with cutbacks in the number of highway patrolmen. The patrolmen had formerly been paid from toll revenues. *New York Times*, October 19, 1994, 22; and *Gannett Suburban Newspapers (Westchester edition)*, February 23, 1997, 16a.

39. Colorado 470 Delegation, *Colorado 470: Building on Progress* (April 1986); Colorado Department of Highways, *Annual Report,* 1976.

40. "Highway Fights," H-Urban Discussion List, www://h-net.msu.edu.

41. Goodstein, 31.

42. Colorado Department of Highways *Interstate 470—A Status Report, January 1975*; Colorado 470 Delegation, *Colorado 470: The Home Stretch* (April 1988).

43. Colorado 470 Delegation, *Colorado 470: Building on Progress* (April 1986); Colorado Department of Highways, *Annual Report, 1979*; *Rocky Mountain News,* June 13, 1979, 9; Colorado Department of Highways, *Colorado State Highway 470 Newsletter*, no. 1.

44. Lewis, 138.

45. Colorado Department of Highways, *Colorado State Highway 470 Newsletter*, nos. 1–3, 10; Colorado Department of Highways, *Colorado Interstate Transfer Funding Requirements* (1981).

46. Dan Hopkins, "C-470: The Centennial Parkway," *Rocky Mountain Motorist* (June 1982): 28–29; Colorado Department of Highways, *Colorado State Highway 470 Newsletter*, no. 4; *Rocky Mountain News*, April 2, 1987, 6; Colorado 470 Delegation, *Colorado 470: The Home Stretch.*

47. Colorado 470 Delegation, *Colorado 470: Building on Progress*; Colorado Department of Highways *C-470 Corridor Land Use Analysis* (1986), 2; George Wallace papers, Western History collection, Denver Public Library; *New York Times*, December 29, 1996, 1; Lewis, 138.

48. C. Kenneth Orski, "Toward a Policy of Suburban Mobility," *Urban Traffic Congestion: What Does the Future Hold?* (Washington, D.C.: Institute of Transportation Engineers, 1986), 9; *Rocky Mountain News*, January 6, 1983, 20; March 17, 1984, 14.

49. Kenneth Small, Clifford Winston, and Carol Evans *Road Work: A New Highway Pricing and Investment Policy* (Washington, D.C.: Brookings Institution, 1989) 3; National Council on Public Works Improvement, 87.

50. Wilfred Owen, in comments on Joel Tarr's "The Evolution of Urban Infrastructure in the Nineteenth and Twentieth Centuries," 62; Roger Vaughan, *Rebuilding America*, vol. 2 of *Financing Public Works in the 1980s* (Washington, D.C.: Council of State Planning Agencies, 1983), 60; Federal Highway Administration, *America on the Move*, 3.

51. *Rocky Mountain News*, February 1, 1984; June 6, 1984, 7.

52. This is a noteworthy departure from the historical pattern, wherein speculators sought to make money by *selling* land, at a profit, to governments building new transportation projects.

53. *Rocky Mountain News*, December 4, 1994, 107A; *Denver Post*, July 20, 1996, 1A.

54. *Rocky Mountain News*, January 22, 1996, 14A; *Bond Buyer*, various numbers; *Rocky Mountain News*, May 28, 1991, 8.

55. Denver Regional Council of Governments, *Transportation Improvement Program, December 1989.*

56. *Denver Business Journal*, January 30, 1989, 1; George Wallace papers, Western History collection, Denver Public Library; *Rocky Mountain News*, December 1, 1994; *Bond Buyer*, February 7, 1996, 2.

57. Denver History Museum, *Facts and Figures*; *Rocky Mountain News*, April 24, 1991, 32.

58. Noel, 21; E.W. Carr, oral history interview, Denver Public Library; Denver History Museum, *Tale of a City*; Mehls et al., 49, 61.

59. Stapleton Airfield Dedication Ceremonies. Friday, August 25, 1944 (Cranmer papers, Denver Public Library); Denver History Museum, *Facts and Figures*; *Rocky Mountain News*, September 2, 1937, 7.

60. George Cranmer, oral history no. 280, Colorado Historical Society.

61. Leonard and Noel, 351.

62. National Highway Users Conference, *Highway Highlights: Automotive Transportation in All Its Phases* (1941).

63. *Denver Post*, October 14, 1951, 21A; Franklin M. Bridge, *Metro-Denver; Mile-High Government* (Bureau of Government Service and Research, University of Colorado, 1963), 34; Goodstein, *Denver Streets*, 31; Leonard and Noel, *Denver: Mining Camp to Metropolis*; Colorado Department of Highways *Interstate 470—A Status Report, January 1975.*

64. Aurora Historical Society, *Newsletter* 5, no. 3 (July 1980); *Denver Post*, June 4, 1971, 25; October 13, 1974, 1E; May 25, 1975, 1E; *Rocky Mountain News*, April 17, 1981, 10; *Denver Business Journal*, January 31, 1997, 14B.

65. Bridge, appendix; George Wallace papers, Western History Collection, Denver Public Libary; *Bond Buyer*, various issues.

66. *Denver Post*, December 24, 1989, 1G; *Rocky Mountain News*, November 4, 1990, 82; *Bond Buyer*, various issues.

67. Lewis, 138.

68. *Rocky Mountain News*, April 24, 1991, 33; December 2, 1986, 6.

69. *Bond Ordinance Records*, Denver City Clerk's Office, room 281; Jeff Miller, "An Airport in Place," *Colorado Heritage* 3 (1984): 10, 16; Noel, "Denver Boosters," 21.

70. Denver History Museum, *Facts and Figures*; Ben Bezoff, oral history interview, Denver Public Library; Lewis, 125; Noel, 23.

71. Technically, Denver was permitted a minimum of one thousand new hotel rooms, and then was thereafter limited to 20 percent of the number of new hotel rooms added to a designated Adams County hotel zone; Lewis, 125, 135; *Rocky Mountain News*, April 24, 1991, 33; December 2, 1986, 6.

72. William Barnes, "Stapleton Gets Ready for Liftoff," *Urban Land* (April 1998): 67–116; Leonard and Noel, 357; *Denver Business Journal*, February 16, 1996, 12C; *New York Times*, September 16, 1998, 12A.

73. Lewis, 92–93, 145; U.S. Census data; *Rocky Mountain News*, September 14, 1987, quoted in Leonard and Noel, 358.

74. Jones and Forrest, 171. Cinderella City eventually couldn't compete against newer malls. By 1997 it had only one remaining tenant, a struggling Montgomery Ward. *Wall Street Journal*, January 6, 1997, 1.

75. *Tower Times: A Periodic Report on Denver's Skyline Urban Development Project, 1966–69*, vol. 1, no. 1. Denver Urban Renewal Authority, *Urban Renewal Goes Forward in Denver* (1965); *Denver Post*, May 5, 1963, sec. AA; Robert Cameron, oral history interview (Hart Library, Colorado Historical Society); Jones and Forrest, 96–97.

76. *Tower Times*, vol. 1, no. 1; Robert Cameron, oral history interview.

77. Leonard and Noel, 409.

78. Regional Transportation District, *A Public Transportation Plan: Summary Report, March 1973*; Thomas, *Regional Transportation District*, *Rocky Mountain News Festival Magazine*, July 29, 1973, 1; *Rocky Mountain News*, November 19, 1977, 6; Regional Transportation District, *RTD Frontier*, vol. 7, no. 8 (December 1977).

79. The total cost was expected to be $53 million, partly funded by the transferred federal aid, with the balance coming from RTD. By the time the mall opened in 1980, the bill amounted to $76 million. *Denver Post*, April 25, 1975, 26; January 28, 1978, 3; *Rocky Mountain News*, May 13, 1978, 8; April 27, 1979, 4; July 27, 1979, 4; Colorado Department of Highways, *1979 Annual Report*.

80. *Rocky Mountain News*, October 5, 1982, 7; March 6, 1984, 1B; July 23, 1985, 10.

81. Leonard and Noel, 409; *Rocky Mountain News*, February 22, 1988, 6; Denver Planning Office, *Tentative Annexation Policy, April 1953*; Nancy Holt, "Remaking Downtown Denver," *Urban Land* (April 1998): 54–113; Lewis, 123.

82. Thomas, 8; Ben Bezoff, oral history interview, Denver Public Library.

83. *Denver Downtowner*, January 30, 1980, 13; April 23, 1980, 2; *Washington Park Profile*, May 1980, 3; *Rocky Mountain News*, December 7, 1982, 8; May 18, 1994; February 2, 1997, 34–a; *Denver Business Journal*, February 16, 1996.

84. Robert Cameron, oral history interview.

85. *Denver Business Journal*, November 2, 2000, page 9–b; *Wall Street Journal*, January 31, 1997, B-12.

86. Holt, "Remaking Downtown Denver," 54–113; Sonia Weiss, "Center City Living," *Urban Land* (April 1998): 61–65; Wellington Webb, "Restoring Denver's South Platte River," *Urban Land* (April 1998): 16.

87. Holt, "Remaking Downtown Denver," 54–113; Weiss, "Center City Living," 61–65.

88. Noel, *WPA Guide to Colorado*, xii.

89. *New York Times*, December 29, 1996, 1; *Rocky Mountain News*, September 12, 1971, 5; Lewis, 146–47; *New York Times*, October 16, 1997, 8.

90. *Denver Post,* November 7, 2000, 1–b; *Rocky Mountain News,* November 7, 2000, 18–A; *Rocky Mountain News,* November 8, 2000, 24–a.

91. *New York Times,* September 16, 1998, A-12.

92. Timothy Egan, "Becoming Los Angeles: Urban Sprawl Strains Western States," *New York Times,* December 29, 1996, 1.

CHAPTER FOUR

1. Village of Middlebury, *Annual Report, 1955,* 9; Thomas Arnold, *200 Years and Counting: Vermont Community Census Totals, 1791–1980* (Burlington: Center for Rural Studies, University of Vermont, 1981); League of Women Voters, "Middlebury, Vermont: Handbook, 1761–1976," 7–9; National Register of Historic Places, *Nomination Form, Middlebury Village;* Peter S. Jennison, *The Roadside History of Vermont* (Missoula, Montana: Mountain Press Publishing Co., 1989), 47; William Upson, "The Cities of America: Middlebury, Vermont," *Saturday Evening Post,* March 22, 1947, 29; League of Women Voters, Middlebury Vermont, pamphlet titled "Know Your Town" (1953).

2. National Register of Historic Places, *Nomination Form, Middlebury Village;* George Mead papers, Sheldon Museum Library; Jeffrey Potash, *Vermont's Burned-Over District: Patterns of Community Development and Religious Activity, 1761–1850* (Brooklyn: Carlson Publishing, 1991), 206.

3. Mead papers, Sheldon Museum Library; Town of Middlebury, *Annual Report, 1865.*

4. Potash, 40.

5. Approximately 41 percent of the shares were bought by 28 different Middlebury residents. Overall, only 2 percent were bought by farmers. Professionals accounted for 49 percent, merchants 31 percent, and artisans 18 percent. Parts of the original route (from Middlebury across the Gap to Hancock, south to Stockbridge, and east to Royalton) were later incorporated into state highways. The last section was turned over to the town of Hancock in 1930. Storrs Lee, *Town Father, A Biography of Gamaliel Painter* (New York: Hastings House, 1952), 212; William Wilgus, *The Role of Transportation in the Development of Vermont* (Montpelier: Vermont Historical Society, 1945), 59; Jilia Kellog, "Vermont Post Roads and Canals," *Proceedings of the Vermont Historical Society* 16, no. 4, 141–42; Potash, 72; Mead papers, Sheldon Museum Library.

6. After the turnpike company abandoned the road, the portion within Middlebury became Seymour Street. The Pulp Mill Bridge has been repeatedly rebuilt by the two towns—in 1871, 1903, and 1938—and is now one of the few active covered bridges left in New England; National Register of Historic Places, *Nomination Form, Middlebury Village;* George Mead papers, Sheldon Museum Library; Jennison, 246; Town of Middlebury, *Annual Report, 1871*

7. Allan Everest, "Early Roads and Taverns in the Champlain Valley," *Vermont History:* 37: 249.

8. Walter Crockett, *Vermont: The Green Mountain State,* vol. 3 (New York: Century House, 1921), 185.

9. Wilgus, 62, 70, 98–99; Mead Papers, Sheldon Museum Library; R. W. Nimke, *The Rutland, Arrivals and Departures: Train Schedules, 1901–1961* (Walpole, 1990).

10. Kellog, 141; T.D. Seymour Bassett, "The Leading Villages in Vermont in 1840," *Vermont History,* vol. 26, 162; Farrington, *History of the Agency of Transportation;* Crockett, vol. 4, 228; Hubert Sargent (Commissioner of Highways), "Vermont Sesquicentennial," *Proceedings of the Vermont Historical Society* 9, no. 3, 230.

11. *The Vermont League for Good Roads: Its Objects, Membership and Officers; Including the Highway Law of 1892* (Montpelier: Vermont League for Good Roads, 1892); Farrington, *History of the Agency of Transportation.*

12. R. S. Currier, *The Vermont State Highway Board* (typed manuscript of recollections, at Vermont Department of Libraries). Currier was the first president of the Vermont Good Roads Association; *The Vermont League for Good Roads;* Vermont State Highway Department, *Biennial Report, 1936,* 45; *Biennial Report, 1942,* 9; Vermont Highway Commission, *Preliminary Report of the State Highway Commissioner* (1904).

13. Crockett, vol. 4, 299.

14. *Middlebury Register,* May 11, 1900, 7; June 29, 1900, 3; August 23, 1901, 4; January 23, 1903, 1; December 1904; May 26, 1906, 12; Sally Dorn, "A Lasting Legacy," *Vermont History,* vol. 33, 448; Federal Writers' Project, *Vermont: A Guide to the Green Mountain State.* (1937), 273. Battell's 30,000–acre property was bequeathed to Middlebury College, which converted it into the well-known Bread Loaf Campus, housing a creative writing retreat and conference facilities.

15. Bernice Wing, "Memories of a Vermont Quaker Farm," *Vermont History,* vol. 22, 110.

16. Farrington, *History of the Agency of Transportation;* Crockett, vol. 4, 379.

17. Farrington, *History of the Agency of Transportation;* Fletcher T. Proctor, "Inaugural Message to General Assembly of the State of Vermont, October 4, 1906," reprinted in *Vermont History News,* vol. 27, 27; Vermont State Highway Department, *Biennial Report, 1942,* 9.

18. "The Automobile in Vermont," *The Vermonter* 10, no. 12 (July 1905): 395; Wilgus, 82; *Good Roads: The Standard Road-Book—Vermont* (Boston: National Publishing Company, 1892).

19. Wilgus, 81.

20. Vermont Good Roads Association, *Proceedings of the First Annual Meeting of the Vermont Good Roads Association, May 5, 1904.*

21. Vermont Department of Highways, *State Aid Laws and General Directions for Building Improved Highways, 1907;* Paul Gillies, *A Short History of Vermont Highway Law: Locating Vermont's Historic Roads and Highways* (Vermont Society of Land Surveyors, 1992), 14; Vermont Agency of Transportation, *Highway Fund Revenue Study, January 1981,* 51; Vermont State Highway Department, *Biennial Report, 1936,* 45; *Biennial Report, 1942,* 9; United States Bureau of Public Roads, *Report of a Survey of Transportation on the State Highways of Vermont, 1927,* 11.

22. Vermont Motor Vehicle Department, *Highway Traffic Facts, 1936,* 20; *Middlebury Register,* April 13, 1915; July 9, 1915, 8; July 23, 1915; Vermont State Highway Department, *Biennial Report, 1942,* 9–15; Town of Middlebury, *Annual Reports;* Village of Middlebury, *Annual Reports;* James Hartness, "Communication from the

Governor to the Senate, February 15, 1921," *Journal of the Senate of the State of Vermont, 1921*, 233–35.

23. *The Highway Problem in Vermont: A Contribution, 1924*; Henry R. Trumbower, *Highway Improvements and Finance in the New England States, with Special Reference to Vermont* (Rutland: Vermont Chamber of Commerce, 1926).

24. U.S. Bureau of Public Roads, *Report of a Survey of Transportation*, 25; Trumbower, 15; Farrington, *History of the Agency of Transportation*.

25. "A Complete History of the Vermont Highway Patrol," *State Police Magazine* 10, no. 1 (April/May 1930): 9.

26. U.S. Bureau of Public Roads, *Report of a Survey of Transportation*, 25; Farrington, *History of the Agency of Transportation*.

27. *Middlebury Register*, April 19, 1926; July 16, 1926; Town of Middlebury, *Annual Reports*; Village of Middlebury, *Annual Reports*.

28. The traffic light's pedestal was finally removed in 1966, when it was cited as a traffic hazard. *Middlebury Register*, July 23, 1926; May 2, 1929, 1; April 2, 1931, 1; *Addison Independent*, January 21, 1966, 19; Nancy Graff, *At Home in Vermont: A Middlebury Album* (Middlebury: Rainbow Books, 1977), 20.

29. The State of Vermont also experimented with a too-good-to-be-true "traffic control device" in the 1920s, installing three hundred gas-fired, flame-throwing warning lights at intersections statewide. After public outcry, the devices were removed by the Gas Accumulator Company, which had donated them to build marketshare.

30. Town of Middlebury, *Annual Report, 1938*; Graff, 19.

31. *Middlebury Register*, April 16, 1931; January 18, 1934.

32. Vermont Department of Highways, *Preliminary Report of the Vermont State-Wide Highway Planning Survey, 1938*, 17; Vermont State Highway Department, *Biennial Report, 1934*, 13.

33. Vermont Motor Vehicle Department, *Wheels,* 39; Wilgus, 98–99; Farrington; Charles Crane, *Let Me Show You Vermont* (New York: Alfred A. Knopf, 1937), 234.

34. Vermont Department of Highways, *Preliminary Report, 1938*, 11, 38; Vermont State Highway Department, *Biennial Report, 1944*, 15–18.

35. Vermont State Highway Department, *Biennial Report, 1954*, 24.

36. Vermont State Highway Department, *Biennial Report, 1934*, 20; *Biennial Report, 1940*, 67; *Biennial Report, 1942*, 9–15; Farrington.

37. Vermont State Highway Department, *Preliminary Report, 1938*, 11, 38, 109; Vermont State Highway Department, *Biennial Report, 1942*, 9–15; Vermont Department of Highways, *Special Report on Needed Highway Improvements, 1941–1950* (Montpelier, 1940), 54, 69.

38. Vermont State Highway Department, *Preliminary Report, 1938*, 11, 38, 109; Vermont State Highway Department, *Biennial Report, 1942*, 9–15; Sargent, Webster, Crenshaw and Foley, *Transportation—State of Vermont* (Montpelier: Office of the Governor, Central Planning Office, 1966), 31.

39. Vermont Department of Highways, *Preliminary Report, 1938*, 89.

40. Vermont Motor Vehicle Department, *Highway Traffic Facts, 1936*, 20; National Highway Users Conference, *Vermont Highway Facts,* 10. All across the state, rail-

based mass transit was replaced with bus lines. While a number of Vermont towns had streetcars and trolleys at the turn of the century, by 1937, all but one (in Springfield, Vermont) had been replaced by rubber-tired bus lines. Federal Writers' Project, *Vermont: A Guide to the Green Mountain State*, 46–50 and 111–12.

41. Town of Middlebury, *Annual Report, 1933*; Town of Middlebury, *Annual Report, 1934*; George Mead papers, Sheldon Museum Library.

42. Town of Middlebury, *Annual Reports*. The town meeting form of government was modified in 1937, when the office of town manager was created, so that the three town selectmen, seven village trustees, and three water commissioners were no longer responsible for the daily administration of local government. However, traditional town meetings (for the town and also for the village) were still held annually, "come rain, snow, or sleet," to vote on taxes, appropriations, election of officials, and other citizen proposals. See League of Women Voters, *Know Your Town*; League of Women Voters, *Middlebury, Vermont: Handbook, 1761–1976*; and Village of Middlebury, *Annual Report, 1937*.

43. Vermont Development Commission, *Financial Statistics of State, County, and Local Government in Vermont, 1932–1946* (Montpelier, 1948), 29; Town of Middlebury, *Annual Reports*.

44. This section, concerning the Green Mountain Parkway, is based on the following sources: Friends of the Parkway, *The Pros vs. the Cons of the Green Mountain Parkway* (pamphlet, 1936); Mead papers, Sheldon Museum Library; James P. Taylor papers, Vermont Historical Society; Hal Goldman, "James Taylor's Progressive Vision: The Green Mountain Parkway" in *Vermont History* 63, no. 3 (Summer 1995): 158–79; Hal Goldman, "'A Desirable Class of People': The Leadership of the Green Mountain Club and Social Exclusivity, 1920–1936," *Vermont History* 65, nos. 3–4 (Summer/Fall 1997): 131–52; Jennison, 246–51; Frank Bryan and Kenneth Bruno, "Black-Topping the Green Mountains: Socio-Economic and Political Correlates of Ecological Decision Making," *Proceedings of the Vermont Historical Society*, vol. 41, no. 4, 224; Hannah Silverstein, "No Parking: Vermont Rejects the Green Mountain Parkway," *Vermont History* 63, no. 3 (Summer 1995): 133–57; Vermont State Highway Department, *Biennial Report, 1934*, 13; Eric Austin, *Political Facts of the United States* (New York: Columbia University Press, 1986).

45. Wilgus was responsible for the plan to build Grand Central Terminal in New York City, cover the railroad tracks north of the new terminal, and develop Park Avenue in the air rights over the trackbed. He had also served as a leading consulting engineer on the innovative Holland Tunnel. There is some disagreement about where the Parkway proposal was first published. According to the 1936 "Friends of the Parkway" pamphlet entitled *The Pros vs. the Cons of the Green Mountain Parkway*, the original suggestion came from the Vermont Commission on Country Life. Peter Jennison, in *The Roadside History of Vermont* (1989), claims that it was first proposed as Proposition Ten in *Rural Vermont: A Program for the Future*, by the Vermont Commission on the Future.

46. Letter from Abbot T. Fenn, January 15, 2001.

47. Vermont State Highway Department, *Biennial Report, 1944,* 27.

CHAPTER FIVE

1. Vermont State Highway Department, *Biennial Reports,* 1946, 1948, 1950; National Highway Users Conference, *Vermont Highway Facts,* 19; Vermont Department of Highways, *Are Toll Roads Feasible in Vermont* (Montpelier, 1952), 1; *Vermont's 1948 Highway Needs: Special Report Supplementing "Needed Highway Improvements in Vermont."*

2. Vermont Department of Highways, *Vermont's 1948 Highway Needs,* 3, 6.

3. Ibid., 3.

4. National Highway Users Conference, *Vermont Highway Facts.*

5. Vermont State Highway Department, *Biennial Report, 1946,* 35; *Biennial Report, 1948,* 19; Western Businessmen's Highway Conference, *Facts and Figures* (1956), 22.

6. Vermont Department of Highways, *Vermont Town Highway Report, 1950,* 23; Town of Middlebury, *Annual Reports.*

7. Wilgus, 89.

8. Vermont Department of Highways, *Preliminary Report of the State-Wide Highway Planning Survey,* 89; William Upson, "Cities of America: Middlebury, Vermont," *Saturday Evening Post,* March 22, 1947; Village of Middlebury, *Annual Report, 1955.*

9. Village of Middlebury, *Annual Reports, 1924–1959* (1955 report), 5.

10. Town of Middlebury, *Annual Report, 1946,* 10.

11. Village of Middlebury, *Annual Report, 1957.*

12. Vermont State Highway Department, *Biennial Report, 1948,* 31; *Biennial Report, 1950,* 11; *Biennial Report, 1952,* 39. This changed the grant ratio on urban extensions from 50–50 to 50–25–25.

13. Vermont State Highway Department, *The Highway Fund in Perspective:* 5.

14. Vermont Department of Highways, *Outline History of Vermont State Highways: National Highway Week, September 19–25, 1965.*

15. Ibid.; Jennison, 7; National Interregional Highway Committee, *Interregional Highways: Report and Recommendations* (Washington, D.C.: Government Printing Office 1944); National Highway Users Conference. *Vermont Highway Facts,* 5.

16. Vermont State Highway Department, *Biennial Report, 1946,* 23.

17. Vermont State Highway Department, *Report to the General Assembly* (Montpelier, 1973), 1.

18. Village of Middlebury, *Annual Report, 1955,* 47–48.

19. Town of Middlebury, *Annual Reports,* (1952, 1953, 1955, 1958); Village of Middlebury, *Annual Reports,* (1955, 1956).

20. Vermont State Highway Department, *Biennial Report, 1954,* 49.

21. Vermont State Highway Department, *Biennial Report, 1950;* Vermont General Assembly, Joint Legislative Committee to Inquire into Highway Financing, *An Inquiry into Highway Financing, February 19, 1968,* E-1; Vermont State Highway Department, *The Highway Fund in Perspective,* 5–6.

22. "Report on H-179, Bond Issue for Construction of Highways," *Journal of the House of the State of Vermont, 1957*: 368–79; Vermont General Assembly, *An Inquiry into Highway Financing*, E-1; Jennison, 7; Vermont Highway Board, *The Highway Fund in Perspective*, 5–6; *Report to the General Assembly*, State Govenor's Special Task Force on Transportation Systems, *Getting There from Here* (Montpelier, 1987), 132. It should be noted that the time frame for this data was not picked arbitrarily. On the one hand, 1955 marked the first highway bond issue by Vermont and was therefore a logical starting point. On the other hand, the energy crisis prompted changes in highway finance in general and Vermont's policies in particular, making 1973 an appropriate ending point.

23. Vermont State Highway Board, *The Highway Fund in Perspective*, 4; Vermont Agency of Transportation, *Highway Fund Revenue Study, January 1981*, 59.

24. Sargent, et al., *Transportation—State of Vermont*, 35, 74; Vermont State Highway Department, *Biennial Report, 1950*, 10, 17.

25. "Report on H-179, Bond Issue for Construction of Highways," 368–79; Vermont Department of Highways, *Financial Report Covering Vermont's Highway Program* (1959); *Vermont's State Highway Needs and Twelve-year Construction Program* (1960); *Vermont's Arterial Highway Plan and Fourteen-year Construction Program on the Federal Aid Primary and Interstate Systems* (1961); *Vermont's Fourteen-year Planning Program on the Federal Aid Highway Systems* (1963); Federal Highway Administration, *Middlebury FF 019–3 (11), Court Street* February 22, 1978.

26. Town of Middlebury, *Annual Report, 1954*.

27. Village of Middlebury, *Annual Report, 1961*, 15.

28. Town of Middlebury, *Annual Report, 1965*.

29. This was the same year that many other metropolitan consolidations were presented to voters nationwide. Most failed, but a noteworthy exception was the amalgamation of the city of Nashville with Davidson County, in Tennessee. For further discussion of this topic, see Jon Teaford, *Post Suburbia: Government and Politics in the Edge Cities* (Baltimore: Johns Hopkins University Press, 1997).

30. Town of Middlebury, *Annual Reports*, 1960–1966; Village of Middlebury, *Annual Reports*, 1960–1966.

31. Unidentified newspaper clipping, August 1968, from Murphy papers, Sheldon Museum; Hans Klunder and Associates, *Comprehensive Plan* (Addison County Regional Planning and Development Commission, 1970), vi-112; Joe Landry, Vermont Highway Department traffic research engineer, memo dated August 3, 1971, to Neil Ralph, Vermont Highway Department location project engineer, as reported in *Selectmen Minutes, Town of Middlebury* for February 22, 1971; Town of Middlebury, *Comprehensive Plan, adopted March 1, 1979*.

32. League of Women Voters, *Know Your Town*; Village of Middlebury, *Annual Report, 1961*; Thomas Arnold, *200 Years and Counting*, appendices 1 and 2.

33. Vermont Department of Highways, *Vermont's 1965 Fourteen-year Planning Program on the Federal Aid Highway Systems* (Montpelier, 1965).

34. R.W. Nimke, *The Rutland, Arrivals and Departures: 1901–1961*; Peter Defoe and Sonny Lewis, *Of Middlebury Town '68* (Middlebury, 1968); Wilgus, 81; and Hans Klunder and Associates, *Comprehensive Plan*, vi–48, vi–50. According to a timetable

in the ephemera collection at the Sheldon Museum Library, a roundtrip fare to NYC in 1953, the last year of regular passenger service, was $13.49 (about $87 in 2000 dollars).

35. Town of Middlebury, *Annual Reports*, 1961, 1962, 1964.

36. Sargent, et al., *Middlebury, Vermont: Master Plan, 1963.*

37. Sargent, et al., *Capital Improvement Program, Town and Village of Middlebury* (1964).

38. Town of Middlebury, *Annual Reports*, 1966–1970; Hans Klunder and Associates, *Comprehensive Plan*; "Public Notice Relating to the Consideration for Adoption of the *Comprehensive Plan* for Addison County." Murphy papers, Sheldon Museum Library. The recurring traffic-light proposal was rejected in 1966, tabled in 1968 (pending a consultant's recommendation), rejected in 1969 (even after the consultants reported favorably), and also voted down in 1970. In 1971 it was narrowly defeated (617 to 524) and was spurned yet again at the 1972 meeting.

39. Vermont Department of Highways, *Long-Range Planning Program on the Arterial Highway System* (Montpelier, 1966), 1.

40. *Vermont Public Investment Plan, Phase II, Part 2: "Twenty Vermont Communities: Public Investment Needs and Capacities"* (Montpelier, ca. 1969), 149.

41. Town of Middlebury, *Annual Report, 1971.*

42. Vermont Department of Highways, *Middlebury Inner Belt Location Report* (1971); *Minutes*, June 22, 1971, and February 22, 1972. Board of Selectmen, Town of Middlebury; *Addison Independent*, July 15, 1971, page 2–c.

43. Ibid.; *Burlington Free Press*, August 17, 1971, 7; undated and unidentified newspaper clipping, Murphy papers, Sheldon Museum Library.

44. Addison County Regional Planning and Development Commission, *Newsletter*, vol. 2, no. 5 (September 1973); Town of Middlebury, *Annual Report, 1973*; Middlebury Development Corp., "Middlebury Industrial Park" (brochure, in Whitehorne papers); Town of Middlebury, *Comprehensive Plan, adopted March 1, 1979*, 4; Harold Meeks, *Time and Change in Vermont* (Chester, Conn.: Globe Pequot Press, 1986), 269; and U.S.-7 Task Force, *Preliminary Progress Report* (Middlebury, 1976).

45. *Addison Independent*, July 15, 1971, 2–c; October 21, 1971, 2–c; Town of Middlebury, *Comprehensive Plan, adopted March 1, 1979*, 3; letter dated March 9, 1972, from Arthur Goss (advanced planning engineer, Vermont Department of Highways) to David Crawford (Middlebury town manager). Whitehorne papers, Sheldon Museum Library; *Middlebury Traffic Survey, 1970*, Whitehorne papers, Sheldon Museum Library; Middlebury Transportation Committee, *Minutes*, August 6, 1974.

46. Vermont Highway Board, *Report to the General Assembly* (Montpelier, Vermont: 1973); John Billheimer, *1974 National Transportation Study, Narrative Report for the Governor's Transportation Coordinating Committee, State of Vermont*, sec. 2, 39; Vermont Department of Highways, *Recommended Highway Construction Program: 1974–1983*, 80.

47. Town of Middlebury, *Annual Reports*; Downtown Task Force, *Proposal*, undated, in Murphy papers, Sheldon Museum Library.

48. U.S. Route 7 Task Force, *Preliminary Progress Report, 1976* (in Walker papers, Sheldon Museum); Town of Middlebury, *Annual Reports*, 1975, 1976; "Comprehensive Plan" (adopted March 1, 1979), 4–5; and U.S. Department of Transportation,

Federal Highway Administration *Draft Environmental Impact Statement, U.S. Route 7, Middlebury (Project #F219–3 [20]),*3.

49. Vermont State Highway Board, *The Highway Fund in Perspective:* 4; *Report to the General Assembly,* "Transportation Plan for Addison County, 1978" (in papers of the Addison County Regional Planning and Development Commission, Sheldon Museum Library), 9.

50. Vermont General Assembly, *An Inquiry into Highway Financing, February 19, 1968;* Vermont State Highway Department, *Biennial Report, 1972,* 11; "Transportation Plan for Addison County, 1978," 9.

51. Vermont State Highway Department, *Report to the General Assembly,* Sargent et al., *Transportation—State of Vermont,* 17–18, 50; Vermont Department of Highways, *Long-Range Planning Program on the Arterial Highway System* (Montpelier, 1966), 1.

52. *Vermont Public Investment Plan, Phase I* (1968), 73; Vermont Department of Highways, *Vermont's 1967 Fourteen-year Planning Program on the Federal Aid Highway Systems;* Vermont Department of Highways, *This Is the Story: Vermont's Highway Needs, 1965–1985;* Vermont State Highway Department, *Biennial Report, 1970,* 11; Billheimer, sec. 2, 38.

53. Vermont Transportation Advisory Board, *Ten-Year State Transportation Plan* (Montpelier: State Planning Office, 1974), II-12, II-19.

54. Vermont Agency of Transportation, *Highway Fund Revenue Study* (January 1981), 36; Addison County Regional Planning and Development Commission, *Newsletter,* vol. 2, no. 7 (December 1973).

55. Vermont Agency of Transportation, *Highway Fund Revenue Study* (January 1981), 8, 16.

56. Vermont Department of Highways, *Recommended Highway Construction Program* (1978), 1.

57. Billheimer, sec. 2, 40; Vermont Agency of Transportation, *An Inventory of Vermont's State-Owned and Supported Transportation System, 1977.*

58. Vermont Transportation Advisory Board, *Ten-Year State Transportation Plan,* I-1, III-28, IV-3; Billheimer, sec. 2, 160.

59. Governor's Special Task Force on Transportation Systems, *Getting There from Here* (1987), 26; Addison County Regional Planning and Development Commission, *Newsletter,* vol. 3, no. 1 (January 1974).

60. Vermont Transportation Advisory Board, *Ten-Year State Transportation Plan,* sec. IV; Vermont Agency of Transportation, *An Inventory.*

61. Town of Middlebury, *Annual Reports,* 1974–1981.

62. Velma Walker papers, Sheldon Museum Library; Town of Middlebury, *Annual Reports,* 1975, 1976; U.S.-7 Task Force, *Preliminary Progress Report* (Middlebury, 1976); U.S. Department of Transportation, Federal Highway Administration, *Middlebury FF 019–3 (11), Court Street: Negative Declaration and Section 4(f) Statement, February 22, 1978;* Town of Middlebury, *Annual Reports,* 1976, 1977.

63. Addison County Regional Planning and Development Commission, *Plan Preface, Town of Middlebury, 1977.*

64. Letter from Harold Curtiss, January 15, 1999.

65. Middlebury Development Corp., "Middlebury Industrial Park" (brochure in Whitehorne papers); Letter from C. J. Neil Kvasnak, vice president and general manager,

Geiger of Austria Incorporated to Board of Selectmen, town of Middlebury, October 10, 1980.

66. Town of Middlebury, *Annual Reports*, 1982–1997; *Addison Independent*, various numbers, 1989–1999.

67. Arnold, *200 Years and Counting: Vermont Community Census Totals, 1791–1980*, appendices 1 and 2; U.S. Census data.

68. *Addison Independent*, June 10, 1999; June 24, 1999; July 12, 1999; December 20, 1999, 1.

69. Town of Middlebury, *Annual Report, 1988*.

70. U.S.-7 Task Force, *Preliminary Progress Report* (Middlebury, 1976); *Comprehensive Plan, Town of Middlebury, Vermont*, adopted February 26, 1987.

71. Town of Middlebury, "Comprehensive Plan," adopted March 1, 1979, 4–5.

72. U.S. Department of Transportation, Federal Highway Administration, *Draft Environmental Impact Statement, U.S. Route 7, Middlebury (Project #F219–3 [20])*, 3; Town of Middlebury, *Annual Report, 1981*; letter from Harold Curtiss, January 15, 1999.

73. Town of Middlebury, *Annual Report, 1981*.

74. Town of Middlebury, *Annual Reports*, 1988, 1989.

75. Vermont Agency of Transportation, *Amended Annual Report to the General Assembly, Amending and Updating the Annual Report dated November 1982* (Montpelier, 1983); Town of Middlebury, *Annual Report, 1982*.

76. Town of Middlebury, *Annual Reports*, 1986, 1987; *Comprehensive Plan*, adopted February 26, 1987.

77. Vermont Transportation Advisory Board, *Ten-Year State Transportation Plan*, sec. III, 30; Richard A. Snelling, *Policy Statement on Capital Debt, February 1978*.

78. Governor's Special Task Force on Transportation Systems, *Getting There from Here* (1987), 42; State of Vermont, *Official Statement: $53,485,000 Series A and B General Obligation Bonds* (1983); *Official Statement: $22,610,000 Public Improvement and Transportation Bonds* (1985); *Official Statement: $41,900,000 General Obligation Bonds 1988 Series A* (1988); Vermont Agency of Transportation, *Vermont on the Move: Policy Plan* (Montpelier, 1992).

79. Town of Middlebury, *Annual Report, 1992*; letter from Harold Curtiss, January 15, 1999.

80. *Addison Independent*, January 11, 1999, 1.

81. *Comprehensive Plan, Town of Middlebury, Vermont*; *Addison Independent*, January 14, 1999, June 1, 2000.

82. Governor's Commission on the Economic Future of Vermont, *Pathways to Prosperity: A Report to Governor Madelein M. Kunin, November 1989*, 17; Arthur G. Woolf, associate professor of economics, University of Vermont. December 3, 1997, on internet discussion list administered by the Center for Research on Vermont, crvnet@list.uvm.edu.

83. Beth Humstone, "Smart Growth or Sprawl? What Will It Be for Vermont?," Center for Research on Vermont Research-in-Progress Seminar 124 (Burlington: University of Vermont, 1997); *Burlington Free Press*, June 13, 1998, 1.

84. *Vermont's Transportation Needs*, Report of the Twentieth Grafton Conference, August 26–28, 1990 (Grafton, Vermont: The Windham Foundation, 1991), 6–9, 11, 13, 14; *Addison Independent*, January 11, 1999, 1.

85. Vermont Economic Progress Council, *A Plan for a Decade of Progress: Actions for Vermont's Economy* (1995), 53.

CHAPTER SIX

1. John Egerton, *Nissan in Tennessee* (Nissan Motor Corporation, USA, 1983), 25; Walter K. Hoover, *A History of the Town of Smyrna* (Nashville: McQuiddy Printing, 1968), 5; Rutherford County Chamber of Commerce, untitled typewritten publication.

2. Federal Writers Project, *Inventory of County Archives of Tennessee, no. 75: Rutherford County,* 5; Carl R. Berquist, "Economic Impact of the Closing of Sewart Air Force Base on the Surrounding Area" (master's thesis, Vanderbilt University, 1967), 23, 27–28.

3. *Census of 1920 for District 3 of Rutherford County, Tennessee* (Smyrna Public Library).

4. For a full account of the Dixie Highway project, see Howard Preston, *Dirt Roads to Dixie,* 52–64.

5. Ibid., 60, 132.

6. Hoover, 27.

7. Federal Writers' Project, *WPA Guide to Tennessee* (University of Tennessee Press, 1986), 398; Hoover, 438.

8. Rutherford County Historical Society, *Bulletin 12,* 5, 24; Egerton, 27.

9. For further discussion about the geographic characteristics of defense spending, see Roger Lotchin, "The Origins of the Sunbelt–Frostbelt Struggle: Defense Spending and City Building," *Searching for the Sunbelt: Historical Perspectives on a Region,* edited by Raymond Mohl (Athens: University of Georgia Press, 1993). Also see Richard Bernard and Bradley Rice, *Sunbelt Cities: Politics and Growth Since World War II* (Austin: University of Texas Press, 1983).

10. Rutherford County Historical Society, *Bulletin 12,* 12–14; Berquist, 3; Hoover, 541.

11. Berquist, 4–5; Rutherford County Historical Society, *Bulletin 12,* 14; *Rutherford County Courier,* March 27, 1951, 1.

12. National Highway Users Conference, *Highway Highlights: Automotive Transportation in All Its Phases,* November 17, 1941.

13. This renovated route was called U.S. 41–70S; Hoover, 31; *Rutherford County Courier,* May 22, 1951; Rutherford County Historical Society, *Bulletin 12,* 14.

14. *Rutherford County Courier,* April 13, 1951, 27.

15. Sewart Air Force Base Redevelopment Committee, *Base Conversion to Civilian Purposes* (1969), 4; Berquist, 8–11.

16. Berquist, 11.

17. Town of Smyrna, *Audit Report,* various years; *Rutherford County Courier,* April 16, 1970, 1.

18. Berquist, 17–22.

19. Town of Smyrna, *Audit Reports,* various years. Smyrna's infrastructure also was subsidized by the Farmers Home Administration, which served as a lender of last resort for small municipal borrowers in agricultural regions. If the capital markets were

unwilling to lend money to Smyrna at low tax-exempt rates, the federal agency would buy town bonds at a similarly subsidized interest rate. Smyrna did not get an investment-grade credit rating until I-24 was built, so bonds issued earlier were bought by local banks or the federal agency. (*Moody's Municipal Manual, 1980*)

20. Berquist, 27–28; *Moody's Municipal and Government Manual,* 1950; Egerton, 22.
21. Town of Smyrna, *Audit Reports,* various years.
22. Berquist, 24; United States Census. The peak population may have been earlier, but 1965 was the first year the base population was counted, following the annexation of the base that same year. (*Tennessean,* January 10, 1971, 12)
23. In addition, there were 200 "semipermanent or temporary" buildings with one million square feet. Sewart Air Force Base Redevelopment Committee, appendix; Berquist, 3, 6.
24. *Rutherford County Courier,* September 10, 1970.
25. *Rutherford County Courier,* April 23, 1970, 1.
26. *Tennessean,* March 7, 1979, 1; oral history interview with Sam Ridley, April 21, 1995.
27. Sam Ridley, oral history interview, April 21, 1995.
28. Berquist, 54.
29. *Nashville Banner,* August 6, 1971.
30. Ricardo Springs, *Pilot Case Study: The Decision by Nissan Motor Manufacturing Corp., U.S.A. to Build a Light Truck Assembly Plant in Smyrna, Tennessee, Volumes I and II* (prepared for U.S. Department of Transportation, Office of the Assistant Secretary for Policy and International Affairs), 71.
31. Berquist, 38; Senator Albert Gore Sr. (Tennessee) was chair of the Senate Roads Subcommittee in the 1950s and played a key role in congressional negotiations concerning the Interstate Highway System legislation.
32. Sewart Air Force Base Redevelopment Committee, 7; Rutherford County Historical Society, *Bulletin 12,* 24–33.
33. *Tennessean,* January 10, 1971, 12.
34. *Tennessean,* March 28, 1973, 42; *Nashville Banner,* December 10, 1974, 3.
35. *Tennessee Statistical Abstract, 1977* (Knoxville: University of Tennessee, 1977); Rutherford County Chamber of Commerce, *Rutherford County, Center of It All.*
36. Rutherford County Historical Society, *Bulletin 12,* 24–33; *Tennessean,* January 10, 1971, 12; November 30, 1977, 18.
37. *Tennessean,* August 8, 1979, 20; *Nashville Banner,* November 22, 1979, 30; *Rutherford County Courier,* June 5, 1980, 1; April 25, 1985, 1; Capital Air filed for bankruptcy in December 1983, just a few months after the Nissan plant opened.
38. *Rutherford County Courier,* May 13, 1980, 1.
39. Sam Ridley interview, April 21, 1995.
40. *Tennessean,* November 17, 1976, 52.
41. *Tennessean,* April 9, 1980, 30.
42. Town of Smyrna, *Annual Audit Reports,* various years.
43. Egerton, 10–20; Springs, 32, 60; *Nashville Banner,* October 30, 1980, 1.
44. *Nashville Banner,* October 31, 1980, 1.
45. Tennessee Department of Transportation, *Report on Proposed I-24 Connector Route* (1981), 4.

46. Egerton, 12; *Tennessean,* January 1, 1982, 43.

47. Egerton, 9–10; *Nashville Banner,* September 20, 1980, 1.

48. *Tennessean,* November 30, 1980, A 17; *Nashville Banner,* November 27, 1980, 30.

49. *Memorandum of Understanding Regarding Payments in Lieu of Taxes between Industrial Development Board of Rutherford County, Nissan Motor Manufacturing Corporation U.S.A., the Rutherford Board of County Commissioners, and the Town of Smyrna.*

50. Letter from Mayor Sam Ridley to Marvin Runyon, Nissan Motor Corp., October 9, 1980; Letter from Mayor Sam Ridley to Marvin Runyon, Nissan Motor Corp., October 20, 1980; Springs, 44; Mike Woods, "A Look at Smyrna: The Nissan Impact," *Public Management,* 66 (June 1984): 4. This is a noteworthy reversal of earlier patterns for the location of automobile production. In the early entrepreneurial years of the industry, no auto manufacturers remained in business for very long in cities with population under 250,000. The industry remained concentrated in a handful of urban areas for many decades thereafter. Ishihara's choice of Smyrna for Nissan marked a distinctly new paradigm. Clay McShane, *Down the Asphalt Path: The Automobile and the American City* (New York City: Columbia University Press, 1994), xi.

51. *Memorandum of Agreement,* October 13, 1980, between the Industrial Development Board of Rutherford County and the Nissan Motor Manufacturing Corporation, U.S.A.; *Memorandum of Understanding Regarding Payments in Lieu of Taxes between Industrial Development Board of Rutherford County, Nissan Motor Corporation, the Rutherford County Commissioners, and Town of Smyrna.*

52. Springs, appendix A, 9.

53. *Tennessean,* May 18, 1983, F2.

54. Egerton, 60. Only thirteen of the plant's permanent workforce (and that of the attached North American headquarters) were transferred from Japan, and Nissan never employed more than fifty Japanese citizens in Smyrna simultaneously. In addition, very few of the workers had ever worked on an automobile assembly line before, even though there were thousands of unemployed and underemployed autoworkers that applied. Nissan officials claimed that they did not want anyone to come with "preconceived notions about how to build a car," although it is possible that they also did not want anyone who had ever been a member of the United Auto Workers. (*U.S. News and World Report,* May 9, 1988 50–57.)

55. *Tennessean,* August 6, 1986, B5; June 12, 1989, E1; *U.S. News and World Report,* May 8, 1988, 54.

56. Rutherford County Chamber of Commerce, *Doing Business with Rutherford County.*

57. Mabel Pittard, *Rutherford County* (Memphis: Memphis State University Press, 1984), 112–114; *U.S. News and World Report,* May 9, 1988, 44, 54. In 1983 the Firestone plant was bought by Japanese tire manufacturer Bridgestone for $52 million.

58. Carroll Van West, *Tennessee's Historic Landscapes: A Traveler's Guide* (Knoxville: University of Tennessee Press, 1995), 17.

59. Town of Smyrna, *Audit Report, 1982; Rutherford County Courier,* December 15, 1994, 1.

60. *Rutherford County Courier,* August 21, 1980, 2; Sam Ridley interview, April 21, 1995.

61. *Rutherford County Courier,* February 12, 1981, 1.

62. Woods, "A Look at Smyrna," 5.

63. *Tennessean,* June 12, 1989, E1.

64. Thomas W. Hanchett, "U.S. Tax Policy and the Shopping-Center Boom of the 1950s and 1960s," *American Historical Review* 101, no. 4 (October 1996): 1082–1110.

65. Woods, "A Look at Smyrna," 4.

66. For a more complete description of federal support for dispersed, mortgage-financed, suburban-style housing, see Jackson, *Crabgrass Frontier.*

67. Ibid., 5.

68. Rutherford County Chamber of Commerce, untitled publication. Not all the surrounding communities wanted to be annexed by Smyrna. In a microcosm of suburban–urban annexation disputes, two different communities attempted to resist annexation by Smyrna. Lake Farm Estates, a subdivision with 320 homes, rejected an annexation referendum in 1985 and again in 1986. Similarly, the town of Florence, midway between Smyrna and Murfreesboro, attempted to incorporate as an anti-annexation defense in 1992. (*Nashville Banner,* April 26, 1992, B2; and *Tennessean,* August 6, 1986, B8)

69. Rutherford County Chamber of Commerce, *Heart of Tennessee,* April 1995, 2; March 1994, 4; *Community Statistics;* U.S. Census data.

70. *Rutherford County Courier,* February 19, 1981, 1.

71. Woods, "A Look at Smyrna," 4.

72. *Tennessean,* December 4, 1988, B8.

73. *Nashville Banner,* June 15, 1989, A20.

74. Town of Smyrna, *Annual Audit Reports,* various years; *Tennessean,* June 11, 1982, 14; September 9, 1982, 62. This practice was perfectly legal, until it was prohibited by the Tax Reform Act of 1986. The "arbitrage" between the rate Smyrna paid on its tax-exempt borrowings and the rate it earned on reinvested loan proceeds was widened in June 1983, when the bond-rating agencies upgraded the town's rating. (*Moody's Municipal and Government Manual, 1985*)

75. Town of Smyrna, *Annual Audit Report,* various years.

76. Ibid.; Rutherford County Chamber of Commerce, untitled publication: "Community Statistics"; "Resource and Site Guide, 1995 Edition," 12; *Tennessean,* September 9, 1986, B3.

77. Rutherford County Chamber of Commerce, "Doing Business in Rutherford County."

78. *Rutherford County Courier,* September 19, 1985, 1.

79. U.S. Census data. In an apparently isolated episode of antigrowth protest, a small group of Smyrna residents scared away an employer that would have been the second largest employer in town, after Nissan: In 1987, when the U.S. Postal Service started its Express Mail overnight mail service, one of the primary subcontractors almost located its hub at the Smyrna Airport. The move would have brought three thousand additional jobs to Smyrna and an initial capital investment of at least $100 million, but a petition with two hundred signatures opposed to increased air traffic (and the resultant noise) derailed the plan. (*Nashville Banner,* May 21, 1987, C10)

80. *Rutherford County Courier,* April 12, 2001; I-24 Expo Center Inc., www.i-24expo.com, December 1997.

81.   Town of Smyrna, traffic maps; Rutherford County Chamber of Commerce, "Resource and Site Guide, 1995 Edition," 14.

82.   *Rutherford County Courier*, February 24, 1994, 1.

83.   Joe Sherman, *In the Rings of Saturn* (New York: Oxford University Press, 1994).

84.   *Tennessean*, December 11, 1986, A1; *Nashville Banner*, November 2, 1987, C1; August 12, 1992, B2; *Rutherford County Courier*, February 1, 2001, 1; April 26, 2001, 1.

Bibliography

I. ARCHIVAL REPOSITORIES

Colorado Historical Society Library, Stephen H. Hart Library
Colorado State Archives
Colorado State History Museum
Colorado State Library
Denver City Clerk's Office
Denver History Museum
Denver Public Library, Western History Department
Linebaugh Public Library, Murfreesboro, Tenn.
Nashville Public Library
Sheldon Museum Library, Middlebury, Vt.
Smyrna Public Library, Smyrna, Tenn.
Starr Library, Middlebury College, Middlebury, Vt.
Smyrna Town Hall
Tennessee State Library and Archives, Manuscript Division
Vermont Department of Libraries
Vermont Historical Society
Vermont State Archives
Wilbur Collection, Bailey/Howe Library, University of Vermont, Burlington, Vt.

II. PRIMARY SOURCES—GENERAL

American Academy of Political and Social Science. *Annals*, vol. 116, no. 205, *The Automobile: Its Province and Problems.* Philadelphia, 1924.

————. *Annals*, vol. 133, no. 222, *Planning for City Traffic*. Philadelphia, 1927.

American Association of State Highway Officials. "A Resolution Adopted December 11, 1919, at the Annual Convention of State Highway Officials held at Louisville, Kentucky." Colorado State Archives.

————. *American Highways*. Vol. 20, no. 1.

————. *Digest of Federal Highway Act, 1-1072, As Approved by Conference Committee of Congress, October 8, 1921*.

American Automobile Association. *Highways and Traffic Bulletin #13*. January 1955.

————. *Why Federal Aid in Roads*. 1916.

American Farm Bureau Federation. "A Few Country Boulevards and Mud Roads vs. Development of a Great Road System." Colorado State Archives, ca. 1919–1920.

American Institute of Planners, Committee on Urban Transportation. *Urban Freeways*. New York, 1946.

Bird, Frederick L. *Revenue Bonds*. Los Angeles: Haynes Foundation, 1941.

Burch, Philip H. Jr. *Highway Revenue and Expenditure Policy in the United States*. New Brunswick, N. J.: Rutgers University Press, 1962.

Catalog of Federal Aids to State and Local Governments. Subcommittee on Intergovernmental Relations of the Committee on Government Operations, United States Senate. April 15, 1964.

Chatburn, George. *Highways and Highway Transportation*. New York: Crowell, 1923.

Chicoine, David, and Norman Walzer, eds. *Financing Local Infrastructure in Nonmetropolitan Areas*. New York: Praeger, 1986.

Council of State Governments. *Transportation Outlays of States & Cities: 1970 Projections*.

Danielson, Michael N. *Federal-Metropolitan Politics and the Commuter Crisis*. New York: Columbia University Press, 1965.

Davies, Richard O. *The Age of Asphalt: The Automobile, the Freeway, and the Condition of Metropolitan America*. Philadelphia: Lippincott, 1975.

Dearing, Charles. *American Highway Policy*. Washington, D.C.: Brookings Institution, 1941.

Dearing, Charles, and Wilfred Owen. *National Transportation Policy*. Washington, D.C.: Brookings Institution, 1949.

Downs, Anthony. "The Law of Peak-Hour Expressway Congestion." *Traffic Quarterly* (July 1962): 393.

Duncan, C.S. *A National Transportation Policy*. New York: Appleton-Century, 1936.

Federal Aid for Post-War Highway Construction: Hearings Before the Committee on Roads, U.S. House of Representatives. Washington, D.C.: Government Printing Office, 1944.

The Federal Aid Road Act and the Rules and Regulations Thereunder, Together with an Article by Secretary of Agriculture David F. Houston on "The Government and Good Roads" (includes "Rules and Regulations of the Secretary of Agriculture for Carrying Out the Federal-Aid Road Act, Issued September 1, 1916"). 64th Congress, First Session, document #548. Washington, D.C.: Government Printing Office, 1916.

Federal Highway Administration. *The Interstate System: Route Log and Finder List*. Washington, D.C., 1978.

————. *The Evolution of the Highway-User Charge Principle*, prepared by N. Kent Bramlett. Highway Users and Finance Branch, Highway Statistics Division. Washington, D.C., 1982.

————. *Journey-to-Work Trends, Based on 1960, 1970, 1980 Decennial Census.* Washington, D.C., 1982.

————. *State Highway Finance Trends.* December 1982.

————. *Financing Federal-Aid Highways.* October 1983.

————. *America on the Move: The Story of the Federal-Aid Highway Program.* Washington, D.C., September 1984.

Financing Highways: Symposium Conducted by the Tax Institute, November 8–9, 1956. Princeton, 1957.

Financing Public Improvements: A Discussion of Public Revenue Bonds. New York: Van Ingen & Co, 1939.

Financing of State Highways. New York: H.W. Wilson, 1929.

Gates Rubber Company. "Building America's First Super-Highway—The Pennsylvania Turnpike." *Industrial News* 10, no. 7 (July 1940). Colorado State Archives.

Highway Research Board. Bulletin no. 64, "Highway Planning and Urban Development." Washington, D.C: National Research Council, 1952.

————. Special Report no. 83, *Law of Turnpikes and Toll Bridges.* Washington, D.C.: National Research Council, 1964.

Hoyt, Homer. "Changing Land-Use Patterns as a Basis for Long-Range Highway Planning." *Highway Planning and Urban Development: Highway Research Board Bulletin no. 24.* Washington, D.C.: 1952.

Joint Committee on Federal-Aid in the Construction of Post Roads. *Federal Aid to Good Roads: Suggested Plan for Intelligent and Practical Expenditure of Three Billions of Dollars During a Period of Fifty Years by the States and the Federal Government in the Construction, Improvement, and Maintenance of Good Roads.* Washington, D.C.: Government Printing Office, 1913.

————. *Good Roads: Hearings Held on January 21, February 10, 11, and 18, 1913.* Washington, D.C.: Government Printing Office, 1913.

————. *Public Road Systems of Foreign Countries and of the Several States.* Washington, D.C.: Government Printing Office, 1913.

Leonoudakis, Stephen. "Financing the Golden Gate Bridge." Paper delivered to American Society of Civil Engineers.

MacDonald, Thomas H. "The Financing of Highways." *Annals* (American Academy of Political and Social Science), vol. 116, no. 205.

————. *The Automobile: Its Province and Problems.* Philadelphia: 1924.

McCarty, John. *Highway Financing by the Toll System.* Berkeley: University of California, 1951.

"Maine Legislature Believes It Has Model Motor Law." *Motor Age,* June 26, 1913.

Meyer, J. R., J. F. Kain, and M. Wohl. *The Urban Transportation Problem.* Cambridge: Harvard University Press, 1965.

Motor Vehicle Manufacturer's Association. *1973/1974 Automobile Facts and Figures.*

Mowbray, A. Q. *The Road to Ruin.* Philadelphia: Lippincott, 1969.

Municipal Finance Officer's Association. *Building Prosperity: Financing Public Infrastructure for Economic Development.* 1983

National Automobile Chamber of Commerce. *Highway Bulletin H-134.* 1921.

National Council on Public Works Improvement. *Fragile Foundations: A Report on America's Public Works*. Washington, D.C.: Government Printing Office, 1988.

National Highway Users Conference. *Highway Users Pay Their Way and More*. 1940.

———. *Highway Highlights: Automotive Transportation in All Its Phases*. November 17, 1941.

———. *Dedication of Special Highway Revenues to Highway Purposes: An Analysis of the Desirability of Protecting Highway Revenues Through Amendments to State Constitutions*. Washington, D.C., 1941.

———. *Highway Development and Financing: Six Aspects of a Vital Problem*. Washington, D.C., 1947.

———. *The Highway Transportation Story, In Facts*. 4th ed. Washington, D.C., 1961.

———. *The Highway Trust Fund: A Historical Review of 11 Years of Operation, 1956–1967*. Washington, D.C., August 1967.

National Interregional Highway Committee. *Interregional Highways: Report and Recommendations*. Washington, D.C.: Government Printing Office, 1944.

National League of Cities and the United States Conference of Mayors. *Capital Budgeting and Infrastructure in American Cities: An Initial Assessment*. April 1983.

National Transportation Committee. *The American Transportation Problem*. Washington, D.C.: Brookings Institution, 1933.

Orski, Kenneth. "Toward a Policy of Suburban Mobility." In *Urban Traffic Congestion: What Does the Future Hold?* Washington, D.C.: Institute of Transportation Engineers, 1986.

Owen, Wilfred. *The Metropolitan Transportation Problem, revised edition*. Washington, D.C.: The Brookings Institution, 1966.

———. *The Accessible City*. Washington, D.C.: The Brookings Institution, 1972.

Pennsylvania Economy League. *Public Capital Improvements Planning and Finance by Major Governments in the Principal Metropolitan Areas*. Pittsburgh, 1956.

Porter, Douglas. *Financing Infrastructure to Support Community Growth*. Urban Land Institute, 1984.

———. *Special Districts*. Urban Land Institute, 1987.

President's Advisory Committee on a National Highway Program. Press release dated October 6, 1954.

Roosevelt, Franklin D. "Interregional Highways: Message from the President Transmitting a Report of the National Interregional Highway Committee Outlining and Recommending a National System of Interregional Highways." Washington, D.C.: Government Printing Office, 1944.

Schmidt, E. L. "Does Additional Federal Aid Solve the Highway Problem?" Convention of the North Atlantic States Highway Officials, February 21, 1950.

Sheets, Frank. *The Development of Primary Roads During the Next Quarter Century: An Address Delivered at the 25th Anniversary Meeting of the American Association of State Highway Officials Held in Richmond, Virginia, October 9–13, 1939*.

Small, Kenneth, Clifford Winston, and Carol Evans. *Road Work: A New Highway Pricing and Investment Policy*. Washington, D.C.: Brookings Institution, 1989.

Smerk, George M. *Urban Transportation: The Federal Role*. Bloomington: Indiana University Press, 1965.

————, ed. *Readings in Urban Transportation*. Bloomington: Indiana University Press, 1968.

Smith, Wilbur, and Norman Hebden. *State-City Relationships in Highway Affairs*. New Haven: Yale University Press, 1950.

Smith, Wilbur and Associates. *Future Highways and Urban Growth*. 1961.

State Highway Funding Methods, 1991. Washington, D.C.: The Road Information Program.

Stocker, Harry. *Transportation and the Public Welfare in War and Peace*. Washington, D.C.: National Highway User's Conference, 1943.

Tax Foundation. *Controlling Government Corporations*. New York, 1955.

Transportation Economics: A Conference of the Universities-National Bureau Committee for Economic Research. New York: Columbia University Press, 1965.

Tri-State Transportation Campaign. *Subsidies for Traffic*. New York, March, 1994.

Tyler, Poyntz, ed. *American Highways Today*. New York: H.W. Wilson, 1957.

United States Department of Commerce. Press release dated August 2, 1956.

United States Department of Commerce. Undersecretary for Transportation. Press release dated October 8, 1954.

United States Department of Transportation. *A Statement on National Transportation Policy*. Washington, D.C., 1971.

Vaughan, Roger. *Rebuilding America: Financing Public Works in the 1980s*. Washington, D.C.: Council of State Planning Agencies, 1983.

Vaughan, Roger, and Robert Pollard. *Rebuilding America: Planning and Managing Public Works in the 1980s*. Washington, D.C.: Council of State Planning Agencies, 1984.

Weeks, Sinclair. *Progress and Feasibility of Toll Roads and Their Relation to the Federal-Aid Program*. Washington, D.C.: Government Printing Office, 1955.

Western Businessmen's Highway Conference. U.S. Chamber of Commerce. *Facts and Figures*. 1956. Denver, Colo., December 6, 1955.

Western Interstate Committee on Highway Policy Problems. *Record of Activities*. 1952.

White, Charles P. *Report on Financing an Expanded Highway Program in Tennessee: A Report to the Tennessee Highway Study Commission, July 1956*. Knoxville: University of Tennessee, 1956.

Wilson, R.S. *Wanted—Another Bong From the Liberty Bell: A Call to the Citizenry to Get into the Fight For Adequate Roads*. Goodyear Tire and Rubber Co., 1952.

III. SMYRNA

"A Japanese Automaker Finds a Home." *Atlantic*, December, 1982, 12–20.

Berquist, Carl R. "Economic Impact of the Closing of Sewart Air Force Base on the Surrounding Area." Master's thesis, Vanderbilt University, 1967.

Berry, Bryan. "Nissan Was First." *Iron Age* (May 16, 1986): 32–35.

————. "An American Work Force Produces Japanese Quality." *Iron Age* (July 18, 1986): 44.

"Census of 1920 for District 3 of Rutherford County, Tennessee." Prepared by Margaret C. Tharckston, Smyrna Public Library, January 2–7, 1920.

Christiansen, Hal. "Smyrna Has Just Begun to Fight." *Nashville Magazine*, April 1970.

Corlew, Robert. *Tennessee, A Short History*. Knoxville: University of Tennessee Press, 1981.

Egerton, John "Nissan in Tennessee." Nissan Motor Corp. U.S.A., 1983.

Federal Writers' Project, Historical Records Survey. *Inventory of County Archives of Tennessee, no. 75: Rutherford County, Tenn.*, 1938.

———. *WPA Guide to Tennessee.* University of Tennessee Press, 1986.

———. *Notes from the Tennessee Guide Project.* Tennessee State Library and Archives, Manuscript Division.

Hoover, Walter. *A History of the Town of Smyrna.* Nashville: McQuiddy Printing, 1968.

"How Japan Is Winning Dixie: The Tennessee Story." *U.S. News and World Report,* May 9, 1988, 43

Kawata, Makoto. "Making It Work: Japanese Direct Investment in the United States." *Journal of Japanese Trade and Industry* 3 (January/February 1984): 25–27.

King, Adeline. "History of Smyrna Air Base." Murfreesboro: Rutherford County Historical Society, 1979.

Martin, Don E. *Housing Study: Town of Smyrna.* Nashville: Tennessee State Planning Office, Middle Tennessee Region, 1977.

Memorandum of Agreement, October 13, 1980 between the Industrial Development Board of Rutherford County and the Nissan Motor Manufacturing Corporation, U.S.A.

Memorandum of Understanding Regarding Payments in Lieu of Taxes between the Industrial Development Board of Rutherford County, Nissan Motor Manufacturing Corporation U.S.A., Rutherford Board of County Commissioners, and Town of Smyrna.

"Nissan Plans to Spend Up to $600 Million on U.S. Engine Plant." *Wall Street Journal,* January 21, 1991, C-10.

Pittard, Mabel. *Rutherford County.* Memphis, Tenn.: Memphis State University Press, 1984.

Proceedings of Conference on Highways of the Future, April 1947. Knoxville: University of Tennessee, 1947.

Proceedings of Conference on the Immediate Highway Program. Knoxville: University of Tennessee, 1946.

Proceedings of Conference on Modernizing the Highway System. Knoxville: University of Tennessee, 1953.

Proceedings of Conference on New Frontiers for Highways. Knoxville: University of Tennessee, 1952.

Published Proceedings of the Highway Conference Held in Knoxville, March 1940. Knoxville: University of Tennessee, 1940.

Published Proceedings of the Highway Conference Held in Knoxville, May 1943. Knoxville: University of Tennessee, 1943.

Rice, Faye. "A Ford Man Tunes Up Nissan." *Fortune* 114 (November 24, 1986): 140.

Ridley, Sam. Interview by the author. April 21, 1995.

———. Letter to Marvin T. Runyon, President, Nissan Motor Manufacturing Corporation U.S.A., October 9, 1980.

———. Letter to Marvin T. Runyon, President, Nissan Motor Manufacturing Corporation U.S.A., October 20, 1980.

Risen, James. "Nissan Plans Big Expansion of U.S. Auto Plant." *Los Angeles Times,* April 4 1989, 1.

Rutherford County Chamber of Commerce. *Heart of Tennessee.* March 1994.

———. *Heart of Tennessee.* April 1995.

———. *Resource and Site Guide.* 1995.

———. *Community Statistics.*

———. *Doing Business with Rutherford County.*

———. *Rutherford County, Tennessee.* 1994.

———. *Rutherford County, Center of It All.*

Rutherford County Historical Society, *Bulletin no. 12.*

Sewart Air Force Base Redevelopment Committee. *Sewart Air Force Base Conversion to Civilian Purposes.* Washington, D.C., 1969.

Sherman, Joe. *In the Rings of Saturn.* New York: Oxford University Press, 1994.

Sims, Carlton, ed. *A History of Rutherford County.* Murfreesboro, Tenn., 1947.

Smyrna/Rutherford County Airport Authority. *Smyrna Airport: Gateway to Middle Tennessee.*

Smyrna, Tennessee. *Annual Audit Reports, 1954–1993.*

Springs, Ricardo. *Pilot Case Study: The Decision by Nissan Motor Manufacturing Corporation to Build a Light Truck Assembly Plant in Smyrna, Tennessee.* Prepared for U.S. Department of Transportation.

Tennessee Department of Transportation. *Report on Proposed I-24 Connector Route, Rutherford County, March 1981.*

———. *City and County Traffic Maps.*

Tennessee Statistical Abstract, 1977. Knoxville: University of Tennessee, 1977.

West, Carroll Van. *Tennessee Historic Landscapes: A Traveler's Guide.* Knoxville: University of Tennessee, 1995.

"Will Nashville Become the Detroit of Dixie?" *U.S. News and World Report,* August 12, 1985, 53–54.

Woods, Mike. "A Look at Smyrna: The Nissan Impact." *Public Management* 66 (June 1984)

———. "The Nissan Impact—One Year Later." *Public Management* 67 (June 1985).

IV. MIDDLEBURY AND VERMONT

Addison County Regional Planning and Development Commission. *Newsletter.*

———. *Comprehensive Plan, 1970.* Prepared by Hans Klunder and Associates.

———. *Plan Preface, 1977.*

———. "Transportation Plan for Addison County, 1978." Sheldon Museum Library.

Arnold, Thomas. *200 Years and Counting: Vermont Community Census Totals, 1791–1980.* Burlington: Center for Rural Studies, University of Vermont, 1981.

Associated Industries of Vermont. *Report of the 1956 Fiscal Study.*

Automobile Club of Vermont. *Yearbook,* 1910, 1912–14.

Bassett, T.D. Seymour. "The Leading Villages in Vermont in 1840." *Vermont History* 26: 162–63.

Billheimer, John. *1974 National Transportation Study, Narrative Report for the Governor's Transportation Coordinating Committee, State of Vermont.*

Breed, Charles B. *Highway Costs and Motor Vehicle Payments in Vermont.* Vermont Railroads Association, 1940.

Bryan, Frank, and Kenneth Bruno. "Black-Topping the Green Mountains: Socio-Economic and Political Correlates of Ecological Decision Making." Proceedings of the Vermont Historical Society, vol. 41, no. 4, 224.

Comprehensive Plan, Town of Middlebury, Vermont. Adopted February 26, 1987.

Crane, Charles. *Let Me Show You Vermont.* New York: Alfred A. Knopf, 1937.

Crockett, Walter. *Vermont: The Green Mountain State.* New York: Century House, 1921.

Currier, R.S. *The Vermont State Highway Board.* Manuscript of recollections. Vermont Department of Libraries.

Defoe, Peter, and Sonny Lewis. *Of Middlebury Town '68.* Middlebury, Vt. 1968.

Dorn, Sally. "A Lasting Legacy." *Vermont History* 33: (Montpelier: Vermont Historical Society) 445–49.

Everest, Allan. "Early Roads and Taverns in the Champlain Valley." *Vermont History* 37: 247–55.

Farrington, Herbert. *History of the Agency of Transportation.* Vermont State Archives.

Federal Writers' Project. *Vermont: A Guide to the Green Mountain State.* Boston: Houghton Mifflin, 1937.

Friends of the Parkway. *The Pros vs. the Cons of the Green Mountain Parkway.* 1936.

Gillies, Paul. *A Short History of Vermont Highway Law: Locating Vermont's Historic Roads and Highways.* Vermont Society of Land Surveyors, 1992.

Goldman, Hal. "James Taylor's Progressive Vision: The Green Mountain Parkway." *Vermont History* 63, no. 3 (Summer 1995): 158–79.

———. "'A Desirable Class of People': The Leadership of the Green Mountain Club and Social Exclusivity, 1920–1936." *Vermont History* 65, nos. 3–4.

Good Roads: The Standard Road-Book—Vermont. Boston: National Publishing, 1892.

Governor's Commission on the Economic Future of Vermont. *Pathways to Prosperity: A Report to Governor Madeleine M. Kunin, November 1989.*

Governor's Special Task Force on Transportation Systems. *Getting There from Here.* Montpelier, 1987.

Graff, Nancy. *At Home in Vermont: A Middlebury Album.* Middlebury, Vt., 1977.

Hartness, James. "Communication from the Governor to the Senate, February 15, 1921." *Journal of the Senate of the State of Vermont, 1921*: 233–35.

The Highway Problem in Vermont: A Contribution, 1924.

Hoffer, Doug, ed. *The History of Sprawl in Chittenden County.* The Champlain Initiative, March 1999.

Huffman, Benjamin. *Getting Around Vermont: A Study of Twenty Years of Highway Building in Vermont, with Respect to Economics, Automobile Travel, Community Patterns, and the Future.* Burlington: University of Vermont, 1974.

Humstone, Beth. "Smart Growth or Sprawl? What Will It Be for Vermont?" Center for Research on Vermont, Research-in-Progress Seminar 124. December 1997. Burlington: University of Vermont, 1997. Videotape.

Jennison, Peter. *The Roadside History of Vermont.* Missoula, Mt: Mountain Press, 1989.

Keese, Susan. "What Is So Rare as a Mall in Vermont." *New York Times,* January 22, 1995, Real Estate section, 7.

Kellog, Jilia. "Vermont Post Roads and Canals." *Proceedings of the Vermont Historical Society* 16, no. 4: 135.

League of Women Voters. "Transportation Problems and Proposals for Solution: A Study of Possible Relocation of U.S. Route 7 in the Middlebury Area." Middlebury, Vermont.

———. "Handbook, 1761–1976." Middlebury, Vermont.

———. "Know Your Town." Middlebury, Vermont, 1953.

Lee, Storrs. *Town Father: A Biography of Gamaliel Painter.* New York: Hastings House, 1952.

Meeks, Harold. *Time and Change in Vermont.* Chester, Conn.: Globe Pequot Press, 1986.

Middlebury Development Corporation. "Middlebury Industrial Park."

National Highway Users Conference. *Vermont Highway Facts: State Statistics on Highway Mileage, Use, Finance, 1947.*

National Register of Historic Places. *Nomination Form—Middlebury Village.* Approved November 13, 1976.

New Hampshire—Vermont Municipal Manual, 1962 Edition. Freeport, Maine: Municipal Manual Publishers, 1961.

Nimke, R.W. *The Rutland, Arrivals and Departures: Train Schedules, 1901–1961.* Walpole, New Hampshire, 1990.

Ogden, Herbert G. "A Superhighway for Vermont? Necessity or Extravagance? Time for a State Wide Referendum." Wilbur Collection, University of Vermont.

Potash, Jeffrey. *Vermont's Burned-Over District: Patterns of Community Development and Religious Activity, 1761–1850.* Brooklyn, N.Y.: Carlson Publishing, 1991.

Proctor, Fletcher T. "Inaugural Message to General Assembly of the State of Vermont, October 4, 1906." Reprinted in *Vermont History News* 27: 27.

"Report on H-179, Bond Issue for Construction of Highways." *Journal of the House of the State of Vermont, 1957*: 368–79.

Sargent, Hubert. "Vermont Sesquicentennial." *Proceedings of the Vermont Historical Society* 9, no. 3: p. 230.

Sanborn Fire Insurance Maps, Middlebury 1879–1959.

Sargent-Webster-Crenshaw and Foley. *Middlebury, Vermont. Master Plan, 1963.*

———. *Capital Improvement Program, Town and Village of Middlebury, 1964.*

———. *Zoning Ordinance, Town of Middlebury, 1964.*

———. *Transportation—State of Vermont.* Montpelier: Office of the Governor, Central Planning Office, 1966.

Silverstein, Hannah. "No Parking: Vermont Rejects the Green Mountain Parkway." *Vermont History* 63, no. 3 (Summer 1995): 133–57.

Snelling, Richard. A. *Policy Statement on Capital Debt, February 1978.*

Sowers, George. *A Study of Toll Roads in Vermont.* Petroleum Industry Committee of Vermont, 1953.

State of Vermont. *Report of the Governor's Committee on Municipal Finances. May 15, 1965.*

———. *Official Statement $34,450,000 Public Improvement and Transportation Bonds, August 1, 1978.*

———. *Population and Local Government.* 1980.

———. *Official Statement $53,485,000 Series A and B General Obligation Bonds, June 9, 1983.*

———. *Official Statement $22,610,000 Public Improvement and Transportation Bonds, August 20, 1985.*

———. *Official Statement $41,900,000 General Obligation Bonds 1988 Series A, October 4, 1988.*

State Police Magazine. "A Complete History of the Vermont Highway Patrol." *State Police Magazine* 10, no. 1 (April/May 1930).

Town of Middlebury. Town Reports, 1864–1990.

———. "Comprehensive Plan, December 14, 1972."

———. "Draft Comprehensive Plan, adopted by Selectmen June 15, 1978 for public hearing July 11, 1978."

———. "Comprehensive Plan, adopted March 1, 1979."

Trumbower, Henry R. *Highway Improvements and Finance in the New England States, with Special Reference to Vermont.* Vermont Chamber of Commerce, 1926.

U.S. Bureau of Public Roads. *Report of a Survey of Transportation on the State Highways of Vermont, 1927.*

U.S. Department of Transportation, Federal Highway Administration. *Middlebury #FF 019-3 (11), Court Street: Negative Declaration and Section 4(f) Statement.* February 22, 1978.

———. *Draft Environmental Impact Statement, U.S. Route 7, Middlebury #F219-3 (20).*

U.S. Route 7 Task Force. *Preliminary Progress Report,* 1976 (in Walker Papers, Sheldon Museum).

Upson, William. "The Cities of America: Middlebury, Vermont." *The Saturday Evening Post,* March 22, 1947.

Vermont Agency of Transportation. *Second Biennial Report: 1976–1978.*

———. *An Inventory of Vermont's State-Owned and Supported Transportation System, 1977.*

———. Annual Reports, 1978–1987.

———. *Highway Fund Revenue Study, January 1981.*

———. *Amended Annual Report to the General Assembly, Amending and Updating the Annual Report dated November 1982.* 1983.

———. *Capital Program and Project Development Plan, 1992–1994.*

———. *Vermont on the Move: Policy Plan, 1992.*

Vermont Central Planning Office. *Highway Development Long-Range Planning 1964.*

Vermont Comprehensive State Planning Program. *What We Are, Where We Are Going.*

———. *Vision and Choice: Vermont's Future.*

Vermont Department of Administration, Budget and Management Division. Expenditures of State Governments in Vermont, 1960–1968, with Projections to 1975.

Vermont Department of Highways. *Long-Range Planning Program, Arterial Highway System.* Montpelier, Vt.

———. *State Aid Laws and General Directions for Building Improved Highways, 1907.*

———. *Survey of Transportation on the State Highways of Vermont, 1927.*

———. *Highway Funds, Fiscal Year 1936/37.*

———. *Preliminary Report of the Vermont State-Wide Highway Planning Survey, 1938.*

———. *Special Report on Needed Highway Improvements 1941–1950.*

———. *Vermont's 1948 Highway Needs: Special Report Supplementing "Needed Highway Improvements in Vermont."* 1948.

———. *Vermont Town Highway Report, 1950.*

———. *Are Toll Roads Feasible in Vermont, 1952.*

————. *Tentative Ten-year Program, November 12, 1952.*

————. *Middlebury Village Highway Report, 1955.*

————. *Financial Report Covering Vermont's Highway Program, July 1, 1948—June 30, 1965.*

————. *Vermont's State Highway Needs and Twelve-year Construction Program, 1960.*

————. *Immediate Economic Benefits Resulting From the Construction of the Interstate System in Vermont.* 1961.

————. *Vermont's Arterial Highway Plan and Fourteen-year Construction Program on the Federal Aid Primary and Interstate Systems, 1961.*

————. *Vermont's Fourteen-year Planning Program on the Federal Aid Highway Systems, 1963.*

————. *Outline History of Vermont State Highways: National Highway Week, September 19–25, 1965.*

————. *Vermont's 1965 Fourteen-year Planning Program on the Federal Aid Highway Systems.* 1965.

————. *Vermont's 1967 Fourteen-year Planning Program on the Federal Aid Highway Systems.* 1967.

————. *Middlebury Inner Belt Location Report, 1971.*

————. *Recommended Highway Construction Program, 1974–1983.*

————. *This Is the Story: Vermont's Highway Needs, 1965–1985.*

Vermont Development Commission. *Financial Statistics of State, County, and Local Government in Vermont, 1932–1946.* Montpelier, 1948.

————. *A Summary of the Reports from the Governor's Postwar Planning Committees.* Montpelier: Vermont State Planning Board, 1944.

Vermont Economic Progress Council. *A Plan for a Decade of Progress: Actions for Vermont's Economy.* 1995.

Vermont General Assembly. Joint Legislative Committee to Inquire into Highway Financing. *An Inquiry into Highway Financing, February 19, 1968.*

Vermont Good Roads Association. *Proceedings of the First Annual Meeting of the Vermont Good Roads Association, May 5, 1904.*

Vermont Highway Commission. *Preliminary Report of the State Highway Commissioner: October 1904.*

Vermont Joint Transportation Commission. *Report, 1941.*

Vermont League for Good Roads. *The Vermont League for Good Roads: Its Objects, Membership and Officers; Including the Highway Law of 1892.* 1892.

Vermont Legislative Council. *Report of the Special Transportation Project Study Committee, January. 10, 1980.*

Vermont Motor Vehicle Department. *List of Registered Motor Vehicles, 1911.*

————. *Motor Vehicle Register* 1920, 1924.

————. *Highway Traffic Facts, 1936.*

————. *Wheels: Vermont Highway and Motor Transport Economics, 1940.*

Vermont Public Investment Plan, Phase I. Prepared for the Vermont Department of Administration and the Northeast Regional Commission, May 1968.

Vermont Public Investment Plan, Phase II, Part 1. "Agenda for the Seventies." Prepared for the Vermont Department of Administration and the Northeast Regional Commission, September 1969.

Vermont Public Investment Plan, Phase II, Part 2. "*Twenty Vermont Communities: Public Investment Needs and Capacities.*" Prepared for the Vermont Department of Administration and the Northeast Regional Commission, 1969.

Vermont Public Investment Plan, Phase III. "*Challenge and Opportunity.*" Prepared for the Vermont Department of Administration and the Northeast Regional Commission, 1970.

Vermont Special Transportation Committee. *Report of the Legislative Committee to Study the Highway Fund, 1981.*

Vermont State Highway Board. *The Highway Fund in Perspective: Past-Present-Future.* Montpelier, 1970.

———. *Report to the General Assembly.* Montpelier, 1973.

Vermont State Highway Department, *Biennial Reports,* 1898–1988.

Vermont Transportation Advisory Board. *Ten-Year State Transportation Plan.* Montpelier: State Planning Office, 1974.

Vermont Transportation Board. *Biennial Reports,* 1974–1988.

Vermont's Transportation Needs. Report of the Twentieth Grafton Conference, August 26–28, 1990. Grafton, Vt: The Windham Foundation, 1991.

The Vermonter. "The Automobile in Vermont," vol. 10, no. 12, July 1905.

———. "Keep Vermont Unspoiled," vol. 40, no. 8, August 1935.

Village of Middlebury. *Annual Reports,* 1924, 1931, 1933–1965.

Wilgus, William. *The Role of Transportation in the Development of Vermont.* Montpelier: Vermont Historical Society, 1945.

Wing, Bernice. "Memories of a Vermont Quaker Farm." *Vermont History* 22: 110–11. N.d.

Women's Auxiliary of Saint Stephen's Episcopal Church. *Middlebury, Vermont and Its Environs.*

V. DENVER

Abbott, Carl, Stephen Leonard, and David McComb. *Colorado: A History of the Centennial State.* Boulder: Colorado Associated University Press, 1982.

Andrus, Milt. *Colorado's Ton-Mile Truck Tax.* Colorado Good Roads Association, 1955.

Aurora Historical Society. *Newsletter,* vol. 5, no. 3, July 1980.

Autobee, Robert. *If You Stick with Barnum: A History of a Denver Neighborhood.* Colorado Historical Society Monograph 8, 1992.

Barnes, William. "Stapleton Gets Ready for Liftoff." *Urban Land* (April 1998): 67–116.

Barth, Gunther. *Instant Cities: Urbanization and the Rise of San Francisco and Denver.* New York: Oxford University Press, 1975.

Bridge, Franklin M. *Metro-Denver; Mile-High Government.* Bureau of Government Service and Research, University of Colorado, 1963.

Bureau of Business and Social Research. "Financing Highways in Colorado." *University of Denver Reports* 16, no. 1, March 1940.

Christensen, Erin. "Lifelines: The Story of Colorado's Public Road System." *Colorado Heritage* 3, 1987.

City and County of Denver, City Service Bureau. *Denver the Distinctive,* ca. 1917.

City and County of Denver. Mayor's 1918–1919 Highways and Transportation Scrapbook.

Collins, Clem. *Taxes and the Taxpayer: How Serious Is the Tax Situation in Denver and the State.* Denver, 1931.

Colorado 470 Delegation. *Colorado 470: Building on Progress.* April 1986.

———. *Colorado 470: The Home Stretch.* April 1988.

Colorado Department of Highways. *Denver–Boulder Turnpike: Final Engineering Report,* 1954.

———. *Paths of Progress.* N.d.

———. *Your Highways: What Does the Future Hold.*

———. *A Report on Colorado's Highway Needs and Highway Finances.* Colorado State Archives, 1945.

———. *Denver–Boulder Turnpike: Engineering Report.* 1949.

———. *Denver–Boulder Turnpike: Report on Economic Feasibility,* July 1950.

———. *The Facts of the Matter: 1953 Annual Report.*

———. *Commemorating the Opening of the Denver Valley Highway.* November 23, 1958.

———. *Colorado Highway User Tax Facts, 1954–1961.*

———. *Denver Metropolitan Area Transportation Study: Land Use Report, Summary Edition.* Denver, 1961.

———. *Commemorating the Opening of the East 46th Avenue Freeway (I-70), Denver, Colorado, September 12, 1964.*

———. *A Guidebook on Highway Funding.* 1970.

———. *Through the Colorado Rockies: I-70.* 1970.

———. *Colorado Interstate 470–A Status Report, January 1975.*

———. *Colorado Interstate Transfer Funding Requirements.* 1981.

———. *Colorado's State Highway Needs.* 1984.

———. *Forecast of the Year 2001 Highway System.* 1985.

———. *C-470 Corridor Land Use Analysis.* 1986.

———. *Colorado State Highway 470 Newsletter* 1–12, [1988–]

———. *Colorado: A Look at Existing Conditions: Transportation from the Socioeconomic and Environmental Perspectives.* December 1989.

———. *Annual Reports,* 1954–1991.

Colorado Department of Motor Vehicles. *Report of the Motor Vehicle Department of the State of Colorado, 1913–1939.*

Colorado Good Roads Association. *Resolutions Adopted and Papers Read at the Fourth Annual Convention of the Colorado Good Roads Association, Colorado Springs, January 15–16, 1914.*

Colorado Highway Planning Committee. *Colorado Highway Needs and Financing.* 1950.

———. *The Committee Reports to John Q. Public on the Long Range Highway Plan.*

———. *Summary of Recommendations of the Highway Planning Committee.* October 19, 1951.

Colorado Highway Planning Survey. *Estimated Cost of Bringing Colorado Roads Up to Desirable Standards Required by Vehicle Use in 1950.* 1941.

———. Correspondence files at Colorado State Archives.

Colorado Information. September 1972, 2–5.

Colorado Municipal League. *The Facts Are Crystal Clear: Town and City Streets Are Highways . . . Vital Links in Colorado's Highway System.* Boulder, 1950.

———. *Financing City Streets and Highways in Colorado: A Preliminary Report.* Boulder, 1950.

———. *Financing City Streets and Highways.* Boulder, 1950.

Colorado Petroleum Industries Committee. *P.I.C. News* 16, no. 10, October 1955.

Colorado State Highway Commission. *Report on the Valley Highway.* 1944.

Colorado State Highway Department, Planning and Traffic Division. *A Report on Colorado's Highway Needs and Highway Finances, 1945.*

Crain, John L. *Review of Denver Metropolitan Area Transportation Study.* 1977.

Crocker and Ryan, Consulting Engineers. *The Valley Highway: A Preliminary Report on a North-South Limited-Access Highway Through Denver, December 9, 1944.*

Dallas, Sandra. *Yesterday's Denver.* Miami: E.A. Seemanns, Inc., 1974.

Denver City Clerk's Office. *Ordinance Records.*

Denver History Museum. *The Interactive Videodisc: Facts and Figures.*

———. *The Interactive Videodisc: Tale of a City.*

Denver Metro Convention and Visitors Bureau. *1996/67 Official Visitors Guide.*

Denver Planning Commission. *The Denver Plan, Volumes 1–8, 1929–1938.*

———. *Denver Planning Primer.*

———. *Planetoid,* Vol. 6, nos. 1–7 (1942–1946).

Denver Planning Office. *General Street Plan, Denver Metro Area (Preliminary),* 1952.

———. *Tentative Annexation Policy, April 1953.*

———. *Urbanized Denver and the Metropolitan Area, January 1953.*

———. *Denver Tomorrow.* 1957.

———. "The Parkway Plan." *Comprehensive Plan Bulletin* 10-3.

———. *Denver 1985: Comprehensive Plan for Community Excellence.*

Denver Regional Council of Governments. *Regional Transportation Plan.*

———. *Transportation Improvement Program.* 1989.

Denver Tramway Corporation. *The Denver Tramway System: Its Past, Present, Future.* 1948.

———. Archives. Denver: Colorado State Archives.

Denver Urban Renewal Authority. *Facts on Urban Renewal.* 1968.

———. *Urban Renewal Goes Forward in Denver.* 1965.

Dorsett, Lyle W. *The Queen City: A History of Denver.* Boulder, Colo.: Pruett Publishing Co., 1977.

Downing, R.L. "Highway Economics." *Papers Presented at the Highway Conference Held at the University of Colorado on January 18–19, 1940.* Boulder: University of Colorado, 1940.

Downtown Denver Master Plan Committee. *Central Area Transportation Study.* 1963.

Etter, Don. *The Denver Park and Parkway System.* Colorado Historical Society, 1986.

Federal Writer's Program. "Denver's Streetcars." Manuscript. Stephen H. Hart Library, Denver, Colo.

Goodstein, Phil. *Denver Streets: Names, Numbers, Locations, Logic.* Denver: New Social Publications, 1994.

Hafen, Leroy. "The Coming of the Automobile and Improved Roads to Colorado." *Colorado Magazine* (January 1931): 1–16.

Halaas, David. "The Legacy of Boom and Bust." *Colorado Heritage* (Winter 2000): 3–5.

Hill, David. *Colorado Urbanization and Planning Context.* Denver: Colorado Historical Society, 1984.

Holt, Nancy. "DIA Takes Off." *Urban Land* (April 1998): 49.

———. "Remaking Downtown Denver." *Urban Land* (April 1998): 54–113.

Hopkins, Dan. "C-470: The Centennial Parkway." *Rocky Mountain Motorist* (June 1982): 28–29.

Hosakawa, Bill. *Thunder in the Rockies: The Incredible Denver Post.* Morrow, 1976.

Johnson, Charles A. *Denver's Mayor Speer.* Denver: Green Mountain Press, 1969.

Jones, William, and Kenton Forrest. *Denver: A Pictorial History, Third Edition.* Golden, Colo.: Colorado Railroad Museum, 1993.

Judd, Dennis. "From Cowtown to Sunbelt City: Boosterism and Economic Growth in Denver." In *Restructuring the City: The Political Economy of Urban Redevelopment,* edited by Susan and Norman Fainstein et al., 167–201. New York: Longman, 1986.

Leonard, Stephen J. "Bloody August: The Denver Tramway Strike of 1920." *Colorado Heritage* (Summer 1995): 18–31.

———. "Denver's Post-War Awakening: Quig Newton, Mayor 1947–1955." *Colorado Heritage* (Spring 1997), 13–24

Leonard, Stephen J., and Thomas J. Noel. *Denver: Mining Camp to Metropolis.* Niwot, Colo.: University Press of Colorado, 1990.

Lewis, Paul G. *Shaping Suburbia: How Political Institutions Organize Urban Development.* Pittsburgh: University of Pittsburgh Press, 1996.

Marshall, Lawrence. *Road Development in Colorado, 1830–1930.* Manuscript. Stephen Hart Library, Denver, Colo. January 17, 1931.

Mayor's Platte River Development Study. *In Response to a Flood.* Denver, 1967.

McCrary, Culley and Carhart. "A City Plan for Half-a-Million Population: Report to City Planning Association, 1924." *Municipal Facts* (May–June, 1924.)

McFadden, Carl, and Leona McFadden. *Early Aurora.* Aurora Technical Center, 1978.

Mehls, Steven, Carol Drake, and James Fell. *Aurora: Gateway to the Rockies.* Aurora: Cordillera Press, 1985.

Metropolitan Transportation Development Commission. *Consensus '91: A Report on the Development of the Transportation System in the Denver Metropolitan Area.* 1991.

Miller, Jeff. "An Airport in Place." *Colorado Heritage* 3 (1984): 2–16.

Miller, Lyle. "Earliest Automobiling in Colorado, 1899–1904." *Colorado Heritage* (Autumn 1999): 22–38.

Narvaes, Emily. "Denver Area Development Markets Fly High." *Urban Land* (April 1998): 45–112.

Noel, Thomas. "Denver Boosters and Their 'Great Braggart City.'" *Colorado Heritage* 3 (1995): 2–29.

Public Improvements: Report of the Special Committee on Pubic Improvements, 1892.

Regional Transportation District. *There Is an Answer.* 1970.

———. *A Public Transportation Plan: Summary Report.* 1973.

———. *RTD Frontier.*

———. *Transit Development Program, 1978–1982.* July 1977.

Robinson, Charles Mulford. *Proposed Plans for the Improvement of the City of Denver.* Denver: Art Commission, City and County of Denver, 1906.

Secrest, Clark. "A Promise Kept: The Denver–Boulder Toll Road." *Colorado Heritage* (Winter 1996): 13–15.

———. "The Valley Highway: The Road That Colorado Loves to Hate." *Colorado Heritage* (Summer 1995): 37–42.

———. "Colorado Fritchie Electric Auto: Cross-Country in 1908." *Colorado Heritage* (Winter 1999): 39–44.

"Stapleton Airfield Dedication Ceremonies. Friday, August 25, 1944." Cranmer Papers, Western History Department, Denver Public Library.

Steele, Lawrence. *Aurora: The Dawning of a 21st Century City.* 1991.

Thomas, Richard. *Regional Transportation District: The Roots, the Ride.* Denver: Regional Transportation District, 1979.

Tower Times: A Periodic Report on Denver's Skyline Urban Development Project, 1966–69.

Webb, Wellington. "Restoring Denver's South Platte River." *Urban Land* (April 1998): 16.

Weiss, Sonia. "Center City Living." *Urban Land* (April 1998): 61–65.

Wilbur Smith Associates. *Colorado Highway Cost Allocation and Tax Alternatives Study.* Columbia, South Carolina, 1988.

Works Projects Administration. *Guide to Colorado.* Lawrence: University Press of Kansas, 1967.

VI. TRADE PUBLICATIONS, PERIODICALS, AND NEWSPAPERS

Addison Independent (1946–Present)

The Bond Buyer, including annual statistical publications

The Bond Buyer 100th Anniversary Edition: A Salute to the Municipal Bond Industry, 1891–1991. New York: Bond Buyer, 1991

Colorado Heritage

Colorado Magazine

Denver Business Journal

Denver Post

Middlebury Record (1900–1930)

Middlebury Register (1850–1946)

Moody's Investors' Service, *Municipal and Government Manual*

Nashville Banner

Nashville Tennessean

Public Roads: A Journal of Highway Research

Rocky Mountain News

Rutherford County Courier

Vermont History

Vermont Life

Vermonter

Wall Street Journal

VII. SECONDARY SOURCES—GENERAL

Abbott, Carl. *The New Urban America: Growth and Politics in Sunbelt Cities.* Chapel Hill: University of North Carolina Press, 1987.

———. *The Metropolitan Frontier: Cities in the Modern American West.* Tuscon: University of Arizona Press, 1993.

Adler, Sy. "The Transformation of the Pacific Electric Railway: Bradford Snell, Roger Rabbit, and the Politics of Transportation in Los Angeles." *Urban Affairs Quarterly* 27, no. 1 (September 1991): 51–86.

Altshuler, Alan A. "The Intercity Freeway." In *Introduction to Planning History in the United States,* edited by Donald A. Krueckeberg. New Brunswick, N.J.: Center for Urban Policy Research, 1983.

American Public Works Association. *History of Public Works in the United States, 1776–1976,* edited by Ellis Armstrong. Kansas City, 1976.

Austin, Eric K. *Political Facts of the United States, Since 1789.* New York: Columbia University Press, 1986.

Barrett, Paul. *The Automobile and Urban Transit: The Formation of Public Policy in Chicago, 1900–1930.* Philadelphia: Temple University Press, 1983.

———. "Cities and Their Airports: Policy Formation, 1926–1952." *Journal of Urban History* 1 (November 1987): 112–37.

Bae, Christine, and Harry Richardson. "Automobiles, the Environment, and Metropolitan Spatial Structure." Working papers, Lincoln Institute of Land Policy, 1994.

Bernard, Richard M., and Bradley R. Rice. *Sunbelt Cities: Politics and Growth Since World War II.* Austin: University of Texas Press, 1983.

Bottles, Scott. *Los Angeles and the Automobile: The Making of the Modern City.* Berkeley: University of California, 1987.

Burnham, John C. "The Gasoline Tax and the Automobile Revolution." *Mississippi Valley Historical Review* 48 (December 1961): 435–56.

Campbell, Ballard C. "Pope, Albert Augustus." *American National Biography Online.* Oxford University Press, February 2000. http://www.anb.org/articles/10/10-01332.html

Choate, Pat, and Susan Walter. *America in Ruins: The Decaying Infrastructure.* Washington, D.C., 1981.

Clow, David. "House Divided: Philadelphia's Controversial Crosstown Expressway." *Society for American Regional Planning History,* Working Paper Series.

Downs, Anthony. *Stuck in Traffic: Coping With Peak-Hour Traffic Congestion.* Washington, D.C.: Brookings Institution, 1992.

Dunn, James A. *Driving Forces: The Automobile, Its Enemies, and the Politics of Mobility.* Washington, D.C.: Brookings Institution, 1998.

Dupuy, Gabriel. "The Automobile System: A Territorial Adapter." *Flux* 21 (July–September 1995): 21–36.

Essays in Public Works History, no. 15. "Planning and Financing Public Works: Three Historical Cases."

Flink, James. *The Automobile Age.* Cambridge: MIT Press, 1990.

Foster, Mark. *From Streetcar to Superhighway: American City Planners and Urban Transportation, 1900–1940.* Philadelphia: Temple University Press, 1981.

———. "The Automobile and the City." *Michigan Quarterly Review* (Fall/Winter 1991).

————. "The Automobile and the Suburbanization of Los Angeles in the 1920s." In *Major Problems in American Urban History*, edited by Howard Chudacoff. Lexington, Mass.: D.C. Heath and Co., 1994.

Fuchs, Esther. *Mayors and Money: Fiscal Policy in New York and Chicago.* Chicago: University of Chicago Press, 1992.

Fuller, Wayne. "Good Roads and Rural Free Delivery of Mail." *Mississippi Valley Historical Review* 42, no. 1 (June 1955): 67–83.

Gaster, Patricia. "Nebraska's Changing Auto Culture, 1900–1930." *Nebraska History* 73 (Winter 1992): 80.

Gifford, Jonathan. "The Saga of American Infrastructure." *Wilson Quarterly* 17, no. 1 (Winter 1993): 40–47.

Gillespie, Angus, and Michael Rockland. *Looking for America on the New Jersey Turnpike.* New Brunswick, N.J.: Rutgers University Press, 1989.

Goddard, Stephen. *Getting There: The Epic Struggle Between Road and Rail in the American Century.* Chicago: University of Chicago Press, 1994.

Hanchett, Thomas. "U.S. Tax Policy and the Shopping-Center Boom of the 1950s and 1960s." *American Historical Review* 101, no. 4 (October 1996): 1082–1110.

"Highway Fights." H-Urban Discussion List. www://h-net.msu.edu

Hokanson, Drake. *The Lincoln Highway: Main Street Across America.* Iowa City: University of Iowa Press, 1988.

Interrante, Joseph. "The Road to Autopia: The Automobile and the Spatial Transformation of American Culture." In *Major Problems in American Urban History*, edited by Howard Chudacoff. Lexington, Mass.: D.C. Heath and Co., 1994.

Jackson, Kenneth T. *Crabgrass Frontier: The Suburbanization of the United States.* New York: Oxford University Press, 1985.

Lazare, Daniel. "Cities Pay for America's Free Ride." *Metropolis*, October 1992, 23.

Leavitt, Helen. *Superhighway—Super Hoax.* New York: Doubleday, 1970.

Lewis, David, and Laurence Goldstein, editors. *The Automobile and American Culture.* Ann Arbor: University of Michigan Press, 1983.

Lisa, Gregory, C. "Bicyclists and Bureaucrats: The League of American Wheelmen and Public Choice Theory Applied." *Georgetown Law Journal* 84 (1995): 373–98.

Lotchin, Roger. "The Origins of the Sunbelt–Frostbelt Struggle: Defense Spending and City Building." In *Searching for the Sunbelt: Historical Perspectives on a Region*, edited by Raymond Mohl. Athens: University of Georgia Press, 1993.

Mallach, Stanley. "The Origins of the Decline of Urban Mass Transportation in the United States, 1890–1930." *Urbanism Past and Present* (Summer 1979): 1–17.

Manchester, Ann, and Albert Manchester. "From D.C. to the Golden Gate: The First Transcontinental Military Motor Convoy." *American History* 32, no. 5 (December 1997): 38–42, 68–69.

Manning, Ian. *Beyond Walking Distance.* Australian National University Press, 1984.

————. *The Open Street: Public Transport, Motor Cars, and Politics in Australian Cities.* Sydney: Transit Australia Publishing, 1991.

McKay, Robert B. *Reapportionment: The Law and Politics of Equal Representation.* New York: Twentieth Century Fund, 1965.

McShane, Clay. *Down the Asphalt Path: The Automobile and the American City.* New York: Columbia University Press, 1994.

———. "Urban Pathways: The Street and Highway, 1900–1940." In *Technology and the Rise of the Networked City in Europe and America,* edited by Joel Tarr. Philadelphia: Temple University Press, 1988.

Meyer, John, and Jose Gomez-Ibanez. *Autos, Transit, and Cities.* Cambridge: Harvard University Press, 1981.

Mohl, Raymond. *The New City: Urban America in the Industrial Age, 1860–1920.* Arlington Heights, Ill.: Harlan Davidson, 1985.

Mohring, Herbert. "Urban Highway Investments." In *Measuring Benefits of Government Investment,* edited by Robert Dorfman. Washington, D.C.: Brookings Institution, 1965.

Moline, Norman T. *Mobility and the Small Town.* University of Chicago, Department of Geography Research Paper, 132, 1971.

Monkkonen, Eric. "The Politics of Municipal Indebtedness and Default, 1850–1936." In *The Politics of Urban Fiscal Policy,* edited by Terrence McDonald and Sally Ward. Beverly Hills: Sage Publications, 1984.

———. *America Becomes Urban: The Development of U.S. Cities and Towns, 1790–1980.* Los Angeles: University of California Press, 1988.

———. *The Local State: Public Money and American Cities.* Stanford University Press, 1996.

Moskowitz, Karl. "Living and Travel Patterns in Automobile-Oriented Cities." Paper presented at "The Dynamics of Urban Transportation" symposium sponsored by Automobile Manufacturer's Association, October 23–24, 1962. Reprinted in *Readings in Urban Transportation,* edited by George Smerck.

Naske, Claus-M. "Alaska and the Federal-Aid Highway Acts." *Pacific Northwest Quarterly* 80 (October 1989): 133–38.

Owen, Wilfred. "The New Highways: Challenge to the Metropolitan Region." Connecticut General Life Insurance Co. Reprinted in *Readings in Urban Transportation,* edited by George Smerck.

Parsons, Kermit C. "Shaping the Regional City: 1950–1990: The Plans of Tracy Augur and Clarence Stein for Dispersing Federal Workers from Washington, D.C." In *Proceedings of the 3rd National Conference on American Planning History, 1989.*

Patton, Phil. *Open Road: A Celebration of the American Highway.* New York: Simon and Schuster, 1986.

Peterson, George E. "Financing the Nation's Infrastructure Requirements." In *Perspectives in Urban Infrastructure,* edited by Royce Hanson. Washington, D.C.: National Academy Press, 1984.

Plowden, William. *The Motor Car and Politics, 1896–1970.* London: Penguin, 1971.

Preston, Howard. *Automobile Age Atlanta: The Making of a Southern Metropolis, 1900–1935.* Athens: University of Georgia Press, 1979.

———. *Dirt Roads to Dixie: Accessibility and Modernization in the South, 1885–1935.* Knoxville: University of Tennessee Press, 1991.

Pucher, John. "Distribution of Federal Transportation Subsidies: Cities, States, and Regions." *Urban Affairs Quarterly* 19, no. 2 (December 1983): 191–216.

Pucher, John, and Ira Hirschman. *Path to Balanced Transportation.* New Brunswick, N.J.: Rutgers University Press, 1993.

Richter, William. *Transportation in America.* ABC-CLIO, 1995.

Rose, Mark. *Interstate: Express Highway Politics, 1939–1989.* Lawrence: University of Kansas Press, 1979.

St. Clair, David. *The Motorization of American Cities.* New York: Praeger, 1986.

Salomon, Ilan, Piet Bovy, and Jeann-Pierre Orfeuil, editors. *A Billion Trips a Day: Tradition and Transition in European Travel Patterns.* Boston: Kluwer Academic Publishers, 1993.

Sanders, Elizabeth. *The Roots of Reform: Farers, Workers, and the American State, 1877–1917.* Chicago: University of Chicago Press, 1999.

Sanders, Heywood T. "Politics and Urban Public Facilities." In *Perspectives in Urban Infrastructure,* edited by Royce Hanson. Washington, D.C.: National Academy Press, 1984.

Sbragia, Alberta M. *Debt Wish: Entrepreneurial Cities, U.S. Federalism, and Economic Development.* Pittsburgh: University of Pittsburgh Press, 1996.

Sclar, Elliot, and K.H. Schaeffer. *Access for All: Transportation and Urban Growth.* Baltimore: Penguin Books, 1975.

Seely, Bruce. *Building the American Highway System: Engineers as Policy Makers.* Philadelphia: Temple University Press, 1987.

———. "A Republic Bound Together." *Wilson Quarterly* 17, no. 1 (Winter 1993): 18–39.

———. "Page, Logan Waller." In *American National Biography Online.* Oxford University Press, February 2000. http://www.anb.org/articles/05/05-00929.html

Tarr, Joel. "The Evolution of Urban Infrastructure in the Nineteenth and Twentieth Centuries." In *Perspectives in Urban Infrastructure,* edited by Royce Hanson. Washington, D.C.: National Academy Press, 1984.

———. "Transportation Innovations and Changing Spatial Patterns in Pittsburgh, 1850–1934." In *Essays in Public Works History,* no. 6. Pittsburgh: Public Works Historical Society.

———. "Infrastructure and City-Building in the Nineteenth and Twentieth Centuries." In *City at the Point: Essays on the Social History of Pittsburgh,* edited by Samuel Hays. Pittsburgh: University of Pittsburgh Press, 1989.

Taylor, Brian D. "When Finance Leads Planning: The Influence of Public Finance on Transportation Planning and Policy in California." Ph.D. diss., University of California at Los Angeles, 1992.

Teaford, Jon. *Post Suburbia: Government and Politics in the Edge Cities.* Baltimore: Johns Hopkins University Press, 1997.

Thomson, J. Michael. *Great Cities and Their Traffic.* London: Victor Gollanez Ltd., 1977.

Vickrey, William. "Pricing in Urban and Suburban Transport." *American Economic Review,* May 1963.

Winston, Clifford. "Efficient Transportation Infrastructure Policy." *Journal of Economic Perspective* 5, no. 1 (Winter 1991): 113–27.

Wolfe, Mark. "How the Lincoln Highway Snubbed Colorado." *Colorado Heritage* (Autumn 1999): 3–21.

Wright, Charles L. *Fast Wheels, Slow Traffic: Urban Transport Choices.* Philadelphia: Temple University Press, 1992.

Yago, Glenn. *The Decline of Transit: Urban Transportation in German and U.S. Cities, 1900–1970.* Madison: University of Wisconsin Press, 1980.

Yago, Glenn, and J. Allen Whitt. "Corporate Strategies and the Decline of Transit in U.S. Cities." *Urban Affairs Quarterly* 21, no. 1 (September 1985): 37–65. See also comments by Duane Windsor and response by Glenn Yago in *Urban Affairs Quarterly* 22, no. 4 (June 1987): 617–24.

All computations involving adjustments for inflation are calculated using "How Much Is That Worth Today" by John J. McKusker, www.eh.net, based on John J. McKusker, How Much Is That in Real Money? A Historical Price Index for Use as a Deflator of Money Values in the Economy of the United States, in *Proceedings of the American Antiquarian Society*, vol. 101, part 2, October 1991. Reprinted. Worcester, Mass.: American Antiquarian Society, 1992.

Index